AMERICAN SKIN

Pop Culture, Big Business,
and the End of White America

Leon E. Wynter

Crown Publishers • New York

Published by Crown Publishers, New York, New York.
Member of the Crown Publishing Group, a division of Random House, Inc.

www.randomhouse.com

CROWN is a trademark and the Crown colophon is a registered trademark of Random House, Inc.

Printed in United States of America

Design by Leonard Henderson

Library of Congress Cataloging-in-Publication Data
Wynter, Leon.
American skin : pop culture, big business, and the end of white America / by Leon Wynter.
1. United States—Race relations.   2. Popular culture—United States—History—20th century.   3. Whites—Race identity—United States. 4. African Americans in popular culture—History.   5. Racism—United States—History—20th century.   6. Racism—Economic aspects— United States—History—20th century.   7. Marketing—Social aspects— United States—History—20th century.   I. Title.

E184.A1 W96 2002
305.8'034073—dc21   2002019365

ISBN 0-609-60489-9

10   9   8   7   6   5   4   3   2   1

First Edition

To all the ones—near, far, and dear—
who told me I could do it.
Especially to the first.
To Yvonne, the last, and Grace, who actually
suffered me through it.

To Jesus Christ, my Lord and Savior.

Acknowledgments

I would like to acknowledge that:

Chris Jackson, my editor, got what I yearned to convey in this book just by reading it, before we ever met. He created a bulletproof bond of trust that made editing it almost a snap.

Jay Mandel, my agent, treated me and my ideas with utmost respect from Day 1, and has represented us well that way ever since.

Jim Sleeper, my friend and fellow traveler. He was the first I heard ask if there was an "American skin" thick enough for us to live in, creating, for me, the presumption that there must be.

The Dark Body Writers Collective shared its unsparing ctitiques, keen literary intellects, and patient wisdom, which energized my work and sustained me to the end.

Contents

Introduction

When I was in junior high school, you could tell the color of another boy's skin by looking at his feet. If he wore sneakers, and they were U.S. Keds or, god forbid, one of the off-label brands lumped into the category called "skips," you could be pretty sure he was white. If you saw Converse All-Stars on his feet, you could bet he was one of the 10 percent or so of kids at Frank D. Whelan Junior High in the north Bronx that was Negro or one of the tiny handful of Puerto Ricans.

It was 1965, and neither the term *black* nor *Hispanic* had been officially adopted. If the boy wore shoes like the kind his father wore to the office you could bet the kid was white, probably Jewish or one of the few Anglo-Saxon Protestants, for whom we had no group names. If the shoes were pointy, with narrow "Cuban" heels and skinny laces, then the kid could very well be Italian or Puerto Rican, although the jokes about the effectiveness of needle-nosed shoes for killing roaches in the corners only fell on the kids with Spanish last names. White boys wore wool hats with flaps on them like Vermont dairy farmers, but only outdoors and in winter. Those in the black in-crowd required a style of round brimmed cap, to be worn year-round, in the building if they could get away with it, and always at the approved rakish angle and attitude. My black friends, aping the styles modeled by the kids from the southern Bronx and Harlem, swore by reptile-skin shoes. "Snakes" and "Lizards" and "Gators" weren't just in the nearby Bronx Zoo, they were authentic "street" brand names that, when possessed, certified authenticity, hipness, and, most important, unquestioned membership in the group identity.

It was the year Malcolm X was assassinated in Harlem. While most of us Negro boys in the north Bronx didn't know what a Black Muslim was, Muhammad Ali's prowess and lippy pride was already on our radar screens. Not that we'd ever seen the Olympic gold medalist on a Wheaties box. Ali wasn't even endorsing roach spray in the ghetto yet, but wherever he was we just knew he was wearing "Gators" and not taking any stuff from white people. JHS 135 was in a very white neighborhood that we entered via public transportation every morning and exited promptly at three. The segregation cohered and intensified an identity found in a shared sense of music, fashion, and style that wasn't necessary in their own black neighborhoods. It was how they knew themselves.

Black kids rooted for the small handful of black major-league sports stars whenever they could. If asked, they would only admit to listening to the "dollar-a-holler" black radio stations at the top of the AM dial. Black girls swore they were Diana Ross or Mary Wells, while black boys aped the moves of "Mr. Dynamite," Jackie Wilson, or James Brown. White kids thought there were no stations in New York besides WABC (home of the "All Americans") or WMCA (the "Good Guys"), and by 1965 there were no groups for white adolescents besides the Beatles and the rest of the British Invasion. To them, Stevie Wonder was just the blind kid who sang a number in one of the beach-blanket movies, a novelty act. To black kids, the name Stevie Wonder was always mentioned with "genius," the only one of their own widely regarded as such. White boys knew of Willie Mays and Roberto Clemente, but there were no gods before white stars like Mickey Mantle. Joe Pepitone, an Italian-American Yankee, was a particular favorite. In basketball every white boy was John Havlicek or Jerry West. And cheerleading on the sidelines, every white girl in JHS 135 was Annette Funicello, the original Italian-American princess, or Sandra Dee. Even the Jewish girls.

It was 1965 and there was no line in most people's minds between the color of one's skin and the content of one's closet. The line was between white and nonwhite and it was crossed at the great peril of losing entirely one's identity in the hyperclannish preteen prison of junior high. Group loyalty was the ultimate value, and loyalty meant conformity, especially for the nonwhite minority; you could get beaten up for deviating by as much as one wrong snap on your cap.

Of course, there was that one white boy in ninety who regularly came to school sporting Converse or lizards, or "Italian" shoes, always topped with a leather jacket, and there were those white boys and girls who sometimes tuned in to the strong black beat under the static at the top of the AM dial. There were white boys who even had one or two of the loud, plush alpaca-wool sweaters we called "blyes" in their closets, just like the most impeccably dressed black kids on the corner. They wouldn't be caught dead in a cheap ski jacket or Buster Brown shoes. Nobody, black or white, thought lightly about messing with those few street fashionable white boys. Nobody knew quite what to make of them, either. We couldn't figure out how they found their way across the line into the wrong race closet. And we couldn't figure out why.

Nobody was openly marketing those $30 sweaters and $60 shoes to the coolest white kids in and around the school. The fashion of hard-core Harlem and the emerging black and Hispanic south Bronx wasn't on display in their neighborhood stores, local newspapers, or magazines. Nobody promoted black radio in media that reached these kids. Yet somehow they found it. Black fashion, music, and style were by definition not part of the mainstream, because mainstream meant white. White kids who embraced the markers of nonwhite cultural identity opted out of the mainstream, as defined, and thus out of whiteness itself.

That, I realize today, was probably the point. Like a subset of white youth in almost every generation before them, these kids had come to understand that cultural whiteness didn't completely capture their reality. The ski jacket didn't fit like a three-quarter-length leather coat. Unlike most of their white peers, they needed what we now understand as the street credibility the nonwhite attitude and style conferred. Association with less reputable Negro role models was a small price to pay, because at some level they understood that despite their white skin, they had more in common with the black kids on the corner than a ski jacket or a corny hat could hide. Not that they were politically conscious liberals, touched by the spirit of brotherhood and civil rights flowing through college-age America in the years after the Freedom Riders and before the Summer of Love. No, these white kids with the look of streets shared something more organic with their fashion mentors than progressive political rhetoric at the putative dawn of the Age of Aquarius. Most of them were leading candidates for dropping out, drugging out, becoming cannon fodder in Vietnam, or all three, and they knew it. In our little corner of the era, they were true rebels without a cause, except perhaps survival. It was the same outlook as the black cohort they emulated.

My old junior high was and still is just across the border that divides the north Bronx from the south, with a clear sense of the edge of where whiteness ends and the ever-encroaching black and Hispanic ghetto on the other side of Bronx Park begins. From that vantage, for these white kids trapped in their own unrecognized, underachieving ghettos, society's margin was the coolest, most unassailable place to appear to be from. It's as if they saw clearly what was coming and dressed accordingly. Like so many in every generation before them, these cooler-than-whites were driven to find a cultural skin that suited them better than the model of the day imposed by their racial skin. But, unlike each of the two generations that have been identified since these white boomers were teens, they didn't have the assembled might of America's corporate giants tripping over themselves to guide, affirm, and especially serve them in their quest across the lines.

Among thirteen-year-olds today, you can no more reliably tell a boy's race by looking at his feet than you can determine his sexual orientation by knowing that he sleeps under an artist-formerly-known-as-Prince poster. In fact, as multiracial America turns the millennial corner, you can't even be sure of someone's race or ethnicity by looking at their face, much less their feet. Exactly a generation after I left JHS 135, whites and nonwhites are still mostly segregated within their neighborhoods in the Bronx. But everyone— young and old, working and upper middle class, college and high school graduates—wears the same sneakers, baseball caps, jeans, boots, and designer names. Not all exactly the same labels at the exact same time, of course, because they are now choosing from hundreds of brands and to suit dozens of shades of lifestyle options mostly unimagined at the time. But, to an extent unprecedented in my lifetime, race and ethnic group membership is no longer the primary screen for filtering decisions on what kind of pants to wear, records to buy, teams or players to root for, or where to take a vacation.

Where once the label on your shirt or jacket amounted to a racial identification, it's now just a label, a fashion. Anything that's mostly cool with one group or subgroup today can and inevitably will become cool with another, socially disparate group tomorrow, if only for a fashion minute. Where headgear amounted to a racial flag in 1965, today young and not-so-young men of all races and ethnicities not only wear the same basic hat—the ubiquitous baseball cap—they wear it at the same attitude, backwards, about half the time. The top cable music services, MTV and VH1, are deliberately not easily categorized by race, and their video playlists, in certain prime viewing hours, are hard to distinguish from the avowedly "black" cable channel, Black Entertainment Television. The "black" radio station is no longer fuzzy near the top of the dial and has at least as many white as nonwhite listeners. Where once our family shopping was segregated by the "neighborhood stores" we frequented, we now mostly shop in the same stores, elbow-to-elbow, in big box branches of regional and national chains including Kmart, PathMark, The Gap, Rite-Aid, Home Depot, and Old Navy. These stores occupy malls that, by definition, are part of no one group's sovereign territory, even when they're an island in the middle of a homogeneous residential area. When you enter a McDonald's, you're in your own neighborhood, no matter where the particular store is located.

It's taken a very long time for the malling of America to reach the New York City. We didn't get our JC Penney in the Bronx until 1996. But now that it's here, it's easy to see what has become true in most metropolitan areas: while we are still divided by race and a dozen ethnic identities in our residential neighborhoods, we're all the same color to Kmart—green—and the same nationality, American. There's been a radical shift in the place of race and ethnicity in American commercial culture since the late 1970s. Near revolutionary developments in advertising, media, marketing, technology, and global trade have in the last two decades of the twentieth century nearly obliterated walls that have stood for generations between nonwhites and the image of the American dream. The mainstream, heretofore synonymous with what is considered average for whites, is now equally defined by the preferences, presence, and perspectives of people of color. The much maligned melting pot, into which generations of European American identities are said to have dissolved, is bubbling again, but on a higher flame; this time whiteness itself is finally being dissolved into a larger identity that includes blacks, Hispanics, and Asians.

On its surface, this book tells the story of how and why big business turned up that flame and a brief history of race and pop culture leading up to this watershed. But at its core, *American Skin* is about the revolution that higher heat on American identity is bringing about: the end of "white" America. This book begins with, and my arguments and insights ultimately rest on, one premise and guiding belief about this country: *We have always been, and will ever be of one race, human, and of one culture, American.* But from its beginning the legal, social, and high cultural institutions of America defined and held American identity to mean white, Anglo-Saxon, and Protestant.

"American" quickly broadened as successive groups of non–Anglo-Saxon Protestant European immigrants were obliged to fit themselves into the nation of slaveholding WASPs in order to lay claim to an American identity. They couldn't become Anglo-Saxons, nor would they convert en masse to Protestant faiths. But they did have the same general pigment and hair texture as the former Englishmen founders. To become American, the Irish and subsequent immigrant groups from Europe were allowed to become "white," though only after a period of sometimes brutal hazing that we now call assimilation. Even then, of course, they were only relatively white; absolute whiteness being reserved for the founding WASPs and their "purebred" descendants. Formerly enslaved Africans, Native Americans, and later immigrants from China and other parts of Asia were barred from assimilation into whiteness, and hence into a recognized share of American identity. Over time, to be sure, Native American people, including those who were indigenous to what is now Mexico, Central America, and South America, could and would enter relative American whiteness through intermixture with Euro-Americans. But no amount of mixture with whites would permit African-Americans to cross the threshold. "White" and "American" were conflated at the nation's birth for a reason: a nation being built on slavery couldn't tolerate the possibility of human property becoming just plain human.

Yet, as it turned out, no one in the young nation was as American as the Africans, free or not, because more than any of the voluntary immigrants from anywhere, they were forced to create themselves from scratch. They became the seminal, disproportionate creators of American culture because, except for the remnants of the displaced Indian societies, they were working, along with their masters, on a blank slate. The climate, topography, and, significantly, economy and technology were unlike anything in the European experience. And no one, not even their masters, was as familiar with its simple pleasures and brutal truths as the Africans who would be Americans. They were excluded from whiteness, and thus from recognition as Americans, even as they led the creation of the culture. The exclusion produced the tension that has driven American popular culture from the start. Whites couldn't abide having Africans inside the definition of American, but as they kept discovering, they couldn't become truly American without them.

Inevitably, something had to give, and that thing was the equation "white = American." It's taken a long time, but American identity has finally begun to reach the truth of its composition. The artificial walls between being American and being *like* an African or Hispanic or Asian American are coming down faster than anyone imagined even ten years ago. Today, we wouldn't think of trying to describe "American" by first excluding what is "nonwhite." The speech impediment that stops a phrase like "as American as Ray Charles" from tripping off the tongue has been almost entirely lifted.

Something had to give, not just because of the contradiction and the aspirations of black and other nonwhite Americans. Something had to give because something was pushing, hard: money.

Today, wherever the real American identity is ready to be expressed in all its miscegenated energy and truth, some capitalist is ready to, as they say, monetize it. And, unlike any time in any generation in American history before, there is no sociopolitical force empowered to stop it. The ultimate irony of the triumph of free-market capitalist ideology in the Reagan revolution is that that the action of the global markets for information and entertainment has demolished the hegemony of the white-bread culture Ronald Reagan epitomized. The truly global market for Hollywood action films has replaced John Wayne with Jackie Chan. And even when it's Bruce Willis shooting up the bad guys, this is not your father's white boy hero anymore. This is that Caucasian-American with the leather jacket and the cigarette on the corner by my junior high in 1965. Or, rather, it represents what he must have wanted to become, because he never misses a movie like *Die Hard II*, in which a cool white guy more than holds his own with a hip African-American. The white Übermensch John Wayne is dead, done in by multinational entertainment firms whose stocks are traded on Wall Street. His replacement is Denzel Washington, or Jackie Chan, or a white icon whose screen persona is much closer to the legacy of the slave than the master. Offscreen and outside the theater, the white film icon and his Caucasian fans are still white and exercise their remaining white-skin privileges as they see fit. But on-screen and inside the theater, and before the television set and hanging out on the street, they live in the skin developed by the ex-slaves and all the world's people they assimilated into our culture: American skin.

In retrospect, I had a lot more in common with the one white boy in ninety with the alpaca sweater on the corner than I knew. Race politics obscured the reality of the connection, but we were both confined and sometimes degraded by being forced constantly to choose between racial group loyalty and our own individual freedom to dress, talk, and associate however we pleased. Now that we've grown up, having survived the late-1960s and early-1970s lethal mix of riots, drugs, Vietnam, and college together, acquiring and/or losing more wealth than we ever imagined, I think race group identity pressure has lost most of its hold over my generation. By the time we came of age as consumers, the only limit we recognized on our lifestyle was how much we could borrow. In the mid-1970s we said, "If it feels good, do it." In the 1980s we were spending money so fast, with so little time to enjoy it, that we shortened our mantra to "Just Do It."

Or, rather, the race-mixing marketing from Nike shortened it for us.

Safe from the race-coded warnings of World War II–generation parents, far from the peer-ethnic group loyalties of segregated adolescence, the boomer generation has been freeing itself, selectively, from the baggage of America's racial past. Armed with hundred-channel cable boxes, we've become free to choose from all the divertissements the media-entertainment-industrial complex can dream up and to experience them in the privacy of our own homes, without being limited by the fact that we are white or black or brown. I can adopt the Golf Channel, buy the clothes, play some occasional rounds, and feel a part of the culture, even though I may not be welcomed at all the courses I see on TV. A white guy living in a mostly white suburb can watch HBO and lap up all the black jive, wit, and wisdom he missed thirty years ago because he didn't have access to our corner, without worrying about whether the people on the screen might be moving in next door. A white woman who grew up in Tennessee, as Oprah Winfrey did, and always wondered what it would be like to share girl talk with the black girls at school when she was a kid, or who lost track of the one or two black girls she knew intimately once puberty and segregated dating drove them apart, can now wallow in Oprah's gabfest on TV or read her magazine.

It may be arbitrary, but I date the emergence of our American skin to January 1979, when Coca-Cola first aired a commercial in which a towheaded white boy approaches former Pittsburgh Steeler defensive end Joe "Mean Joe" Greene, perhaps for an autograph, in the stadium tunnel after a tough game. "Mean Joe," a fearsome black gridiron warrior, is tired, soiled, and sore and is no mood for fans. But, in a moment of advertising magic, "the Kid" offers up his bottle of Coke to the thirsty athlete, who downs it with gusto and a palpable sigh of release. "The Kid" had already begun walking away. "Hey, kid," the future Hall of Famer calls to him, and with that pulls the sweaty jersey off his shoulder and tosses it to him. "Gee, thanks Mean Joe," "the Kid" beams. This was before professional team sport jerseys were a day in/day out wardrobe fixture. This was before pro football players like Tony Dorsett, Walter Payton, Jerry Rice, and dozens more black stars came to epitomize the marketing image of the game, permanently taking a hefty slice of the limelight from the white quarterbacks in the process. "Hey, Kid" was a watershed moment in commercial culture, ten years after the peak of the civil rights movement. Because it was one thing to legislate the integration of the races and quite another thing for a generation of white youths to begin openly idolizing the sweat off a black man's back and to have their idolatry validated and amplified by the power of a multinational marketer on national television.

Call it the first American skin graft. The commercial, which went on to win numerous awards, moved its intended boomer target audience because it touched the child in them that wanted to love Joe Greene that way too, but never got to see him with his helmet off, big, black, larger than life and human at the same time. I have been amazed at the high percentage of thirty-five-to-fiftysomething people who instantly recall the ad. But the commercial was more important as a sign of what was coming for the youngsters of Generation X, many of whom were adolescents at the time, and especially for the infant Generation Y. These young consumers, who drive today's commercial culture, hadn't yet learned that All-American football stars are white by definition: the commercial caught them when it still seemed perfectly natural to identify with the best football player, or the most exciting basketball player, not necessarily the white one. The media, fashion, and entertainment choices of Generation X reflect the fact that they've never really known an America that didn't allow them to try on and be comfortable in multicolored American skin.

Now, imagine the vision of the American dream through the eyes of Generation Y, who mostly weren't even born when "Hey, Kid" first aired. Their image of "movie star" is as much Eddie Murphy as Tom Hanks. Their image of "star athlete" is Michael Jordan (or any of a dozen black or Hispanic basketball, baseball, football, or boxing standouts) as much or more than *any* white athlete. They were born into a world in which Michael Jackson and Whitney Houston defined "pop star," and white skin was no longer a prerequisite. And, as far as Gen-Y knows, hip-hop is not just black culture; it's the most distinctive characteristic of their generation. Boomers can act out their American dreams in color today because, starting in the 1980s, commercial popular culture began catching up to America's transracial collective unconscious. But Gen-Y's multicolored vision is its collective consciousness as well as the national id. Even if he is white, lives in an all-white community, and identifies with mostly white celebrities, the Gen-Y consumer is acutely aware of the fact that his preferences, his very whiteness, are not preeminently American, and in some contexts (e.g., when he ventures from the suburbs into Chicago, New York, Los Angeles, etc.) are not even average.

All this has come about, I believe, because of a simple, powerful truth that's finally in the spotlight: *American* does not mean "white." If it wasn't true, then the list of people we have ordained as great Americans since World War II would have to be halved. If it wasn't true, no corporate media marketing program in the world could on its own muscle confer the retroactive all-American hero status Muhammad Ali enjoys today. The truth is that Americans are "a composite that is part Yankee, part backwoodsman and Indian, part Negro,"[1] part schtetl Jew, part Sicilian: part every group that ever came here, not just the white Anglo-Saxon Protestants. But "the truth that makes men free is for the most part the truth which men prefer not to hear."[2] The challenge of writing this book is convincing people not of this truth or that it is on the the way, but that it has arrived. American industry has produced a lifelike artificial skin of commercial culture that's supple yet strong enough to cover us all. We understand what Oprah means as an American industry. But can we understand the meaning of "as American as Oprah"?

1

The Color and the Dream

Predjudiced, I am not, and have never been, otherwise than in favour of the United States. I have many friends in America, I feel a grateful interest in the country, I hope and believe it will successfully work out a problem of the highest importance to the whole human race.

—Charles Dickens, from the preface to
American Notes and Pictures from Italy

Charles Dickens, a visiting author of some note, was especially interested in the state of entertainments to be found in New York City. After just a few days, in so many more eloquent words, Dickens wondered at length about the one thing visitors to New York in his or any day since most want to know before they've properly unpacked their bags: Where's the party? His handlers, including some hip cops and no doubt a few other swells out for a good time on somebody else's tab, take him to a spot in the Lower East Side near the intersection of what are now Baxter and Worth streets, just north of City Hall. There the famed English guest might get his eyes full, his money's worth, his whistle and maybe other, more private parts, wet. The party of fashionable gentlemen arrive at the steps to the after-hours club and are guided to the cellar-door entrance to Almack's place. The streets are dark and filthy, filled with pigs and mud. But the door is opened by "a buxom, fat mulatto woman, with sparkling eyes, whose head is daintily ornamented with a handkerchief of many colours."[1] The party is warmly greeted by this woman and her husband, Pete Williams, resplendent in "a smart blue jacket, like a ship's steward, with a thick gold ring upon his little finger, and round his neck a gleaming golden watch-guard."[2]

Think Cab Calloway, welcoming a white celebrity looking for "the real thing" in the hottest joint in Harlem in the 1930s. Only it's 1841, in ante-bellum America, not quite three generations after the Revolution.

> How glad is he to see us! What will we please to call for? A dance? It shall be done directly, Sir: "a regular break-down." The corpu-lent black fiddler and his friend who plays the tambourine, stamp upon the boarding of the small raised orchestra in which they sit, and play a lively measure. Five or six couples come upon the floor, marshaled by a lively young Negro, who is the wit of the assembly, and the greatest dancer known. . . . And in what walk of life, or dance of life, does man ever get such stimulating applause as thun-ders about him, when, having danced his partner off her feet, and himself too, he finishes by leaping gloriously on the bar-counter, and calling for something to drink, with the chuckle of a million counterfeit Jim Crows, in one inimitable sound!

It's not clear what problem Dickens thought America was destined to work out for the world, a problem he thought important enough to place at the heart of an omnibus apology preceding the account of his travels in the young nation in 1834. But it's clear that the interrelations between all the "races" he saw mingling and becoming Americans was among his most keen "grateful" interests.

Almack's, rechristened "Dicken's Place" in honor of the author's visit, was near the heart of the Five Points, known in its day as perhaps the most squalid, crime- and vice-filled district in the world. Needless to say, Almack's was the place to see, if not to be seen in, as it would be for spots in the South Side of Chicago or Harlem or Beale Street in Memphis or the red light dis-trict of Kansas City one hundred years later. The very concept of "slumming," tourism lined with a certain mixture of fear, lust, and revulsion, was born to explain the attraction to New York's Five Points. As dangerous as it was, the Five Points, America's first urban ghetto, fairly burned in the imagination of the nation's earliest interpreters. No less a seminal American than Davy Crockett made a point of a pilgrimage to Almack's in 1834 about seven years before Dickens and two years before the Alamo. The Five Points was a catchment for the most wretched of the earliest non-Anglo-Saxon immigrants to come to the United States in great numbers before the Civil War. They were mostly Irish, along with many Poles and Germans. But what really set the Five Points apart as a tourist attraction, and places it at the start of a serious inquiry into American popular culture, was its sizable black population, a kind of ghetto within the ghetto.

When they weren't competing for mere survival, the Irish- and African-Americans competed for supremacy in New York's earliest street cultures, especially dancing. The mixture of Irish jigs and steps to more African beats at Almack's are said to have given birth to tap dancing and other forms that would evolve through minstrelsy and emerge in the Jazz Age as cakewalk and fox-trot and Charleston. The songs heard at Almack's and other lower Manhattan haunts, mixing Irish ballad melodies with lyrical parodies of the African-American life and worldview in demeaning—but revealing—"blackface dialect," gave rise to Stephen Foster's great American songbook, which in turn begat Tin Pan Alley, the future center of the American pop music industry. Crockett himself had a collection of such songs in circulation under his name when he visited Almack's. He also turned up as a hip character in some early blackface songs. The shamelessly self-promoted backwoodsman and populist congressman also counted himself as a proficient fiddler and blackface performer. Disney's 1950s revival of the Crockett legend didn't do the Alamo martyr justice: he should also go down in history as the first American pop star to sport a bit of a "white Negro" persona.

More than the music, the dance, or the danger, it was the very concept of mixture itself, the seductive spectacle of miscegenation in fact (Pete Williams was said to be "coal black" but the father of several "yellow boys" and "mulatto" girls)[3] and by implication that installed the culture born in places like Almack's at the foundation of the American identity. Here's what Davy Crockett saw:

It appeared as if the cellars were jam full of people; and such fid-
dling and dancing nobody ever before saw in this world. I thought
they were the true "heaven-borns." Black and white, white and
black, all hugemsnug together, happy as lords and ladies, sitting
sometimes round in a ring, with a jug of liquor between them: and
I do think I saw more drunken folks, men and women, that day
than I ever saw before.[4]

While Americans are all too accurately perceived as living in black and
white, America has always dreamed of itself in color. Our dreams haven't
always been pretty, and in some ways they have been a reflection of our
vices, especially racism, more than our virtues. Color was essential to American identity long before German immigrants inculcated the apple pie in our
consciousness, and indeed long before there was an American nation.

Though built on the labor of enslaved Africans, on the usurpation of previously colonized natives (whom we now call Mexican-Americans), and on the
near elimination of the Indians, the nation was founded on the dreamy principle that all men are created equal. This fundamental contradiction between the
practice of white supremacy and the principle of egalitarianism is the most
consistent and distinguishing feature of American history. Whiteness found its
place at the center of American identity well before the Declaration of Independence. It was codified in law and federal administrative practice in one of
the earliest acts of Congress in 1790, when the first law governing the natural-
ization of immigrants into the status of American citizens specified that only
"free white persons" qualified for admission. Article I, section 2, of the Constitution of 1787, in establishing the basis for taking the decennial census, specified the "three-fifths of a man" rule for counting slaves (as most of us recall
from American history class) and excluded Indians but said nothing about
"whites" as such. Yet in the first census in 1790, enumerators were instructed
to count by the following categories: free white males above and below the age
of sixteen, free white females, all other free people by sex and color, and slaves.
Whiteness (i.e., free-male-over-age-sixteen whiteness) was set apart in the first
census "to assess the country's industrial and military potential," according to
the Census Bureau's account of its own history. It offers no reason why counting by racial categories, ever more elaborate in specification as the decades

wore on, was continued for over two hundred years; in theory there was no federal legal justification for such counting until the affirmative action era of the 1970s. But the practice was consistent with the assumption of Anglo-Americans that they had not only launched the American nation: after a half-dozen generations, they constituted an American race.

The term *white* began to account for Americans of English descent and for those northern Europeans, mainly Irish and German at first, who were deemed assimilable into the Anglo-Protestant identity that would become American whiteness. The census in practice codified the truth that those whom the Anglo-American fathers had considered unquestionably beyond the pale as candidates for assimilation—so-called free blacks, Jews, Indians, and others—were presumed permanent outsiders with no legitimate role in American economic or martial potential, much less in American cultural stock. Yet these outsiders were present from the start, preceding the offical beginning of a political whiteness that held them to be culturally inert when in fact they were catalytic.

When you take the fictitious construct of American whiteness and place it back-to-back with the true transracial nature of America, in principle and in blood, you get the two differently charged poles from which the cultural energy of American identity flows. It is the electricity that makes American popular culture crackle. Born in the decades preceding the great civil war over slavery, American popular culture has always closely tracked the place of color in the social mainstream. Our popular culture institutions have always embodied the very contradictions that gave and continue to give America life. The seminal creators of truly American culture have always struggled to contain and mediate the manipulated conflict between white and nonwhite in their own personal, intellectual, and creative lives.

The music, dance, popular style, and language in which Walt Whitman heard America singing in the decades after the Civil War were inherently miscegenetic, in a land where miscegenation was legally outlawed yet widely practiced, in his lifetime and increasingly in every generation to follow. Virulent (and often violent) denial of color in the social and political mainstream only added to the energy of attraction of a race-mixing popular culture. In hindsight it should have been obvious that our everyday culture—our vernacular style, popular artistic expression, and creative vitality—would eventually come to be dominated outright by the descendants of slaves and of colonized peoples from the Caribbean and Latin America.

Color was the binding aspect of American popular commercial culture from its pre–Civil War dawn to the advent of a true national mass media culture at the start of the twentieth century. In this period the production of popular culture went from a noncommercial folk craft to a struggling cottage industry to a big business driving not only the sale of entertainments but the powerful engine of American mass consumption itself. Indeed, by the 1920s the American dream was defined not by the political heirs of the founding fathers of whiteness but by the dominant players in commercial pop culture: Madison Avenue, Hollywood, radio, and Tin Pan Alley. The creators and innovators (and in the case of Hollywood and Tin Pan Alley, the managers and owners) were overwhelmingly not the Anglo-American Protestants whom the founding fathers assumed would always be synonymous with "the American people."

But first we must define our terms. What is *whiteness*? What is *color*?

The original American whiteness consisted primarily in being of Anglo-Saxon descent and Protestant faith, like the Founding Fathers themselves. The *w* in *white Anglo-Saxon Protestant* was little needed, almost redundant, and in any case a much more limited concept when it was entered into the founding documents of the Republic. *White* wasn't necessary to distinguish these Americans from free blacks, much less from slaves or Indians, because such nonwhites were already presumed to be less than human, much less Anglo-Saxon. The term *white* became necessary to account for a small non-Anglo-Saxon but still European minority and to provide for their ongoing immigration into the new nation. White grew in stature as their numbers grew, from a concept needed to include a minority to the specification of the American majority. The founders' acceptance of a creeping pan-European whiteness as the national center was grudging at best. "Jefferson himself was opposed to the introduction of a 'heterogeneous, incoherent, distracted mass' of European immigrants" into the WASP republic, says Michael Lind in his history of American nationalism, *The Next American Nation*.[5]

Benjamin Franklin, Lind notes, favored the exclusion of all the "tawny" peoples of Europe in favor of "the lovely red and white" of certain, but not all northern Europeans.

Franklin's notion of "tawnys" included most Caucasians: "In Europe the Spaniards, Italians, French, Russians and Swedes are generally of what we call a swarthy complexion; as are the Germans also, the Saxons only excepted, who with the English make up the principal body of white people on the face of the earth."[6]

The founding elites, like the society of citizen farmers they imagined America to be, saw themselves as the progenitors not of America's *white* people but simply of America's people. In a widely discussed 1991 treatise, Peggy McIntosh of the Wellesley College Center for Research on Women listed fifty primary attributes of what we now identify as white privilege, but the normative assumption of whiteness-as-peoplehood is the most privileging of all. It's also the hardest for white Americans to objectify and thus to recognize, because unlike, say, preference in housing or employment, the assumption that white people are just people is ineffable, not easily quantified in the field, and nowhere near illegal. It's not even politically incorrect, because while not part of the unconscious mind, it operates below the level of choice or deliberation. It's like the way we can only calibrate our experience of time in minutes and hours, or the way most Americans just can't reckon in metric units. White is not only the baseline, the plane against which everything and everyone else is measured, it's a baseline that's never examined, any more than we examine the x-axis on a graph. Whiteness is a given. This normative quality of whiteness privileges white people to "normally" be immersed in an institution, society, or state of their own construction except when they choose otherwise. From this vantage, whites may freely ponder all things in their depths without ever objectively considering the medium in which their world is suspended, any more than a fish in the ocean considers the seawater.

Whiteness, to those who created it and for those who unthinkingly swim in its inherited abyss, is not limited in its authority to what is particular to white people. Whiteness assumes the coverings of humanity in general, and in that guise, under normal conditions, like Windexed glass, it tends to disappear. In *White*, his meticulously researched critique of whiteness in Western culture, Richard Dyer details the sociocultural consequences of white privilege and the image of whiteness in visual media.

For those in power in the West, as long as whiteness is felt to be the human condition, then it alone both defines normality and fully inhabits it. . . . [T]he equation of being white with being human secures a position of power. White people have power and believe that they think, feel and act like and for all people. . . . White people, unable to see their particularity . . . create the dominant images of the world and don't quite see that they thus construct the world in their own image. . . . White people set standards of humanity by which they are bound to succeed and others [are] bound to fail.[7]

A special case of the white privilege to "inhabit" all of humanity is the power to don the cultural garb of any particular so-called ethnic group or race as needs dictate. This corollary of the whiteness-as-humanity principle, actively applied in America since the nineteenth century, is directly responsible for the miscegenetic and ultimately transracial nature of American popular culture and identity. The English, our most dominant cultural forefathers, had a particular gift for assuming they could achieve mastery over the cultural heritage of any place or people they colonized, while still remaining English. When, after colonizing America, they decided they were really natives and revolted against the Crown, they laid the cornerstone of institutional American whiteness. But the edifice had a weak foundation from the start.

The self-concealing quality of white privilege was developed to its full potential in the United States because the country was founded not as an ethnic nation or race, like France or Poland or Japan, but in an idea: All men are created equal and free. From the beginning, WASP social privilege here had to hide itself not only from America's stated ideals of equality but from the growing tide of other-than-English immigrants from Europe. It did so through a process of political assimilation. As more and more Irish and German newcomers began covering the surface of the Anglo-white sea, pragmatic democracy pulled them into the depths, incorporating their distinctiveness (as *Star Trek*'s Borg would say) into a larger white identity, while obliterating their awareness of whiteness itself. The intent of the heirs of the founding Anglo fathers was to force the new immigrants into a fixed standard of Anglo-American identity centered on Protestantism, federal republicanism (i.e., what came to be known as "states' rights"), and, of course, whiteness. But as it turned out, instead of merely bolstering a national Anglo-American identity, the politics of accommodating the new European immigrants demolished Anglo-American identity and replaced it with something the Anglo fathers hadn't anticipated: Euro-American identity, and a political whiteness that not only had no place for blacks but had no use for slavery, either.

In the decades preceding the Civil War, as the Anglophilic Franklin and Jefferson likely turned over in their graves, modern (as in up through the 1960s civil rights era) political whiteness—the melding of a dozen or more European "races" like German, Irish, and Swedish into a single, implicitly white polity calling itself "the American people"—cohered. In political history, what Lind calls "Euro America" began with the coalition of antislavery, pro-northern industrial and pro-western expansion constituencies in 1854, under the banner of the new Republican Party. America's first sectional political party, its mandate came overwhelmingly from the North and included most of the burgeoning Irish and German immigrant populations that would provide much of the Union Army's cannon fodder. In a sense, modern American social identity is rooted in the bloody contradiction of immigrants giving their lives to free from slavery the very blacks they feared and despised. It was the price of their admission into an American political whiteness that, ironically, had originally been created for the benefit of Anglo-American slaveholders and other beneficiaries of a slave-based economy. The emergent Euro-American North rose up against the South not so much to free the slaves as to remove enslaved Africans from labor competition once and for all. These northerners had no intention of allowing freed slaves to compete for work or social place as equals. But it also had no program to account for their continued presence in the late-adolescent nation. At the same time, the Euro-American polity was uniquely susceptible to the cultural influence of the black minority, in part because it had no clear Euro-American culture of its own.

The seeds of American popular culture and those of pre–Civil War whiteness were sewn in the same hole, giving rise to closely entwined vines. But the central theme of this book is that over time the growth from the seeds of American popular culture has proven to be the more vigorous and now the more dominant of the two. That produce, cultural *Americanness*, has been

specially nurtured by generations of demographic, technological, and economic change to develop into a variegated, robust fruit that's the envy of the
world. The fruit of the system rooted in pre–Civil War political whiteness,
white cultural identity, is now exposed as stunted and possibly withering on
the vine. Cultural whiteness was always well-watered and protected from
the elements by the politics of whiteness. But its seed was weak from the
start. It's not that Euro-whites had no culture; they had all the cultures of
northern, and eventually all of Europe, at their collective command. But
once they set foot on these shores, they had no separate and distinct white
culture that unified them in the American experience.

As political whites, immigrant Irishmen and Germans very quickly
bonded in opposing the entry of ex-slaves into their workplaces, churches,
and neighborhoods. But as cultural whites the only thing they had in common was their shared role as consumers of the cultural output, in American
English, of the towns that grew into cities where they tended to concentrate.
Try as they might, they had no way to exclude the substantial contributions
of African-Americans, whose cultural cohesion, after many generations of
shared experience with Anglo-Americans, displayed itself in a far more distinct, potent, and uniquely American identity. Even in the slave South, with
its strictest codes of political whitenesses, the case for pure cultural whiteness was a fraud because of the great reliance on slaves for sport and entertainment of all kinds. Everything else was a pale—no pun intended—imitation of
the English. It was little different in the post–Civil War North. At the end of a
hard day of segregated labor, one of the few things the Irishman and the German could do together was frequent the places—usually drinking places—
where uniquely American culture was being created, and see what the blacks,
or those whites who specialized in aping blacks, were up to.

From the start, pop culture has been constructed on the facts as well as
white fantasies of nonwhites and their cultural forms. American identity
within this pop culture, history shows, is in large part projected onto the
culture at large through certain mass-marketed, commodified projections
of nonwhite identity. To loosely paraphrase President Bill Clinton's 1998
appearance on a prime-time television tribute to Motown Records, white
America has always depended on nonwhite America to know itself. But white
men—even Bill Clinton—have not obtained their identities as white men
from Marvin Gaye or Smokey Robinson. Whiteness, in both American and

European identity, comes from a careful construction of what the African or African-American is *not*. These assumptions about nonwhite people began taking their modern shape during the expansion of European empires into Africa and Asia. By the eighteenth century, European and later American scholars of biology and what is now anthropology were hard at work on devising scientific explanations for the differences between northern Europeans and other "races." These thinkers were especially interested in the black race because it seemed most opposite, and because of the intimate involvement in the slave trade and slavery itself. Most of this pseudoscientific inquiry was founded on the premise that the "civilized" enslavers of and colonizers of the world must be not just superior to all the rest but so unique and evolved as to be a class unto themselves, true representatives of humanity.

So whiteness begins with a fundamental denial of commonality with the nonwhite other. From the start there was no denying the fact of common physiognomy and the fact that, were it up to mere physical prowess alone, white men could never rest easy in their assumption of superiority. And from the start it was evident that nonwhite men were not only capable of brilliance within the context of their indigenous cultures but could be educated to full fluency in Western culture, too. The search for whiteness was thus forced from location in the white body to placement in the white spirit. This displacement from the corporeal to the essential in the white archetype goes so far as to take the form of a denial of the body itself, along with any number of qualities associated with the bodies of lesser races. A proper white man was the embodiment of a withdrawal or disconnection from the body that lesser races just couldn't make. Not that white men were not to have bodies; from Davy Crockett to Paul Bunyan to Johnny "Tarzan" Weismuller to Arnold Schwarzenegger, they had lots of hard lean muscle mass and "universal" recognition for what those bodies could do. But when they did it, it wasn't the same as when nonwhite bodies did the exact same thing or even did it better. In the whiteness archetype, white men merely operate bodies that themselves are products of discipline and evidence of virtue. On the other hand, the assumption follows, nonwhite men *are* their bodies, which are products of nature and evidence of nothing more.

White men, in this archetype, do not naturally sweat but only perspire under extraordinary conditions that are a challenge to the white nature—like doing the work of slaves. White women do not sweat at all. To sweat would be to *shine*, and the literature of female whiteness calls of white women to glow, according to Dyer, another reflection of the ineffable essence of whiteness that is in the skin but more than skin deep. In his discussion of the construction of the white female beauty archetype in photograpy and advertising, Dyer notes:

> Idealised white women are bathed in and permeated by light. . . . They glow rather than shine. The light within or from above appears to suffuse the body. Shine, on the other hand, is light bouncing back off the surface of the skin. It is the mirror effect of sweat, itself connoting physicality, the emissions of the body and unladylike labour. . . . In a well-known Victorian saw, animals sweated and even gentlemen perspired, but ladies merely glowed. Dark skin too, when it does not absorb the light, may bounce it back. Non-white and sometimes working class white women are liable to shine rather than glow in photographs and films.[8]

Whiteness in females idealized an absence of sex drive entirely (think classic, Scarlett O'Hara, Anglo-American southern belle), while

> . . . white men are seen as divided, with more powerful sex drives but also a greater will power. The sexual dramas of white men have to do with not being able to resist the drives or with struggling to master them. The drives are typically characterized as dark.[9]

The institution of whiteness requires dissociation from much of the essence of the American experience, if not the human experience. Whiteness is about racial purity; we are relentlessy mixed. Whiteness is about how whites do not smell, do not act on impulse (like talking over the sound track at the movies), and do not normally give in to baser instincts or the influence of lesser cultures. From the beginning this dissociation created a vacuum that people and cultures of color have been conscripted to fill and in which they have voluntarily sought opportunity under conditions of white political hegemony. Everything about African-Americans—their bodies, dances, songs, dialects, passions, worldview, and so on, real and especially as imagined by whites (and eventually imagined by other blacks, too)—became the base material for the popular entertainments that matured into mass culture. The black condition became a canvas for projecting all that the whiteness ideal sublimated; black cultural output became the paint.

❒   ❒   ❒

All the archetypes, contradictions, stereotypes, and conflicts of black and white in American commercial culture were laid down before the Civil War, when the white American need for identity and expression forced itself into bed with black and pseudoblack culture and style. Specifically, the musical and theatrical institutions of blackface and minstrelsy, born in the 1830s, inculcated the various stereotypes of the happy, happy-go-lucky, or just plain hapless nigger, the grinning, foot-shuffling, tap-dancing, bug-eyed coon, and the lustful black buck, his mangled English dialect consistent with his sub-human intelligence and the dark Negro world from which he came, in which violence was a way of life but mostly death.

A not-too-cynical reading of this history can support the argument that while much has changed in 170 years, the pattern of appropriation, exploitation, distortion, and ultimate marginalization of black and other nonwhite cultures in mainstream entertainment remains the same today, and with the same effect: the reaffirmation of white supremacy.

The dismissive charge that the more things have changed, the more they have in fact remained the same resonates because American culture can no more walk away from its basis in slavery, white supremacy, and minstrelsy than a tree can walk away from its roots. Mainstream popular culture, wordlessly construed as "white," developed dependent on people and cultures of color for raw material on one hand, while constrained by the requirements of white social hegemony on the other. A pattern of interplay developed that is cyclical but, most important, dynamic over time. In the beginning the cycle was simple, because it essentially turned in only one direction. Whites could appropriate—literally—the identity of a mostly enslaved group of people in society, distort it to fit the limitations of their own creative imaginations (or constricting racial self-definitions) and the prevailing racist expectations in the market, and exploit it for gain without ever paying any social, political, or monetary tribute to the source. Blacks had almost no input into the process, either in reaction to the cultural expropriation or through recognized independent innovation. But that state of one-sided simplicity would only grow more multilateral and complex over time. While the archetypes that made their debut in antebellum America are still with us, they have slipped the social and economic shackles that initially defined them, giving rise to complex variations barely recognizable in the original themes.

American popular music begins with songs in the "blackface style" in the early 1800s. One of the earliest was inspired by a successful (for the Americans) War of 1812 naval battle against the British in upstate New York. In his biography of the seminal American songwriter Stephen Foster, Ken Emerson writes that "the War of 1812 inspired not only our national anthem but the first American song of note in blackface dialect. Indeed, the two songs were synchronized so closely that it's almost as if blackface were inseparable from our national identity."[10] "Backside Albany" commemorates the Battle of Plattsburgh, which took place around Lake Champlain in 1814 just days before the bombardment of Fort McHenry in Baltimore harbor inspired the poem "The Star-Spangled Banner." Not by coincidence, Emerson notes, while the Francis Scott Key poem was set to a traditional English melody and written in standard Anglo-American English, "Backside Albany" was put to an Irish melody and written in a dialect imagined to come out of the mouth of one of many black sailors who actually fought in the war. The comical account of the battle remained popular for more than thirty-five years. The song's author, a New York City innkeeper named Micah Hawkins, went on to write "Massa Georgee Washington and General LaFayette" in the appropriated voice of a black Revolutionary War soldier. It was performed on New York stages, and its original sheet music bore the face of a white actor in blackface makeup, an illustration that looked more like "a European nutcracker . . . than an American racial caricature," Emerson says.

> [I]t fell to George Washington Dixon to take blackface several crucial steps further. In 1829 if not earlier, Dixon, a Virginian by birth, performed "Coal Black Rose," in New York City. The song's very first lines announce the arrival of full-blown blackface: "Lubly Rosa, Sambo cum, / Don't you hear de Banjo, tum, tum, tum. . . ."
> A travesty of a troubadour, Sambo came a-courtin', serenading the beauteous Rosa . . . promising her "possum fat and hominey, and

some rice, / Cow heel and sugar and ebery ting nice." Sambo, the banjo, the phonetic spelling, and the vagrant consonants became stocks-in-trade of the "Ethiopian delineators," as the blackface entertainers who followed Dixon were initially called.[11]

Dixon went on to create and popularize in performance more blackface standards, like "Zip Coon," which introduced the character of the "uppity" black buffoon who dared to ape the manner and dress of his white superiors. "[A] lithograph illustrating an early edition of the sheet music immortalized a blackface Beau Brummel, twirling a lorgnette on one extended finger, his other hand pulling aside his long-tail blue [coat] to expose watch fobs and a key that dangle[d] from his waist like an extra cock and balls."[12]

In addition to its enduring incarnation as "Turkey in the Straw," "Zip Coon," or at least its nonsensical chorus—"O zip a duden duden duden zip a duden day"—also survives in "Zip-A-Dee-Doo-Dah," from the soundtrack for *Song of the South*, Walt Disney's animated version of Joel Chandler Harris's "Uncle Remus" tales. This is but one of many echoes of blackface in Disney. Mickey Mouse himself, who first appeared in the aptly titled *Steamboat Willie*, was a cartoon of a cartoon, his black skin, exaggerated facial features, white gloves, and big feet an updated Ethiopian delineation.[13]

In *Doo-Dah: Stephen Foster and the Rise of American Popular Culture*, Emerson offers considerable evidence that Foster's most important compositions represent some of the seminal acts of miscegenation from which American popular entertainment was born. Foster directly influenced a long chain of innovators, mostly non-WASPs, from the self-styled "Father of the Blues" W. C. Handy to Irving Berlin to George Gershwin and Duke Ellington. A handful of Foster songs, like "Old Folks at Home," "Oh! Susanna," "De Camptown Races," and "Dixie," are not just standards of the American canon; they are, in whole but especially in their parts, a good measure of the essential musical DNA that these composers used to form the quintessentially American music of the twentieth century As a child, Al Jolson sang the Stephen Foster catalog in the streets for spare change. Jolson reached the height of his stardom in blackface, in the title role of *The Jazz Singer*, the film that introduced the world to movies with sound. Berlin's "Alexander's Ragtime Band," the first modern megahit, musically quoted both "Old Folks at Home" and "Dixie" while mentioning the "Swanee River" by name. Berlin, a turn-of-the-century Russian-Jewish immigrant, kept on his office wall a portrait of Foster, a WASP of an antebellum era when even Irish immigrants weren't entirely seen as white. Emerson says it might have been from gratitude, as "Foster blazed the trail that eventually led to Tin Pan Alley."

The trail from Foster to modern popular, mass-market entertainment connects much more than musical forms. Foster is the original "white boy" who finds his distinct voice, and stardom, only after channeling the apparent forms and styles of African-Americans through the filter of his own conflicted experience of blacks and their distinct cultural contributions. At the start his relationship with blacks was fairly simple. Africans in America were mostly enslaved and socially marginalized, but their very presence in great numbers was the only thing that distinguished the emerging identity of Euro-Americans from their predominantly English forebears. Indeed, until it began incorporating into its identity a distorted reflection of the African and Native American presence, American culture remained far beneath Europe's notice. In *Doo-Dah* Emerson reminds us that just before blackface gained wild popularity in the 1830s:

> "In the four quarters of the globe" a British critic had sniffed . . . "who reads an American book? or goes to an American play?" It would be a while before American literature enjoyed an international audience, longer still before American theater and sculpture achieved global renown, but by 1836 the world was pricking up its ears to American popular music. It was in this year that the United States began trafficking in its most successful cultural export before the movies. Thomas Dartmouth "Daddy" Rice wheeled about and "jumped Jim Crow" in two English theaters nightly, bowling over Britain and creating such a stir with his grotesque gyrations—120 years before Elvis—that the celebrated Shakespearean actor William Charles Macready cut short his London engagement.[14]

The first book, it should be noted, that defined the American experience in a way that gripped the world as well as the young nation would be *Uncle Tom's Cabin,* some twenty years after the British critic's conclusions were published. Whatever is distinctly American yet somehow universally appealing in our most immortal works of popular culture flows from the alchemy of racial amalgamation peculiar to the United States. Whenever whites of any provenance have gone looking for collective archetypes that reflect their American experience, they inevitably begin by selectively eliding more and more of their specific European cultural inheritance, then escaping cultural whiteness altogether. That's how pop cultural *Americanness*—from the frontiersman to the cowboy buckaroo (a word whose orgins are in *vaquero,* the word Mexicans coined for "cowboy") to the hipsters of the Jazz Age and beyond—was born and raised. The discovery of the American pop culture archetypes—now simply "icons"—in the tropes of the ultimate outsiders provided meaning for the people of the young nation that purely white mythologies (really Anglo-white mythologies) like that of the gentleman farmer (Thomas Jefferson), genius tinkerer (Thomas Edison), or self-made *legitimate* business tycoon could not. There was an aspect of the imagination of American identity that they just didn't capture for the people in the bars where Micah Hawkins's early blackface songs were sung. Oh, one could aspire to becoming a president or a land baron while working in grinding industrial poverty or rural isolation. But there was no release from hopelessness, no respite from economic pressure or social insecurity, in putting on Thomas Jefferson or J. P. Morgan in your few leisure hours, and very little appreciation from your peers. No, cultural Americanness is about getting together with that old gang of yours and putting on the slaves while quietly aspiring to be the masters, especially the rebellious, creative slaves who have what it takes to outdo or overturn the master. It's the unmistakably American dream of making it to the top of the ladder while still seeing yourself as one of the guys or girls from the block or the rural front porch you came from, preferably one with the hippest of them. That's how far back, and how deep, the fusion between nonwhiteness and popular cultural Americanness goes.

It wasn't hard to slip through the porous, poorly guarded borders of American *cultural whiteness.* For the majority of Americans, it was easier, and far more exciting, to assume the reflection of a nonwhite persona and imagine themselves successful, as long as their grip on the priviliges of *political white-ness*, while loosened for a moment in a carefully guarded place, was still firm. The nineteenth-century white producers of popular culture instinctively disguised their creative flights from whiteness with conventions that simultaneously reinforced the audience's sense of white supremacy. The escape from Europeanness, and from the femininity of its formal culture, has also been incorporated in American identity by the embrace of the frontier-savage mythology. Davy Crockett, a Foster contemporary who was already passing into legend even before dying at the Alamo in 1836, came down to baby boomers as the grizzly bear wrestling, "blood brother to the wild Indian," and "King of the Wild Frontier."[15] But historically the African-American has provided the most natural and heavily traveled route out of whiteness and into true Americanness, not by accident of history or of physical proximity but by design, because whiteness, in all its oppressive spiritual, sexual, and political constrictions, was constructed to be the antithesis of blackness. But the American culture could not easily reach that necessary place of meaning without somehow acknowledging the unavoidable political contradictions it was building into the road—even if only, in the convention that began most famously with Foster, by combining slavish mimicry with racist disparagement of the mimicked. Emerson says the contradiction was vital to no less a purpose than national unity.

> Why did blackface take off so dramatically in the 1830's? For starters, blackface was clearly an expression of nationalism. It may appear paradoxical that patriotism and blackface would be so closely linked. "Daddy" Rice in burnt cork and rags would seem a source of national shame rather than pride. On the other hand, a shared feeling of superiority to blacks was one of the few things that united a nation of immigrants, many of them more recent arrivals than the African-Americans they mocked. By the late 1830's, for example, more than half of Pittsburgh's population had been born abroad. Blackface helped immigrants acculturate and assimilate by inculcating a common racism.[16]

In other words, popular culture transmitted the kernel of white American identity through racist put-ons of a semifictional black persona. But as would be more apparent (though not necessarily better understood) by the Jazz Age, what white America would put on for its convenient amusement, over generations and under increasing pressure of commercialization, would eventually begin to fit like a second skin.

❐　　❐　　❐

Stephen Foster was born near Pittsburgh on July 4, 1826, the day the slave-holding Thomas Jefferson and Jefferson's antagonist, the proto-abolitionist John Adams, died. Foster's family were not southerners or slaveholders like Jefferson, but they were staunch supporters of his Democratic-Republican Party, as it was on its way to becoming the political home of the Anglo-American South in the decades leading up to the Civil War. Blackface was cultivated and nurtured into bloom in the Northeast and Ohio River Valley by writers and entertainers who knew little of the slave South, for consumption by socially and economically insecure white audiences at a time of industrial upheaval. The only thing the immigrant masses of the North, America's first mass audience, feared more than competition with free blacks before the Civil War was competition with the masters of enslaved blacks. In fact, but especially in the imagination of the Irish or Norwegian immigrant in New York or Philadelphia dreaming of farming a little land on the praire, there was no competing with vast plantations full of slaves in the opening territories of the West. Blackface performances, putting on the black man to put him down, provided a release from racial tensions and sometimes something more. Some blackface lyrics and traditions, by capturing a reflection of the slave's plight, generated a sympathetic resonance and distant identification in white consumers. Foster's family, writes Emerson, was not immune:

> They'd never met a "massa," but more and more of them had a boss. If they couldn't be whipped, they could be broken on the wheel of the economic cycle. Their families could not be divided and sold, but the panic of 1837 devastated households. It certainly scarred the Fosters. It was during the 1830s and 1840s that the terms "white slavery" and "slavery of wages" entered American discourse.[17]

Foster's father, William, a less-than-successful political opportunist and mediocre businessman, lost the family estate not long after Stephen, his last child, was born. Stephen Foster would spend most of his life moving between temporary homes, living with various combinations of family and friends. Foster, like his family and most whites in the border state of Pennsylvania, was lukewarm on the issue of slavery. White Pennsylvanians didn't condone slavery, but they would never be confused with abolitionists. Yet from the start Foster's earliest blackface songs were marked by a more musically respectful and, compared with the average for the genre at the time, relatively sentimental evocation of enslaved African-Americans. Consider the lyrics of "Old Uncle Ned," one of Foster's first hits:

> Dere was an old Nigga, dey call'd him Uncle Ned
> He's dead long ago, long ago
> He had no wool on de top ob his head
> De place whar de wool ought to grow.
> Den lay down de shubble and de hoe
> Hang up de fiddle and de bow
> No more hard work for poor uncle Ned
> He's gone whar de good Niggas go.[18]

No less an abolitionist icon than Frederick Douglass approved of "Old Uncle Ned" as the kind of blackface song that "can make the heart sad as well as merry, and can call forth a tear as well as a smile . . . [and] awaken the sympathies for the slave, in which anti-slavery principles take root and flourish."[19]

Black folks, as Emerson points out, tended to die at an alarming rate in Foster's most famous and commercially successful songs. Take this forgotten second verse of "Oh! Susanna":

> I jump'd aboard the telegraph
> And trabbled down de ribber,
> De lectrick fluid magnified,
> And kill'd 500 Nigga

Emerson suggests these lines may be a frustrated wish that blacks would just vanish, taking the problem of slavery and the insecurity of white American identity with them. At that time even many abolitionists, Abe Lincoln among them, supported the idea of returning blacks to Africa. Whatever it meant to

Foster's conflicted racial feelings, I think Foster's lyrical body count also pre-figures the commercial usefulness of African-American cultural themes as a vehicle for delivering the sensationalism of violence and death to mass audiences. Consciously or not, Foster discovered a mass audience demand for stylized and sometimes stark violence. It would season the base broth of popular music from the knifings and stabbings of Bessie Smith–era blues to the more potent, gun-soaked mayhem in the gangsta rap of the 1990s.

Throughout his career Foster had tried hard to score with compositions outside the blackface dialect and genre. While he had some creative successes, like the classic "Jeanie with the Light Brown Hair," the fact was that his blackface songs earned ten times the royalties that songs in standard English did. Nevertheless, one result of Foster's divided loyalty was a merger between "Jeanie's" universal sentimentality and key elements of the blackface aesthetic in Foster's most enduring works. Take "Old Folks at Home," perhaps his most famous composition, for example. Haunted to the end by the feeling of being exiled from the bosom of his childhood domestic bliss by his hapless father's failures, Foster broke new ground by inhabiting a blackface song with nostalgia and a personal sense of loss.

> It's as if Foster's pencil were teetering on the brink between black-face and a deeper identification with African Americans, an identification at once more personal and more universal. He had tried in earlier songs to cross the great divide between blackface and parlor ballad, black and white, them and us. Now he was inching closer than ever before.[20]

An instant hit, Emerson writes, "Old Folks at Home" was sung everywhere, by everyone, from slaves in Georgia to immigrant street gangs in lower Manhattan, where it was also heard in saloons and other venues that were the forerunners of New York's musical theater. At Foster's death, in the middle of the Civil War, the American "old folks" united in popular song were bitterly riven politically, North from South, immigrant from native, and black from white. Nevertheless, Foster's compositions had established the basic formula for a crude but powerful cultural glue, a sense of Americanness, that would be continuously refined and enriched by the further contributions of non–Anglo-Saxon Protestant Americans into the binding element of modern American popular culture. The formula's equation is a function of the language of African-American suffering and striving as it rushes to fill the vacuum of whiteness removed from Europeanness, raised to the power of African rhythms (perhaps the one element Foster's contribution lacked).

Never secure, financially or emotionally, even at the height of his success, Foster died a lonely and near penniless drunk in New York City in January 1864 at age thirty-seven. In his last summer he witnessed New York's draft riots of 1863, the worst in American history, when Irish immigrants, the core of the mass audience for the blackface culture he pioneered, vented their wrath on civil authority and especially on New York's black community. The role of New York City as the red-hot forge of American pop culture cannot be overstressed. Mass popular culture began with the music publishing industry, which has been based in Manhattan since Foster's time. It was from New York's swirling tide of immigrants and migrants—from Reconstruction through the Roaring Twenties—that the mass-market products of popular entertainment and style that are uniquely American first emerged. Well after the birth of mass media, New York remained the nearly unchallenged leader in the production of commercial popular culture, much of it mined and refined from the great mélange of human raw material on its teeming sidewalks. Indeed (as will be discussed later), New York's only competition in this regard, Hollywood, can be seen as a mere extension of the city, since Hollywood was founded by Jewish immigrants who first made it big in New York's movie theater business. New York, argues documentary filmmaker Ric Burns, unlike any other city in the world, was born to market the product of people rubbing against people, especially people of different races, ethnicities, and origins. Not more than a decade after Foster's death, Burns's documentary history of New York notes, the interplay between European immigrants and African-Americans, on almost the exact same streets that originate rap and hip-hop culture today, struck Walt Whitman with a prescient vision of the emerging American cultural identity: "Watching African-Americans and Irish immigrants dancing and mimicking and parodying each other in minstrel shows along the Bowery, Walt Whitman predicted it would one day give rise to a native grand opera, in America."[21]

❑   ❑   ❑

If American popular culture can be compared to a computer software program, then by World War I blackness (and later, to a lesser extent, Hispanic and Asianness) can be seen as what computer programmers call the back door code. Nonwhiteness is the inside route to understanding the direct instructions to the computer's brain, the commands that make the lights flash, the bells chime, and the whistles blow, even if all the characters doing the blowing, flashing, and chiming are white. The contributions of African-America to music are the best documented and most often cited examples of the integral role of color in American mass culture. But the black source code goes far deeper than the melodies, harmonies, and even the rhythms. It's more than the music; it's the meaning.

When you decrypt Irving Berlin's immortal "Alexander's Ragtime Band," for example, using this blackness-in-whiteness key, you learn that the song was an extension of a tradition that Berlin biographer Laurence Bergreen calls an "Alexander song":

> The Alexander song . . . taps into a very tragic, sad part of our nation's racial history because an Alexander song was a type of song that was meant to refer to black vaudeville often in a disparaging way. Alexander was thought to be a comically grand name for a black vaudeville actor to take.[22]

In other words, it was a deep echo of Dixon's 1830s "Zip Coon" songs. Berlin plugged into the text and subtext of minstrelsy, and its essential relationship to Americanness, to animate the first true superhit of the modern pop music age. And he figured out the code just eighteen years after setting foot on these shores from czarist Russia. He sharpened his ear while working as a singing waiter at a Chinatown restaurant called Nigger Mike's, where he "sang with equal facility as an Italian, an Irishman, a German, a Jew, or, as the saloon's title promised, a nigger," writes cultural historian Ann Douglas in her history of New York in the 1920s, *Terrible Honesty*.[23] The virus that incubated in Stephen Foster had, barely a generation after his death, implanted its instructions in the brain of American identity.

By the turn of the twentieth century, the cycle of racist appropriation and exploitation that marked the commercial growth of this miscegenated culture had grown more complex, due to the participation not only of nominally free blacks in creating it, but of new waves of immigrants from southern and eastern Europe. Slowly but surely African-American creators were able to accommodate the distorted images of their identities in the marketplace, incorporate more European-derived forms, and, using the opportunities commercial minstrelsy created, innovate and improvise their way to periodic positions of leadership, if not of control. Ragtime music, for example, began in the late 1800s as the sole province of black pianists in the Midwest and Southwest—and only then made its way to New York's melting pot. There it was exploited by the sheet music industry, the burgeoning business known as Tin Pan Alley. Ragtime's acknowledged master innovator, Douglas reminds us, was the legendary black pianist and composer Scott Joplin.

> Ragtime inspired a rash of schools pledged to teach anyone to play it . . . but many amateurs found it beyond their skills; although they bought the sheet music in droves—in 1904 Joplin's "Maple Leaf Rag" was the first piece of sheet music to sell more than a million copies—they preferred to buy player pianos . . . so that they could listen to ragtime played by genuine [black] masters—Joplin, Eubie Blake, James P. Johnson.[24]

Joplin, like Stephen Foster, also died sick and nearly penniless in New York, in 1917. Nevertheless, with every period of success, African-American innovators incrementally advanced a long, labored campaign to move the terms of trade for their contributions into their favor. America's transracial culture gained in intricacy as a function of America's rapidly growing complexity. The arrival of a wider variety of immigrants to New York, including migrants from Latin America, greatly increased the possibilities and permutations of interaction among peoples and cultures. Every new technology and refinement further loosened the grip of antebellum social conventions and eventually even post-Reconstruction taboos against race mixing in popular culture. Every halting political advance by blacks, mostly as individuals before World War II, pushed the envelope a bit further.

❑　　　❑　　　❑

There is an undeniable link among, say, a white minstrel comedian in blackface making white audiences laugh with a joke putting down black skin color in 1890; Frank Sinatra and the Rat Pack on stage with Sammy Davis Jr. making "colored" jokes at Davis's grinning expense in 1959; and black comedian Damon Wayans baiting a skinny, ebony-skinned foil with "Anybody ever tell you that you look like a struck match?" in the mainstream action-comedy movie *Bulletproof* in 1996.[25] The link is the most enduring aspect of American identity itself. We are racist, but built on race mixing. We deny the "other's" humanity even as we overtly and covertly lust and often mate across racial and ethnic lines. Then we still go on, through various strains of racial and ethnic self-hatred, or white self-abnegation, to live in a schizophrenic, dysfunctional relationship with our own mongrelized identities. Unlike any other nationality, tribe, or ethnicity in the world, Americans are people who look in the mirror of identity and, confounded by the truth, make up their own reflections in an effort to reconcile their social contradictions. The result is the essential root of uniquely American dramatic literature. Most American comedy, for example, is patterned after the self-deprecating, self-pitying, insult-laden humor of black and Jewish Americans. The reason, I think, is that blacks and Jews have been most keenly aware of the ironic, the tragic, and the just plain ridiculous contradictions that are nevertheless integral to their experience of being American.

When Wayans compared a man of my own coloring to a skinny cinder, I cracked up instantly, without bothering to process the political incorrectness of the joke. I was not inhibited by the latent, painful memory of being put down by black and white kids with very similar cracks when I was in grade school. I imagine that many white people of good will who ought to know better laughed hard, too, because the film grossed a respectable $22 million in its first seven weeks without a massive ad campaign in a traditionally slow period for new relases. My only explanation, in our defense, is that that was then and this is now. Americans' well-known historical amnesia perhaps has a perversely benign side effect: optimism. We tend not to let the imperfections of even the recent past interrupt our faith in the possibilities for the future, which is where we really live. Even in 1980 no one could imagine hearing young white people casually calling each other "nigger" as a term of endearment, but that was then; today many nonblack hip-hop-influenced youth do it without thinking. That fashion, as it fits in today's culture, would have been as unfathomable and impossible in the 1890s as gay liberation.

Sammy Davis Jr. grinned and took the Rat Pack putdowns even as he was opening up, under Sinatra's protection, nightclub stages where blacks had never set foot. That was then. He grinned and sacrificed so that Damon Wayans could now take black putdown jokes into the mainstream on Wayans's own terms, for the kind of paycheck that even the legendary Davis could only have dreamed about. Wayans today is just like Sinatra or Dean Martin doing "wop" jokes in the 1960s, when they were Italian-American pop superstars, confidently installed in the American mainstream. Only Wayans, of course, is still politically black, while Sinatra and Martin were fully white by then.

For that reason, politically, it would *still* be very difficult, but by no means impossible, for a white character to deliver that Wayans zinger today. Black-face itself has been disowned by America for at least sixty years. But Wayans can do it, perhaps to the horror of black entertainers just a half generation his elder, because he is an African-American pop star who couldn't have existed as recently as 1980. The part of the old cycle of transracial American culture in which the nonwhite originator is pushed to the sidelines in favor of the white emulator (à la Pat Boone "covering" Little Richard or the crowning of Elvis Presley as the "king" of rock and roll in the 1950s) and the identification with nonwhite communities is suppressed or severed, has been permanently broken. As black filmmaker Reginald Hudlin is fond of pointing out, hip-hop with a mostly black face has been a growing force in popular culture for nearly twenty years, "and there still is no Elvis." Even as a handful of white rappers gained stardom at the end of the 1990s, they remain circumspect with respect to their place in what is now a commercially mainstream genre (i.e., the majority of its buyers are white), almost to the point of self-parody. Interestingly, wrote music critic Jody Rosen, much of their deference is self-imposed in self-defense.

> At its core, rap authenticity is based on a commitment to giving musical and poetic expression to urban African-American experience, to reflecting the changing slang, styles and values of black youth. White rappers have naturally had a difficult time finding a voice. . . . The infamous Vanilla Ice brought hip-hop to an all-time low with his flimsy rhymes, imaginary criminal record and prepos-

terous pants. In the post–Vanilla Ice era, white rappers' most potent strategy has been defensive: to avoid being the butt of others' jokes, they have embraced irony, accentuating the artifice of, and maintaining a winking distance from, their rap personas.

The discomfort of white rappers about their place in hip-hop stands in marked contrast to the cavalier attitude of an earlier generation of white musicians toward black music. It is doubtless a sign of social progress that white rappers feel conflicted about the propriety of cultural piracy.[26]

Indeed, as Rosen writes, "The notion of a white rapper is no more inherently foolish than a bunch of middle-class Englishmen singing the blues," as they have for two generations. But the legacy of race in America that includes blackface and minstrelsy complicates the issue for white rappers in a way that Elvis was not obliged to respect in his time. With deep irony Rosen's article is titled "Rapping in Whiteface (for Laughs)." To be sure, there are now (and will be more) white rap acts comfortable enough in their transracial skin to take themselves seriously and to be believed as such by the market. But the bar for authentic participation in the American experience that generates hip-hop culture is much higher than it was, say, for a white jazz musician in the 1950s. The majority of the audience—the white majority—demands it. Where the old chain of white cultural appropriation has been broken, the role of whiteness in popular culture is fast being transformed. Unlike the nineteenth century, pop culture no longer needs an overlay of white supremacy to cover the tracks of shameless appropriation. Unlike the first three quarters of the twentieth century, with a few notable exceptions, a white face is no longer mandatory to make an artist, performer, or product "pop." The value in entertainment is inexorably shifting from what is "white" to what is deemed "real."

For the moment, black, Hispanic, and Asian-Americans have a certain edge as authentic signifiers for the real, but they can't afford to be complacent or ignore the fact that the implosion of whiteness puts black, Hispanic, and Asian-American cultural identity into play, too. A final, critical distinction between then and now is the way today's commercial culture has finally turned minstrelsy's underlying precept of white supremacy nearly inside out. Outside hard-core rap itself, there are too many white performers whose "blackening up" on stage is as reverent as the pope and as natural as their own skin. Think of Mick Hucknall, former lead singer of the British pop-soul group Simply Red. There's a video of young white pop star Britney Spears covering a Bille Holiday song *in a high school talent show* that would make your hair stand on end it's so good and true to the blues. At the same time, too many nonwhite artists are making commercial hay by enfolding so-called white and black pop culture in one talented embrace, in effect, having careers to which, as recently as 1980, only white performers could routinely aspire. Listen to reigning Broadway diva Audra McDonald sing a classic Harold Arlen composition, "Any Place I Hang My Hat Is Home," from the 1940s all-black musical *St. Louis Woman*. It's on McDonald's hot-selling 2000 CD *How Glory Goes*. In the liner notes, longtime former *New York Times* theater critic Frank Rich exclaims:

> If the American musical didn't already exist, it would have to be invented for Audra McDonald. The musical was dreamed up by artists eager to break free, to honor the old world cultural past and yet transcend it, to create a new form as varied and exciting and of-the-moment as their new melting-pot country. In McDonald, the form has found a singer whose voice, history . . . embody all its contradictory joys. She's a black woman who first captivated New York audiences by playing the once white Mrs. Snow in *Carousel*. . . . It would be foolish as well as impossible to predict what the full breadth of [her] career is meant to be.[27]

Rich has the melody right, but, as is usual in mainstream criticism, he's muffed some of the lyrics of context. American musicals were "dreamed up" as much by black artists in the 1890s who had recently broken chains of slavery and escaped the post-Reconstruction South as by melting-pot immigrants. As will be touched upon in the next chapter, these minstrelsy derived, ragtime-driven black musicals were squeezed off Broadway by works by new Americans of southern and eastern European descent like Al Jolson, Irving Berlin, and Fanny Brice during the 1910s, only to come roaring back with the 1920s. Only this time, they insisted on wearing tuxedos and tails.

It was in 1946 that Harold Arlen (dubbed "Brother Harold" in a black magazine appreciation piece because he understood the blues so well) wrote the music for *St. Louis Woman*. Johnny Mercer's lyrics are perfumed with the essence of the blackface dialect popularized by Stephen Foster, much refined by a kind of linguistic minimalism. Just enough final consonants are dropped to be true to the hybrid culture without disrespecting it. Listen to McDonald slide and glide over the sound of the miscegenated American soul:

> Free an' easy—that's my style . . .
> Sweetnin' water, cherry wine
> Thank you kindly, suits me fine . . .
> Birds roostin' in the tree
> Pick up an' go . . .
> There's a voice in the lonesome win' that keeps whisperin' roam!

McDonald combines the unmistakable sound of a black woman's voice with the perfect operatic (i.e., white) articulation and authority that Frank Rich says classical American music deserves. The original production of *St. Louis Woman* met with tepid reviews and ran only 113 performances. But that was then. Stephen Foster would scarcely have recognized himself, or any of his beloved, pathetic darkies in this great-great-grandchild of his. This is now, and the irony could not be more complete.

2

Color Under Cover from the Great War to the Cold War

A white music producer, working with a talented white singer, was having trouble with the way she was putting over a new song in rehearsal. The song, intended as a star vehicle for the singer's Broadway debut, was written in the latest, hippest black street expression and style, having been commissioned from a hot young black composer. It was the kind of song already being sung by black singers to great success, and the producer expected his new vocalist, as a white woman, to be able to take the song deeper into mainstream audiences that black performers couldn't reach. The problem was that his singer was insisting on sounding *too* black, dropping not just final consonants but final syllables from the verses, so words like *sure* and *more* came out of her mouth as *sho* and *mo*. The singer's insistence jeopardized the success of her Broadway debut, the producer feared, because white audiences wouldn't accept that kind of black sound coming out of her mouth.

The confrontation could have been playing out as recently as the 1970s, because even then there was still an important racial distinction about who was pop and who was not. A white singer, particularly a white female, who overshot the mark and came off sounding too black could end up like the phenomenal soprano diva Teena Marie, who after a spectacular debut found herself strangely locked out of the pop charts and top-forty radio airplay.

That you couldn't tell that Marie wasn't black until you saw her could not have been a coincidence.

The producer story might more likely date from the 1950s, when parents were thoroughly mortified by their teenagers' embrace of raw rhythm and blues and early black rock-and-roll shouters like Little Richard. The music industry frequently responded by turning out cleaned-up "covers" of black rock-and-roll songs, recorded by white artists, in which the driving rhythms were muted and the lyrics' slurring and slanging were cleaned up to acceptable white standards. No 1950s producer would let Doris Day sing something like:

> He can do some lovin' and some lovin' sho'
> An' when he starts to love me I jes hollers "Mo"!

For her part Day, who gave us "Sentimental Journey," would probably not have wanted to sing the song "Lovie Joe" as it was written. But to our producer's consternation, the legendary Fanny Brice did insist, in 1910, that she couldn't sing it any other way. The story is retold in *Terrible Honesty: Mongrel Manhattan in the 1920's,* Ann Douglas's authoritative account of the interplay of black and white artists in New York at the dawn of mass commercial popular culture.

> During rehearsals, the producer Abe Erlanger tried to get Brice to Anglicize the words of the song. . . . He wanted the Anglo-American "sure" and "more," but Brice insisted on singing "sho" and "mo." "I live . . . on the edge of Harlem," she explained. "They all talk that way. No Negro would pronounce these words the way you did. I can't sing them any other way."[1]

Brice's insistence on authenticity, says Douglas, was "prophetic." The future star of the famed *Ziegfeld Follies* realized that the idiom of the reviled Negroes, as put across by leading black entertainers and cultural innovators of the day, was "pav[ing] the way for the real black-and-white American vernacular in the 1920's." What's important here is that it is inconceivable that Abe Erlanger's complaint could have surfaced since the 1980s. The objective of nonblack performers and creators of much pop culture—from Britney Spears to Ricky Martin (when he isn't trying to sound Latino) to the Backstreet Boys to Christina Aguilera et al.—is to sound as close to the current standard of pop vocal style as possible, and that standard is usually set by black artists. Interestingly, little or no appetite seems to remain for distinctly "white" innovation in mainstream pop, no Elvis or Tony Bennett or Frank Sinatra who, while firmly grounded in the underlying African-American idioms, stands apart with a unique and unambiguously nonblack character to his or her performance persona. For the current and aspiring class of hot nonblack pop acts, the danger is that they will not sound black *enough* to withstand the critical scrutiny of a mass audience that knows the difference between feeling the culture's African-American essence and merely flavoring a performance with it. That's why, tellingly, a majority of today's top "white" pop acts are actually molded by black producers.

In a sense, though it's taken nearly a century, we have come full circle in the relationship of color to pop culture, back to Fanny Brice's naïve yet sage conviction that political whiteness should have no bearing on what she sang or how she sang it. But then again, what did Brice, or Irving Berlin, Eddie Cantor, Al Jolson, or any number of relatively new Americans of eastern and southern European extraction know about American whiteness? Their very presence at the portals of American cultural and social influence, as part of the unprecedented tide of immigrants from other-than-northern European countries, was itself posing a massive challenge to the nature of white identity. The first and second generation of these new immigrants arrived just in time to tint American identity at the dawn of mass market culture. In fact, it can be argued, in their effort to navigate and assimilate the cultures they found around them where they landed—primarily in New York—they created modern commercial pop culture. And as Douglas and other cultural historians have shown, the new Jewish, Italian, and other "swarthy" Europeans, who were not immediately accepted into prevailing standards of whiteness anyway, began their assimilation by first incorporating black musical and stylistic idioms to succeed where racism still barred African-American advancement. Only later did they worry about about their incorporation into whiteness.

The celebrated American immigrant stew first began bubbling in the rich broth produced as minstrelsy was melting into ragtime and the modern

Broadway show. Again, it is important to remember that commercial minstrelsy had its main roots not in the Deep South but in New York and, to a lesser extent, other East Coast port cities like Baltimore and Philadelphia. With relatively little formal segregation to separate the groups at the bottom of the social heap, the newest immigrants were almost forced into intimate cultural intercourse with urban blacks on the streets and to a lesser extent in the workplace. Thus, much like many of today's Asian and Hispanic newcomers, their first teachers of what it means to be American—from vernacular English to the informal, familiar, and secular manners of social congress we think of as typically American—were African-Americans. Blacks became primary reference points, if not actual role models, because in African-Americans the new immigrants saw the essence of what distinguished "native" white Americans—mainly WASPs of northern European descent and the more assimilated Irish Catholics among them—from the real Europeans they had left behind. Blacks were especially essential to the assimilation of American musical and theatrical culture.

This is not to say that the newcomers brought nothing of their own cultural identities to the melting pot. In most cases they brought a traditional appreciation for European classical music and often some formal training. More important for the music, the Jewish immigrants' liturgical music canons would find an amazing kinship with the emerging blues-gospel foundation of modern popular music. The complementary musical reflections of the only two groups of Americans with the experience of slavery at the core of their identities would reach its highest expression in the works of George Gershwin. To this day, in fact, partisan music scholars argue about whether the true source of some of the signature vamps in *Porgy and Bess* is the "field hollers" of the southern cotton patch or a particular Jewish tradition of chanting prayer.

> "Ragging," or syncopating, came easily to [Irving] Berlin, as to all
> Jewish composers, because Jewish music, with its Eastern and
> Mediterranean sources, its complex rhythms and preference for
> minor keys, had something in common with the African-American
> sound. Harold Arlen, who wrote "I've Got the World on a String"
> and "Stormy Weather," once played a Louis Armstrong record for
> his father, a Louisville cantor; after one riff, or "hot lick" as Arlen
> called it, his father asked, amazed, "Where did *he* get it??"[2]

I doubt the issue will ever be resolved in favor of one side or the other, because it cannot; nor should it be. The exercise is just another furtive but futile attempt to evade the truth of the transracial synthesis that shifted into a higher gear in the first two decades of the twentieth century. As eastern and southern Europeans merged into American whiteness, they brought not only their Mediterranean, Balkan, and Levantine genetic and cultural markers into the American identity genome. At the point of entry, they also brought some of the African-American cultural DNA they naïvely acquired while their new American identities were still being formed.

> Sophie Tucker, the earthy, tough-minded . . . Jewish singer who made it big in the early 1910s . . . was billed as the "Last of the Red-hot Mamas." . . . She had come with her family from Russia in 1887 at the age of three; [Irving] Berlin was an ally and a friend. A product of the Yiddish theater, Tucker moved effortlessly from her Yiddish numbers to slangy American songs like the bluesy "Some of These Days," her greatest hit, recorded in 1911. Significantly, when she crossed over from the Yiddish theater to English-speaking burlesque, she began as a blackface performer and coon shouter; the lyricist-composer of "Some of These Days" was the Negro songwriter Shelton Brooks. . . . Her career was proof that Jewish and Negro musical styles and influences could and often did flow seamlessly together.[3]

Ragtime grew out of the "coon songs" of the minstrel shows that were themselves the immediate forebears of the modern American musical. They were typically sung in blackface by both black and white performers. While black songwriters were among the most prominent creators of the songs, with titles like the smash hit "All Coons Look Alike to Me," white songwriters jumped into the business at the turn of the century, when the music became the rage. Ragtime relied on the African-American experience for more than the raw material that was shamelessly exploited in the typical "coon song" (e.g., "You May Be a Hawaiian on Old Broadway, But You're Just Another Nigger to Me"). Ragtime composers needed the colorfully direct, ragged-edged black vernacular English phrasing and syntax to dance with the syncopated rhythms that were displacing traditional waltz and march beats in popular music. The "Negro dialect," as Douglas calls it, of emerging popular music was to a large extent a commercial confection, drawn from but by no means the same as the language of postslavery African-Americans that some scholars call Black English. Ragtime English, if you will, was improvised by blackface performers—black and white—to meet the expectations of an expanding commercial audience while entertaining them. The incorporation of this language into popular culture during the first hot blush of ragtime, well after Reconstruction but almost twenty years before the Jazz Age had properly begun, has an interesting parallel with the browning of pop culture at the end of the twentieth century. Then as now, in the minds of the culture's consumers, what was undeniably black was unquestionably authentic.

First, in ragtime, even white guys had to do it in blackface—that is, they had to display the color of their art up front. Nobody tried to deny the black roots of the stuff, as they would by the late 1920s. The measure of a performer in the first decade of the twentieth century wasn't so much how effectively he could degrade the black man in his act but how faithfully he could appear to inhabit the black man's idiom. A century later we see a similarly unabashed putting on of unmistakably African-American tropes by nonblack performers, especially in the required usage of today's version of "Negro dialect" and the de rigueur "ghetto style" costuming and posing of teen pop stars. You almost have to look twice at some popular "boy bands," with their assortment of close-cropped heads and image-darkening facial hair, to be sure they're all white and non-Hispanic. As soon as a nonblack purveyor of today's pop culture, whether on stage or just on the bus or subway, turns his baseball cap backward, he strikes a pose of the the new blackface.

Second, the years between 1900 and 1920 marked the opening of a rare window through which white Americans could be seen in open rebellion against the quite recently prevailing standards of the WASP, Calvinist middle-class culture epitomized by the reign of Queen Victoria. Two generations of straitlaced Victorian morality, and what Douglas identifies as a thoroughly feminized popular culture had produced a pent-up demand to bury the matriarch. Ragtime culture was the perfect tool for the task, and it was consciously wielded by cultural entrepreneurs like Irving Berlin. Though his roots were in the street patois of immigrant New York, he knew very well how to write a song like "God Bless America" in standard English. But that was in 1916, a few years after his first big mass market hits, when the socially ambitious Berlin probably saw a great opportunity for musical patriotism, as it was clear that the war raging in Europe would soon involve the United States. He had something else in mind when he wrote "Ain't you goin'?" to hear Alexander's Ragtime Band in 1911.

> Berlin had targeted "Alexander's Ragtime Band" for a wider mar-
> ket than his own ethnic group; he was writing for mainstream
> middle-class audiences who did not naturally talk in black and/or
> ethnic idioms but were apparently eager to begin. The moment the
> speakers of a special race or ethnic group aimed at . . . a trans-class,
> trans-race mass audience, an ethnic and/or racial dialect became
> [popular] slang. . . . Slang was deliberate disguise and pretense . . .
> art passionately interested in downward mobility as the source of
> new forms of elite expression.[4]

Today's rap and hip-hop culture, from its core Gen-X and Gen-Y market to its more diffuse hold on many baby boomers, has also served a sense of rebellion in the market. Openly displayed, the fetishes of hip-hop are a portable pledge of allegiance against both 1960s rock-and-roll liberalism and 1980s conservative culture-mongering. The broad success of the 1999–2000 Budweiser beer campaign, featuring four black men and some high-context male bonding around the catchphrase "Whassup?!," provides a good example of the contemporary value of commercial blackface as a liberating force. Even thirty-something white guys want to blacken up in public today, and they see little contradiction in doing it.

"I knew we were in trouble with its popularity," says hip-hop entrepreneur and record producer Bill Stephney, who is black, "when I was going up the escalator at a [New York] Knicks [professional basketball] game, and these four white stockbroker types in suits are behind me going 'Whassuup, whassuup, whassuup!' I'm like 'Oh no, Chuck [filmmaker Charles Stone III, who created the commercials] has started a revolution.'"

Finally, in the first decade of the twentieth century, the open rejection of whiteness, up to a point, was at or near the cutting edge of making money in the new "information economy" of the day. It marked the very first opening of a period during which African-Americans would clearly dominate the sales of popular music, even the before the recording industry had properly been born. It was the first time they were in a position to be in on the ground floor of a commercial pop culture trend. Pianos were the dominant hardware; sheet music and piano rolls were the software.

Ragtime created unprecedented opportunities for black creators and performers to capitalize on the appeal of their work in the marketplace. While it might be a stretch to say that Joplin was the Sean "Puffy" Combs of his day, he was acknowledged as the master of the most popular musical form of his age in his own (tragically short) productive lifetime and, to an extent, was remunerated as such. This was a revolutionary advance for black cultural entrepreneurs (even though it would soon be partially reversed).

Ragtime didn't create a host of young millionaires, as hip-hop and rap have done in a remarkably short period of time. But it did create an entirely new class of African-American entrepreneur: the entertainment professional. The bulk of the black population was still in the South, bound in semifeudalism, just a generation and a half out of slavery. Ragtime gave the slow but steady stream of African-American would-be artists moving north and into cities something to sell to whites besides menial and semiskilled labor. But while today hip-hop provides continuing expansion of commercial opportunities for nonwhite cultural entrepreneurs, ragtime's black exponents found their aspirations to greater acceptance by the white mainstream unfulfilled. Today it seems the only limit on the frequency or extent to which a nonwhite cultural lick can be quickly popularized and then taken to the bank is the imagination of the creator or marketer (or increasingly the lack thereof). The Baha Men didn't have to be Scott Joplin or even "Puffy" Combs to come up with the "Who Let the Dogs Out" anthem of a moment in the summer of 2000. And race was no barrier to attaching it to a succession of baseball teams through the playoffs and into the World Series. All it required was the kind of transracial marketing environment that was unimaginable in 1908, forty years before baseball broke its own color line.[5]

By 1912, according to Douglas, people had started calling Irving Berlin the "Ragtime King," not without good reason. It began a pattern that would persist at least until the 1980s. African-Americans or other minorities would innovate and for a time capitalize on a commercial pop trend, only to have it "covered" by more acceptable, more marketable white (or whiter) creators and performers; often a new name would be attached to the product to signify its whiteness. So for example in 1917, as ragtime gave way to jazz, some white New Orleans musicians soon to be well known as the "Original Dixieland Jazz Band" arrived in New York playing their own version of the musical brew that nurtured Louis Armstrong. Jazz, of course, had been played by blacks and a few whites in New Orleans since the turn of the century. But until the ODJB hit New York, writes Laurence Bergreen in his biography of Armstrong, "it hadn't occurred to anyone that jazz could make much money."[6]

> On March 25, 1918 . . . they waxed a tight, furious recording of "Tiger Rag," that instantly took the country by storm. . . . Releasing one hit song after another, the band ignited a craze for jazz and incited college boys everywhere to take up the coronet and form jazz combos. The fact that they were white smoothed the way for the widespread acceptance of their style of music. The commercial success quickly spawned scores of other white jazz bands. . . . Jimmy Durante, a musician before he became a comedian, concocted a so-called "New Orleans Jazz Band" in Harlem, a white man bringing black music to a white neighborhood that would soon become a black one. This type of cross-cultural exchange became part of the uproarious era that F. Scott Fitzgerald christened "the Jazz Age."[7]

Again, it's no coincidence that the young Durante, like the more prominent members of the ODJB, was a so-called white ethnic of recent immigrant provenance. They were perfect conduits for infusing color into the WASP mainstream of the day. As these "almost white" interpreters of black-based cultural forms rose in the 1910s, African-Americans were sidelined for a time from the pop culture spotlight. Most notably, black shows almost disappeared from Broadway. The rise of the pivotal blackface performer Al Jolson in the 1910s, writes Douglas,

> coincided with the so-called years of exile for black musical theater, when an all-white Broadway made possible the success of white blackface performers like Jolson, Eddie Cantor. . . . Inevitably, the

return of the black musical to Broadway . . . spelled the decline of white blackface.[8]

The black return to Broadway was marked by the opening of *Shuffle Along*, a musical review by Eubie Blake and Noble Sissle. It was significant not only for being on Broadway but for reviving and reinventing the black-face minstrelsy idioms and ragtime music; its black creators seemed bound by few cares about the sensitivities of the recent past, white or black. In its inspired outrageousness, *Shuffle Along*'s creative and commercial impact on Broadway in 1922 was strikingly similar to the impact of the television show *In Living Color* on television comedy in 1990. From the sexually provocative choreography of the hottest new black dances to the renovation of stereotyped caricatures to the over-the-top (for the day) mockery of any and every prevailing social convention they could get away with, both *In Living Color* and *Shuffle Along* served notice that, among other things, African-American creators were ready and able to "outblack" white usurpers to compete in the pop culture marketplace, without necessarily pandering to what whites found acceptable or even funny. The difference, of course, is that the milieu that Sissle and Blake created on stage held out no presumption that blacks were now competing as cultural equals with whites, much less as social or political equals. Even on Broadway blacks coming to see *Shuffle* were segregated in the balcony seats. Nevertheless, *Shuffle* and subsequent Sissle and Blake shows in the next decade established a beachhead from which black artists would capture new pop culture ground and market share by freely claiming and/or reclaiming all the cultural inheritances available to them as Americans. Sissle and Blake, Douglas writes,

> like their white slangster peers, had open to them a linguistic and musical range that went from high white to low-down black, and a power of choice in selecting from it that their predecessors had not had: they had the chance to produce an exuberantly and self-consciously mongrel art, to do, in other words, what no non-American could hope to do.[9]

And like *In Living Color* (at least at the beginning of its run), the phenomenal success of Sissle and Blake's work with the broader audiences, in what we now call "crossover," was hailed as a milestone in the realization of a truly American, albeit New York–American, culture. As Douglas cites a critic from the *New York Herald Tribune* in 1924:

> Let it be said that it was an American Negro revue which first started . . . New Yorkers going to the same show a dozen times or more. After all, in this cosmopolitan city, and this heterogeneous nation, what can be more to the taste of New Yorkers than the productions such as the American Negro, with all his versatility and innate music, can present.[10]

Following World War I, the market for African-American expression was irrevocably and profoundly transformed by the opening of Europe as an outlet. In fact, though few observers recognized it at the time, jazz, along with its related fashion and lifestyle accessories, was the first American cultural export to go over big in world markets, preceding the film industry. America's most reviled group succeeded in opening up the Euro-fatherland, which had been mostly closed to its child's cultural products for more than a hundred years, to the first fruits of American popular culture. While this development was entirely lost on provincial mainstream American awareness, it was a commercial, political, and psychic watershed for black cultural entrepreneurs, if not all African-Americans who could read of the unimaginably favorable receptions that members of their own race were getting from the rest of the "white" world. It must have been like waking up to discover that the world was not flat but round. Now there was an alternative, a commercial, political, and psychic option. And that option had come into being because Europeans saw blacks as the culturally essential Americans, even if domestic whites couldn't.

The First World War dramatically increased black American exposure to Europe, especially to France, and vice versa. Afterward African-American bands, Broadway-type shows, and then individual performers were in many ways more widely welcomed abroad than at home. Josephine Baker's barebreasted *danse sauvage* in Paris sparked a Europe-wide craze for all things "Josephine" (one of the first performers recognizable by just one name) in 1925, including dolls and even the products she used to slick back her hair in the style that would become emblematic of Roaring Twenties fashion. "The white imagination is sure something when it comes to blacks," Baker has been widely quoted as saying in reaction to all the attention she received. But even Baker failed to appreciate that the object of their imagination was as much her Americanness as her blackness, which were, of course, inseparable. Europeans, after all, had known black Africans and Afro-Caribbeans for generations through colonial relationships—but they weren't trying to do their hair like black Congolese or Jamaicans.

◘   ◘   ◘

It's hard to understate the role of new technologies in the browning of popular culture in the 1920s. Phonograph records, as they became standardized on the 78 rpm format, enabled the work of African-American musicians to reach worldwide audiences, as Duke Ellington pointed out, far in advance of appearances by the artists themselves. More important, in the domestic market, where formal and informal segregation severely limited social interaction between the races, the widespread ownership of phonograph records allowed whites to freely choose from an expanding array of black musical voices and bring them into their living rooms. The young recording industry was booming in 1923, when Louis Armstrong made his first records, and the music driving the sales of both phonographs and disks was jazz and the blues.

> At the time Louis [Armstrong] entered the studio, there were as many as two hundred recording companies generating annual sales of over one hundred million dollars, and *Variety* had recently begun to chart bestselling records. Victor, especially, reaped vast profits from its recordings of jazz performed by both black and white bands.... The popularity of jazz on disc caught everyone by surprise. Intended primarily for black listeners, jazz recordings instantly appealed to whites, as well, and "race records" quickly became desirable commodities, even collectors' items. For this reason, *record companies were avid to record black talent wherever they could find it and market it to everyone.*[11]

In short, the arrival of modern phonograph technology, at the dawn of mass culture, both enabled and compelled the record industry to become an engine pushing the browning of American pop culture. In the great many neighborhoods that blacks simply couldn't enter, except perhaps by the back door as servants, jazzmen like Louis Armstrong and Joe "King" Oliver could come in the front door under the arm of a white homeowner hot to hear the latest sounds. Blues music, largely relegated to the fringes of commercial pop culture since its beginnings in the post–Civil War South, exploded with the 1920 recording of "Crazy Blues" by singer Mamie Smith.[12] It sold one million copies in just seven months, and though its consumers were mostly black and working class, it validated a vast and profitable African-American market for what would be called "race records." "Crazy Blues" in fact saved Okeh Records, a division of Columbia, from bankruptcy. Afterward "the music industry . . . discovered the Negro as artist and consumer and held on for dear life," according to Douglas. The success also inspired a rush of commercial "blues" of suspect authenticity by white singers and composers. Interestingly, unlike jazz, the long isolation of the blues made it seem too black—that is, too independent of Euro-American cultural experience—to gain a popular white following. Jazz was born a miscegenated, transracial music; blues has always been a separate, pure black vein that is mined and then alloyed with Euro-American additives to enter the mainstream.

> As the blues rooted in the northern cities, their rural and folk nature was altered, refined, whitened. The songs were written down; the lyrics were cleaned up and elaborated, and the music was . . . jazzed and ragged, more often Europeanized into conventional harmonies and turned into Tin Pan Alley Pop. Black blues and jazz musicians and singers who tended to stay closer to the original "classic blues" format never sold with white audiences in the numbers their white imitators and peers did.[13]

Nevertheless, the establishment of the "race music" branch of the music industry especially for the blues created a viable commercial space in which black talent could flourish primarily for the consumption of black audiences without regard to white sensibilities. From this platform, starting in the late 1920s and increasing through World War II, a generation of black artists, primarily singers like Ethel Waters and Alberta Hunter, were able to cross over into the broader market as blues itself was insinuated into the mainstream as Tin Pan Alley pop. It is from this space, this commercial well of the blues, that in the 1950s the "rhythm and blues" category would emerge and finally conquer pop, under the white brand label "rock and roll."

While the recording industry developed the first technology to enable the physical crossover of color into white American homes on a massive scale, the records quickly became secondary to a new medium for mass distribution of recorded content and much more: radio. Radio was the first and perhaps the most important communications technology in the creation of a mass market for a multidimensional, multicultural, and thus multiracial common American identity. To an even greater degree than the phonograph, it allowed Americans to freely identify with their individual interests and desires without regard to barriers of class, gender, ethnicity, or race. It could convene an unprecedented audience for a simultaneous experience of mass community around a concert, a comedy show, or a prizefight. While bringing Americans together, radio also sliced the existing social groups by popular culture interests and recombined them as large subgroups of listeners that communications professor Susan Douglas calls "imagined communities." Today, of course, jazz lovers, sports fans, news junkies, and a host of other pop culture submarkets are recognized simply as commercial market niches. Radio didn't just change Americans' relationship to popular culture; it transformed our sense of relationship to other Americans by making the individual potentially part of one or any number of validated wholes that never existed before.

The role of race in the dynamic of radio was consistent with all that had gone before. The story and song of the African-American, whether told and sung by him or borrowed and bent by whites for their own purposes, occupied a disproportionately large space in the national imagination. In the radio age, just as in the culture of minstrelsy, nothing tied Americans of all backgrounds together like their fear and loathing of black people—except perhaps their profound dependence on the black experience for cohering a distinct American identity. Radio almost insidiously expanded the possibilities for this transracial identification by whites, while simultaneously embedding the fundamental, volatile contradiction of American race much deeper in the individual and national psyches. Susan Douglas describes how the new technology both revved up and de-tuned the cultural engine of white supremacy.

> Radio ... simultaneously reinforced and profoundly destabilized white supremacy and racial segregation in the United States throughout the century. . . . [R]adio has supplied white people that private place, that trapdoor into a culture many whites imagine to be more authentic, more vibrant, and richer than their own. Through radio whites could partake of the spirit of black culture without being forced to witness or experience its deprivations and injustices. . . . On radio, white ridicule of black culture and of African-Americans mixed with envy, desire, and imitation. . . . Radio may have been used through its history to reaffirm the supposed superiority of whiteness. But it has also been used, since the 1920's, to challenge, laugh at, and undermine this flimsy conceit.[14]

In its early years, before the hegemony of the networks, radio's eclectic, democratic offerings shocked the social establishment by making "hot" jazz and the blues, performed by a wide range of black artists, easily accessible to American households. The ensuing debate, coupled with the maturing (or monopolizing) of the airwaves as a corporate commercial medium, eventually curtailed the exposure available to African-American artists on radio. By the end of the 1920s, mainstream airtime was mostly limited to a relative handful of the most undeniable stars like Duke Ellington, Louis Armstrong, and Fats Waller. Nevertheless, Susan Douglas writes in *Listening In: Radio and the American Imagination,*

> A critical symbiotic relationship began between African-American music and radio. The timbre and tempo of jazz made the most of the limited fidelity and sound ranges of radio in the 1920's; more to the point, two-beat and four-beat jazz enlivened radio. . . . [Louis] Armstrong was a genius at combining African-American rhythms, vocalization, and blues chords with Western harmonies, embodying the quixotic notion that black and white music—and thus culture—could happily coexist. . . . And radio . . . gave Armstrong,

Duke Ellington, and others exposure to a huge audience they would never have had otherwise. Radio made them international stars.[15]

In the 1930s increased corporate control led to more segregation in prime-time radio, although a wide range of black expression was still available on less commercial, late-night broadcasts. But the essence of African-American musical expression, however co-opted, diluted, and standardized to pacify reactionary critics, had become firmly embedded in mainstream culture; what had been unambiguously black in 1923 was acceptably "mainstream," especially when performed by whites, in 1933. Blackface makeup and the conscious, schizophrenic nod toward the American racial contradiction that had been the essence of minstrelsy was no longer required. Radio technology enabled the first, irreversible step toward the virtual reality that I call "dreaming in color." The dream rose up from a very deep sleep, but at a time when the theories of the unconscious and collective unconscious were gaining their first widespread currency, conservative social critics recognized that radio's influence on identity was far more than skin deep. As Susan Douglas writes:

> As early as the the 1920's . . . people understood that concentrated music listening—memorizing lyrics, putting dance steps to certain songs, trying to copy chords or harmonies on one's own instrument at home—shaped individual and group identity as never before. . . . Much of the white bourgeois panic about jazz was based on this understanding . . . of *how powerfully music listening was constituting identity,* and that now, at least with black jazz and blues, some of that identity, especially among the young, would be constituted in and through black culture. This emotional identification with African-American culture, however partial and complicated by racism, spawned fears of psychic miscegenation and informed the reactions against white youth's using radio to tap into black music.[16]

The show that established radio as the dominant medium for comedic entertainment, setting the national habit of tuning in to a specific broadcast station at a predetermined hour that exists to this day, was a sitcom about two hapless black men living in Harlem. From its start months before the 1929 stock market crash, *Amos 'n' Andy* was a national phenomenon, with an audience of up to 40 million, or one-third of the American population. With the characters played by two white actors trading on stereotypes about lazy, gullible, mendacious, and ignorant black males, it was a clear throwback to minstrelsy. But as with music on radio, technology eliminated the need for black greasepaint. Still, *Amos 'n' Andy* used its black characters and milieu to covey something far more meaningful if not compelling to mainstream white America than racist putdowns. At one level, the show provided white audiences with a window into the most vital source of American vernacular language and its application to social conditions affecting average Americans of all colors. Just as in the antebellum dawn of American pop, putting on the hip, if hapless, survivor slave had a utility and meaning for listeners that went much deeper than the surface racism. As Susan Douglas points out,

> The fact that so many catch phrases from *Amos 'n' Andy* were used by millions of white listeners is testimony to people's affection for the show's version of Black English: people borrow linguistically from those they admire, not those they scorn, however forbidden it is to admit that admiration. . . . The malapropisms also ridiculed mainstream, white America, especially the arbitrariness and high handedness of government bureaucracy and big business. . . . This use of blacks—or faux blacks—to attack the pretensions, snobbery, and frequent inhumanity of the upper classes had begun in minstrel shows, in which the Dandy Jim caricature lampooned not just the urban black dandy but also the prissy and pompous upper-class *white* dandy.[17]

The early maturity of radio, like the mainstreaming of jazz, took place in the context of the Depression's profound economic and social upheaval, an era of bitter social repression of blacks and, to a lesser extent, the newest European immigrants. The color that had burst forth in the first and third decades of the century couldn't be denied, but it could be forced under cover. *Amos 'n' Andy*'s writers were white, of course, and while the show invented radio comedy, with protagonists who sounded black enough to easily suspend white disbelief, only one black actor, Eddie "Rochester" Anderson, ever made it big in the new medium's early heyday. Pop culture also worked to compel the "less than white" Euro-immigrants, whose influx was cut off by law in 1924, to cover their ethnic roots, as well as the early influence of African-Americans on their acculturation, with political whiteness. The culture doled out a kind of ethnic hazing that the newest Americans had to accept as the price of their ultimate assimilation. But unlike blacks, this hazing was often led by one of their own who had already crossed over, like the Jewish Jack Benny sending up the stereotype of the penny-pinching Jew, or the Jewish Eddie Cantor's radio show that featured a wide variety of what Susan Douglas calls "ethnic jokesters," whose "exaggerated accents . . . [and] inability to master proper English marked them as men still outside the fold, yet their ability to zing Cantor verbally showed that recent immigrants could hold their own."[18]

In the 1930s and 1940s, the door to absorption into American political whiteness was, of course, still firmly closed to blacks and other people who were clearly nonwhite. The Mexican roots of southwestern culture never made it into cowboy movies of the period. The cultural contributions of Asian-Americans were buried under stereotypes of Asians as indelibly foreign, exotic, and unknowable, as exemplified by the *Charlie Chan* detective movies. In the 1930s, as the culture cast a wary eye on the rise of imperial Japan, Asian features became the personification of extraterrestrial evil, in the character Emperor Ming of the popular *Flash Gordon* series. (The image would persist to an extent as late as the 1960s, even on the original, otherwise antiracist *Star Trek* television series.) And as with Mexicans and Native Americans, when the story occasionally called for a sympathetic or heroic portrayal of Asian people, a white actor played the role, as was the case with *Charlie Chan*.

Nevertheless, during this period the new European immigrants and, to a lesser extent, people of Latin American descent—none of whom had been considered 100 percent "white" when the century began—started fraying the edges of political whiteness by integrating, assimilating, or outright passing for "white." And in the course of bringing their cultural distinctiveness into the mainstream, they frequently brought along the African-American cultural tropes they had acquired in big cities, tropes that could not enter the mainstream in black skin. Professional baseball's color bar, for example, did not apply to Latin Americans, provided they were sufficiently "white" in appearance. In the 1930s and 1940s Xavier Cougat, an acceptably "white" Hispanic,[19] could freely ply Afro-Cuban rhythms before white audiences in white ballrooms and on white radio stations while staying at hotels and dining in restaurants where Duke Ellington couldn't. Carmen Miranda was able to create the persona of the exotic Latina in mainstream films that, while limiting, was still several steps closer to the full humanity that was the privilege of whiteness than anything black actresses could hope for. Rita Hayworth, born Margarita Carmen Dolores Cansino, was able to escape being Hispanic altogether. She became a "white" star by hair dye, electrolysis, and a name change, white enough to have her face on the side of the bomber that launched the Atomic Age over Hiroshima in 1945.

In movie culture the gateway to mainstream exposure to color was controlled by a half-dozen Hollywood executives who were mostly Jewish immigrants. Their own status as outsiders to American whiteness was both ironic and determinative in the ultimate impact of their decisions. They had come to the United States as children in the decades just before the invention of the motion picture, in families fleeing impoverished, persecuted communities in Poland, Russia, Germany, and Hungary. When their parents' fantasies of acceptance in the American mainstream were frustrated by discrimination and an inability to adjust to the crushing competition in the urban immigrant slums, the future "Hollywood Jews" became even more determined to make it in whatever business they could get a toehold. As detailed in the 1998 documentary *Hollywoodism: Jews, Movies and the American Dream*, these outsiders, with generational memories of racial oppression, ended up casting the mold for the central pillar of the American mass culture industry.

"Hollywood was a dream dreamt by Jews who were fleeing a nightmare," wrote Neal Gabler, author of *An Empire of Their Own*, on which the documentary was based.[20] From an early start in various kinds of petty retailing, many Jewish businessmen found a place in exhibiting early movies, a product that, in the years before World War I, was seen as slightly disreputable, working-class entertainment. The early films themselves promulgated an image of America consistent with the turn-of-the-century racist assumption that proper American identity inhered only to certain northern European, Protestant nationalities.

> [They] reflected the vision of America shared by Thomas Edison and the other men who invented the film industry . . . these old stock Protestants . . . presented negative images of hooked nosed Jews, blacks and others. They championed an idea of an America where the white upper classes ruled and immigrants knew their place.[21]

When when Carl Laemmle, a German-born Jew, seemed to forget his place by first importing and then making his own films, Edison and the other WASP film and film equipment makers tried to drive him and the other Jews out of the business, but they succeeded only in forcing Laemmle to leave New York for Los Angeles in 1912. Other future moguls, like Louis B. Mayer and the Warner brothers, soon followed and proceeded to invent, by trial, error, and intuition, the mass media myth of America that we've come to know as the American dream. As Gabler sums it up in *Hollywoodism*:

> They created their own America, an America which is not the real America [but] their own version of America. . . . Ultimately this shadow America becomes so popular, and so widely disseminated that its images and values come to devour the real America. And so the grand irony . . . is that Americans come to define themselves by the shadow America that was created by eastern European Jewish immigrants who weren't admitted to the precincts of the real America.[22]

In the documentary Gabler's remarks come right before the sound and sight of a pigtailed Judy Garland singing "Over the Rainbow" about a land that she had "heard of once, in a lullaby," where "the dreams that you dare to dream really do come true." A montage of newsreel-type film clips then proceeds from the familiar historical footage of steerage-class immigrants making their way through Ellis Island and herding themselves into ghetto squalor. The sequence ends with the immigrant moguls feting themselves at openings and the award ceremonies they invented in the 1930s, when 75 percent of Americans went to the movies at least once a week. While the movies they made covered all the genres, from Westerns to historical dramas, they generally portrayed America as a family tied together not by common race or ethnicity but by common values shared by common people. "Hollywoodism," with its spirit of optimism and virtue in the teeth of the Depression, became a secular near religion.

One value that the Hollywood religion expressed was the virtue of upward class mobility, usually punctuated by interethnic romance and intermarriage, paralleling the moguls' own tendency to acquire WASP second wives. Another was the recasting of the role of African-Americans in the great American family. As the critic J. Hoberman notes in the documentary, the Jewish moguls saw blacks as "quintessential" Americans and the wellspring of what made America itself, the core of American identity. From a practical standpoint, black popular culture was the perfect raw material for reprocessing as the most active ingredient in the Hollywood pop formula. It could be acquired cheaply and, with some creative packaging, molded into extremely popular product.

After clips of Lena Horne singing "Stormy Weather," composed by cantor's son Harold Arlen for the 20th Century–Fox film of the same name, historian Hasia Dier summarizes the critical middleman role between black and mainstream white America that the Hollywood Jews began perfecting by the 1930s:

> Jews served as messengers . . . of black culture. They took it, consumed it, integrated it into their own cultural repertoire . . . and then introduced it to a white America that was willing to listen to Jews and partake of what they had to offer in a way that they never would from blacks.[23]

In retrospect, if the African-American experience and the position of black culture in America had not existed, the historical record suggests that Hollywood Jews would have had to invent it. African-American music was the perfect lyrical vehicle to convey the yearning for redemption, acceptance, and release from oppression that was a deep emotional concern of the Jewish moguls. Black culture, with its recent memory of slavery and continuing torture under Jim Crow, held uncannily durable parallels with the most recent generations of Jewish oppression in Europe. Most important, black cultural expression was already hardwired into the American idiom. It was as instantly commercial as found money, as long as it was Hollywood speaking through blacks and not blacks speaking for themselves.

Some Hollywood Jews, while trying to pass as Gentiles, went so far as to mine the dramatic possibilities (if not the realities) of blacks passing as whites. The film adaptation of the 1927 musical *Showboat* actually made the controversial suggestion that the literal mixing of bloods, the ultimate assimilation, was a legitimate interpretation of the American destiny. To be sure, most Hollywood output settled for themes about the struggles of white ethnic and class outsiders to reach acceptance in the mainstream. And while the Hollywood Jews added a conscious twist to the complexity of nonwhite characters and their relationship to the larger themes, they were still cast in overwhelmingly servile and unsophisticated positions, with the notable exception of jazz musicians like Duke Ellington and other entertainers identified with the "youth music" of the generation about to go to World War II: swing.

◻   ◻   ◻

Powered by the mix of massive immigration from southern and eastern Europe and the emergence of American Negroes pioneering jazz and style in the North, color exploded in mainstream American consciousness, as the 1920s roared themselves hoarse into the Depression. But by the Japanese bombing of Pearl Harbor at the end of 1941, the children and grandchildren of the swarthy, non-Protestant newcomers were well on their way to melting into all-American whiteness. The passage from their old nations, the bridge to their parents' identities, had been shut down by the Immigration Acts of 1921 and 1924. By December 1941, Hitler's armies had obliterated most of whatever traces of Polish or Hungarian or Lithuanian failing ancestral memories hadn't already lost.

The ultimate nonwhites, meanwhile, blacks who predated the great immigrant flood, found themselves going off to war with little real equity in the modern pop culture they'd created. The mobilization did create new, unprecedented opportunities for industrial employment, and though they remained segregated, black soldiers eventually seized chances to distinguish themselves in combat. But in mainstream commercial culture, the browning wave that had been washing over the culture since the century's turn was in some ways receding. Color was once again going "under cover," in the national

Zeitgeist, in a lull very similar to the pause in the 1910s. To be sure, music and popular style with clear origins in black communities had penetrated to an unprecedented depth. In the midst of the Roaring Twenties, for example, black slang traveled informally from Harlem and Chicago's South Side into the larger white world, carried primarily by a gin-soaked class of white high rollers, bohemian intellectuals, and mob-related lowlifes. Near the end of the 1930s, as "swing" jazz became the fulcrum for the first truly commercial youth culture in American history, Cab Calloway, the flamboyant Harlem bandleader, was able to lease his name to a guidebook for the new style called *The Hepster's Dictionary*, published very much above ground. Much like hip-hop in the mid-1990s, swing in the late 1930s was growing exponentially by swallowing whatever it wanted from previous musical generations, "swinging the classics—rifling well-known works by everyone from Bach to Stephen Foster in search of familiar airs that could be turned into danceable hits."[24] But at the height of the swing era, the net effect of such creative cannibalism on the color of commercial culture was much more like what happened at the zenith of disco in the late 1970s, when it was possible to make a top-ten hit out of the opening theme of Beethoven's Fifth Symphony ("A Fifth of Beethoven") just by adding some disco rhythm arrangements. The popular product's penetration into the nonblack mainstream had diluted it past the point of requiring unambiguous African-American idiomatic content to succeed. Under those circumstances, in the late 1930s as well as forty years later, black cultural entrepreneurs lost their earlier competitive advantage in the marketplace, while white creators—whether genuinely acculturated to the black idiom or not—regained all the advantage conferred by their skin color. That advantage, in the pre–civil rights era, was still prodigious.

Musically, swing was the distillation of certain jazz elements of the early 1930s into arrangements that took on a vibrant and, most important, danceable life of their own. Its most seminal developer was the black orchestra leader Fletcher Henderson, and its proving ground was the dance floor wherever it was played, especially New York's Roseland Ballroom, downtown, and the Savoy Ballroom uptown in Harlem. Commercially, however, swing's emergence as a pop phenomenon is directly tied to the racism of political whiteness that shaped the career of the legendary Benny Goodman, also known as the "King of Swing." It was a title fairly earned, but only after segregation effectively sidelined legitimate black contenders. In 1934 Goodman won a chance to lead a band playing the hottest youth-oriented dance music on a national CBS network show called *Let's Dance*. As Ken Burns and Geoffrey Ward write in *Jazz*, Goodman's unrelenting ambition to lead the most successful jazz band, playing the best and most authentic jazz, had never been hampered by considerations of race. Years later he would be instrumental in breaking color lines on the bandstand, but at the time of his big break in 1934, network studios were mostly closed to black orchestras, especially the kind playing hot, stomping music for which, it would soon be discovered, there was a huge pent-up demand among white youth. Goodman put together the best white players he could find, including the drummer Gene Krupa, but quickly realized he needed a "Harlem book," a library of arrangements, of which Henderson was the best creator. Henderson especially excelled at taking ordinary pop standards and "swinging" them into the style that Benny Goodman's white orchestra was about to drive into the soul of a generation.

Goodman and *Let's Dance* were an instant hit, and from its national coming-out party on the radio in 1934 through its fade from phenomenal popularity by 1950 swing was noted for a vigorous interaction between black and white bands, in an almost equal but always separate state of respect and rivalry. Determined to play on the rhythmic edge, Goodman quickly drove the popularity of the music, a brand most closely associated with himself, to places black performers couldn't go. In the years just before before the Second World War, the browning of popular culture had simply run a bit too far ahead of the pace of racial politics, which was still glacial. Music of color quickly kindled a broad mainstream youth culture under the banner of swing—and was just as quickly forced to defend itself against political attacks whose racist underpinnings were only lightly veiled.

> Dr. A. A. Brill, a Manhattan psychiatrist, went before newsreel cameras to declare that "Swing music represents our regression to the primitive tom-tom-tom, a rhythmic sound that pleases savages and children. . . . The sight of white youths enthusiastically adopting dances that had been born in the black community had always alarmed their elders. 'If they'd been told it was a Balkan folk dance,' Duke Ellington said, 'they'd think it was wonderful.'"[25]

But defending swing against such attacks had the effect, partially intentional, of covering the color of swing culture with whiteness. Swing's defense rested on promoting the perception that it was as natural to its mostly young white fan base as if they had invented it entirely within their own communities. As long as they were, in fact, "swinging it" in overwhelmingly segregated venues, under the influence and control of overwhelmingly white cultural icons and musicians, the prosecution's case was doomed. In truth, the "bobbysoxers" were the first generation born into a mass commercial culture of color. But securing their claim to that birthright, ironically, required complicity in disavowing to a significant extent the larger claims to independent recognition and social respect of the culture's black innovators.

Swing's case for legitimacy also required a new model of white pop culture icon. Much as Irving Berlin had been seen as America's "Ragtime King" as World War I began in Europe, Benny Goodman was the unchallenged "King of Swing" at the start of World War II. Both Goodman and Berlin were American Jews, but they came to their African-American acculturation by different means, from different generations. By World War II, when both were widely celebrated as cultural heroes supporting the war effort, they represented very different senses of American cultural identity as far as color was concerned. By the late 1930s, the Russian-born Berlin, who began as a "coon shouter" at Nigger Mike's infamous Lower East Side saloon, was beginning to see himself as a national treasure and found it necessary to distance himself from all things colored or, for that matter, Jewish. As Ann Douglas writes in *Terrible Honesty*:

> Over the years, Berlin grew increasingly quick to deny the black sources of his music. Sounding much like [Paul] Whiteman, he explained that "our popular songwriters . . . are not Negroes" but "of pure white blood . . . many of Russian . . . ancestry"; he had avoided the word "Jew" and expunged the Negro.[26]

Not content to identify with the miscegenated American identity that he had been instrumental in tinting, Berlin aimed to pass for WASP. Where he was once consciously smashing European cultural molds and writing songs perfect for fellow Russian Jew Al Jolson to immortalize, Berlin was by World War II a conscious Anglophile who most wanted to write songs for the "casually patrician and Nordic Fred Astaire," according to Douglas. Berlin's self-whitewashing campaign is symbolic of the larger moment in the intersection of race, commercial culture, and American identity. Essentially, in the Nazi-clouded predawn of the war, the politics of whiteness caught up and for a time overtook the economics of color in commercial culture. America couldn't handle the unavoidable summons to answer Hitler's "master race" doctrines and at the same time address the glaring, chronic issue posed by institutional white supremacy at home. As America rose to meet its greatest test of nationhood, still mired in its worst-ever economic collapse, the order of the day was pulling together. Letting miscegenated cultural Americanness trump political whiteness could only pull us apart, especially in the South. Though Berlin may have overdone it, his migration reflected the fact that less-than-white immigrants, whose old homes were looking permanently cut off from them, needed to fully fit in.

It was already too much that white mainstream America suddenly found its physical and moral manhood carried on the legs of Jesse Owens in the 1936 Olympics, then resting on the black shoulders of Joe Louis in 1938, when he fought for the championship against Hitler's favorite son, Max Schmeling. Louis's early professional victories, including one over Mussolini protégé Primo Carnera in 1935, revitalized the business of boxing. But as good as Louis was, in the ring as well as in managing an immaculately wholesome, nonthreatening image outside the ring, America wasn't ready to let this new opening of color run its course in commercial culture. Boxing, like baseball, Susan Douglas writes, was different from jazz:

> As with so many black talents, Louis became the object of white envy and admiration, and of white resentment and fear. Celebratory songs about him—mostly blues and swing—intermixed with race, referring to his punches as "dark dynamite," insisting on calling him "coffee-colored" or "the Tan Tornado."
>
> But his fights on the radio made boxing profitable again. In fact, Joe Louis prize fights . . . attracted the largest audiences in U.S. radio history, with the exception of two prewar addresses by FDR. It wasn't just that white fans were eager to see which "great white hope" might take him out, although clearly many were. James T. Farrell, writing for *The Nation* in 1936, reported that many white

fans were rooting for Schmeling during their first bout, yelling, "Kill him, Max," and cheering wildly when the German beat Louis against heavy odds.[27]

Nazism began to pose a grave challenge to the meaning of political white-ness in American identity at the same time that black labor and political organization began to make demands that could, and eventually would, rock the foundation of American political culture. The segregation of professional baseball at the time provides a perfect example of the stalemate between pol-itics and the commercial mass culture that was just reaching economic ado-lescence. It's hard to understand today, but in 1939 the integration of the major leagues was still unthinkable because, even though it was also a busi-ness, baseball was much more closely identified with American national identity. Not long before, the "national pastime" had even been granted a special dispensation from prevailing rules of economic competition by the U.S. Supreme Court, the same court that established "separate but equal" as the law of the land and upheld it against all challenges for forty years. Base-ball was a business, but its whiteness was seen as a white man's political right, one that even its owners could not lightly brush aside merely to make more money. Baseball's integration was still a very long decade away. Com-mercial mass culture, like swing and the movies, belonged to an entirely dif-ferent category of consumption from baseball and other professional sports. Sport had simply not yet fallen to the level of just another entertainment product; or depending on your point of view, sport had not yet begun its rise to preeminence in the commercial pop culture hierarchy. Swing, by contrast (and the larger, jazz-influenced, Hollywood-validated pop culture), wasn't as formally tied to strict segregation as baseball but was still very much a cul-tural upstart without tenure that, in wartime, had to be mindful of its place and the place of the African-America that inspired it.

Modern advertising culture, for example, grew up with the jazz-swing age, and the advertising industry would eventually find itself not only the primary sponsor of mass entertainment culture but a faithful extension of that culture. But in the 1930s and for some years after the war, advertising and jazz could not have been farther apart, either in spirit or in substance. Jazz was a bottom-up cultural expansion, spreading from Deep South black communities into the poor black and immigrant precincts of a few big northern cities. Its leading icons and commercializers were overwhelmingly African-Americans as well as Jewish immigrants and their children. Advertising was the consciously top-down communication of a separate stream of commercial culture: the marketing of manufactured goods. Advertising worked by identifying everything from washing machines to instant coffee with a vision of progress and modernity that was inconsistent with even the presence, much less the cultural influence, of nonwhites. The ultimate irony, as I'll discuss in Chapter 5, is that in the 1990s even the most conservative manufacturing and service corporations seized on the tactic of using racial and ethnically inclusive images to signal their technological prowess and to identify themselves as being in step with the new global economy.

Advertising's creators were a direct reflection of the upper-middle- and upper-class WASP male corporate executives who paid the bills. A study found that only ninety-two of the five thousand men in the 1931 *Who's Who in Advertising* were identifiably Jewish, and less than 10 percent of them worked for large New York agencies. Similar studies found "virtually no names of agency personnel that are manifestly Italian or Polish, or of other Eastern or Southern European origin," and "no evidence that blacks did anything other than janitorial work" for agencies during the 1920s and 1930s.[28] Paradoxically, while near and actual nonwhites were shut out of the business of stimulating sales with ad culture, they were creating the entertainment culture that would eventually become the primary driver of all mass consumption. While WASPs were inventing the Arrow Shirt Man, Jews were inventing Hollywood and the record industry, using liberal quantities of nonwhite cultural input.

While incorporating many subtle variations between sex roles, American advertising confined its depictions of America, and the emerging American way of life, to upper-middle-class "nonethnic" white urbanites. The advertising profession thereby consciously excluded up to 65 percent of the American consumer "electorate" from the franchise of direct advertising attention, according Roland Marchand's study of the industry between 1920 and 1940, *Advertising and the American Dream.*

> Ethnic and racial minorities found virtually no employment in the advertisements of the 1920's and 1930's. The names and facial features of the central and supporting figures [in the ads] never suggested Southern or Eastern European origins. Asians found no role

whatsoever in the ads; one "Mexican" washer woman and an Eskimo wash lady made single appearances as archaic foils for modern washing methods in a Procter and Gamble series. Categorically, ethnic and racial minorities failed to qualify as modern. "Advertisments" largely confined [blacks] to roles as contented porters, janitors, wash-women, and house boys. A few black trademark figures, such as Aunt Jemima and Rastus, the Cream of Wheat cook, at least managed to preserve a measure of humble dignity. Blacks never appeared as consumers, or as fellow workers with whites, or as skilled workers.[29]

In the 1960s, while still following the latest trends at a safe distance, advertising slowly began to leverage pop cultural and even social realism to sell goods. In the 1980s it began closing its gap with the trailing edge of commercial pop culture. In the 1990s, as "edginess" itself became a commercial cultural value, advertising entirely closed the gap and increasingly began to *lead* the popular culture on which it was now utterly dependent and from which it was virtually indistinguishable. But in its early adolescence in the 1930s, advertising was more inclined to exploit negative perceptions of pop trends and fears of social change driven by the mix of new technologies, especially mass communication technology, and the seeming ascendance of racial and ethnic "outsiders." As Marchand writes:

> The exhilaration created by the new pace of technological change . . . coexisted with deep anxieties about social disorder— anxieties symbolized by prohibition, immigration restrictions, and warnings of the dangers posed by the "new woman" and "flaming youth." Jazz . . . the hip flask, and sexual frankness all flouted traditional moral standards and seemed to threaten family stability and [white male] paternal authority. Ad creators seized on the public's sense of an exciting yet disconcerting new tempo, reinforcing and amplifying this perception for their own purposes.[30]

Unconsciously, perhaps, advertising knew that America wasn't ready to gaze full-face into the reflection of the identity makeover wrought by technology and browning popular culture between the wars. The country needed a breather just to assimilate it all. World War II provided more than sufficient distraction. Unity behind the war effort had the amazing effect of simultaneously blunting the surge of African-Americans toward the foreground of popular and political culture while camouflaging the tentative beginnings of integration and the coming assault on segregation. The armed forces remained segregated, but the total mobilization of American industry, technology, and human talent pulled some blacks not only into factories employing the most advanced production techniques to make planes but into cockpits in limited but critical roles as fighter pilots. Young America went to war united under the aural banner of swing, a culture that seemed conveniently born out of the ether, not black like its father Louis Armstrong or its godfather Fletcher Henderson, but not white like the WASP-supremacist presumptions celebrated in Thomas Edison or D. W. Griffith's prewar film industry. If swing had a face as we went to war with the Axis, it was Benny Goodman's bespectacled visage. Goodman, born in a poor Jewish ghetto in Chicago, the first to integrate a major bandstand of the era, proud of his slightly affected black hipster accent, was the poster child of the new American identity.

To be sure, that mandate, coupled with a level of combined artistic and commercial ambition that perhaps has never again been matched in jazz, led Goodman to play an important role as a pioneer in mixing races on the bandstand. Even before his groundbreaking January 1938 concert at Carnegie Hall that incorporated the talents of both Duke Ellington and Count Basie and his band, Benny Goodman had been making America safe for the "All-Star," racially integrated jam session. He had, of course, made history just a few years earlier by making black musicians like vibraphonist Lionel Hampton and pianist Teddy Wilson a regular part of his small group concerts and recording sessions. Unlike Irving Berlin, Goodman had no problem owning up to the African-American talents he had mined to forge his crown as the "King of Swing." He wasn't necessarily a crusading integrationist—often his race-mixing moves were driven by his influential patron John Hammond— but Goodman was a perfectionist and tended famously to place what a musician could do for his band above race, to the extent that the strictest rules of political whitness did not preclude it.

By 1940, according to the authors of *Jazz*, the companion book to the 2000 PBS documentary series, the slow, Goodman-inspired integration of commercial jazz made it the best and worst of times for black bands and their seminal leaders. Those with marquee names—earned by dint of talent, hard work, and the luck to be validated by a powerful white figure like Goodman or Hammond—were making good money even as the country was still shaking off the last of the Depression. But the average black band increasingly found itself without a seat at the sumptuous swing feast. Whatever advantage the unheralded but authentic black musical group had was now erased as white bands could legitimately claim at least equal ownership of the style—especially when, like Goodman and Artie Shaw, they literally paid for their stake by employing black talent. As early as 1932, *Jazz* notes, lyricist Andy Razaf anticipated the threat of marginal status for black artists posed by the steady acculturation of white American bands like Goodman's, and by white America in general.

> You're a novelty no longer,
> They have copied all your tricks;
> 'Til white bands can pass for colored
> With "gut-bucket" blues and "licks"
>
> Once they marveled at your ragtime
> And you gladly showed them how,
> So they've mastered all your rhythms;
> They don't really need you now.[31]

As color went under cover in the early 1940s, the marketplace, or rather its arbiters in the critical community, declared partial independence from black America for a new kind of swing that was "'sweet hot' or 'swing sweet,' a white man's style of swing, retaining the Negroid bounce but coupling it to more respect for the melody."[32] Goodman and other leading figures paid no attention to such nonsense; they continued to hire away the most talented veterans away from black bandleaders like Duke Ellington and Count Basie, sweet hot or not.

Thus the long wave of miscegenation creating American culture—from minstrelsy to ragtime to Louis Armstrong and now Benny Goodman—resolved itself into a new, tighter pattern of commercial expression, one with shorter cycles that were much more closely tied to American social and political struggles around race. The swing era opened a permanent commercial pipeline, or network of pipelines, between the talent of black and other non-white creators of culture and the American mainstream. In the 1950s white disk jockeys and seminal white artists like Elvis Presley would tap the pipeline near the wellhead to let rock and roll spring forth. At first it came out crude and wholly transracial in its essence and audience appeal. You couldn't hear any whiteness in early Elvis; nor could you distinguish by race his first fans from those of Little Richard. In less than a decade, compared to the nearly thirty years it took for swing to declare independence, rock and roll was a mainstream American (still read: white) pop culture in which African-Americans *participated,* usually as equals and sometimes as first among equals. Through the 1960s the pattern grew more complicated as Europe and then the rest of the world began exerting more and more influence, as consumers as well as creators, over the shape of American popular culture. Rock and rock culture became the ubiquitous backdrop to the baby boomers' young adulthood. It peaked as pop in the early 1970s, but its recession has been slowed and obscured by the sheer size and dominance of the boomer cohort, and rock's tenacity (in contrast to jazz) in incorporating anything new to stay culturally and commercially relevant.

In the early 1970s, a more sophisticated pop culture industry again tapped the African-American pipeline near its source, and out gushed James Brown's funk into the commercial mainstream. Funk enabled disco, disco became white, and then it passed to yet another incarnation of youth culture in just over five years. But hip-hop/rap, the fifth and latest draw on the black well in the forty years since and including swing, would be categorically different, beginning a new pattern whose frequency and period are still not fully known. To date, after nearly twenty years, hip-hop has had no Benny Goodman, no Elvis, no Beatles, and no BeeGees. The closest rap has come to having a white face is the recent success of the rapper Eminem. But the exponentially dysfunctional, antisocial Eminem cannot possibly be a place-holder for white identity in an ever-browning American culture. When white parents see their children watching him on MTV, they surely cringe and pray they'll change the channel to someone more all-American wholesome—like LL Cool J. That's how much commercial popular culture has changed American identity since the boomers' parents first found themselves in Benny Goodman.

3

The 1950s Set Up the 1960s and 1970s: American Is As Americans Buy

The 1950s set up the social political and technological upheavals of the 1960s and 1970s. But in many ways the period from the election of Eisenhower through the assassination of Kennedy was as much a preview of the Reagan-Bush 1980s-to-early-1990s America than the precursor of race riots, Woodstock, and affirmative action. As invested as we baby boomers are in having experienced the glory of the 1960s, a fresh look at the 1950s reveals that that period is much more representative of the long-term pattern of American identity formation and thus perhaps is more important in understanding the meaning of the 1980s. A look at the 1950s from this angle also raises a very interesting question: If the 1950s are really blood brother to the 1980s, are the Clinton-Bush II years the 1960s again? The answer, as we will see later in this chapter, is a little yes, but mostly no. The 1960s, as my more soberly reflective boomer friends are fond of pointing out with a sigh, will never happen again. Not just in the obvious sense that one never steps into time's river in the same place twice. The 1960s and 1970s were the first wild fruit of seeds sown in the decade or so that preceded them. But those seeds also gave rise to new growth in the 1980s and 1990s, growth that was rooted in a much older and more enduring pattern of struggle to accommodate our transracial identity and to live in our hybrid skin. As much as I'd like to buy into the myth of boomer exceptionalism, I will say that as race and culture go, the latter part of the 1960s and early 1970s was a significant and perhaps invaluable digression from the central story of transracial American identity. "Black power" and all the group identity cultural politics it inspired did not mean the end of the long story of a maturing multiracial American identity. That story, about all that we have dreamed in common despite the sins of white male supremacy, was a novel, a love story we were forced to put aside the day John Kennedy was killed. We had to deal some serious history and other nonfiction about the pain and accumulated rage from those sins for a decade or so. But eventually, and all the wiser for it, we picked up again from where we left off, the chapter about the possibilities of a generation awakened together by Elvis and Little Richard . . . and television.

With all due deference to the legacy of Beatlemania, the breakout moment of the color forced under cover during World War II was not when America saw and heard "I Want to Hold Your Hand" on *The Ed Sullivan Show* in 1964, the year that would be more lastingly associated with the landmark Civil Rights Act. That moment, and the British invasion that would follow, was just the latest, greatest new layer of American skin on our popular culture. Though imported, it was American skin because it was grafted from samples of Carl Perkins and Chuck Berry that John Lennon and Paul McCartney and the others had taken in the 1950s. The real breakout moment had occurred with Little Richard's "Tuti Frutti" and Elvis's "Blue Suede Shoes," both released in 1956. The very idea of a triumphant civil rights movement at the time seemed farther away from reality than a man on the moon. Still, caught up as the new generation was in the energy of the beat, the truth of the rhythm and the uniquely American attitude of: *Do anything that you wanna do/But aww haw honey stay offa' my shoes,* anything seemed possible.

The 1950s, like the Roaring Twenties, began with a kind of social and economic clean slate, largely a result of the immediately preceding wars. While Europe was digging out from its ruins, a booming America was happily self-absorbed in invention and reinvention. What crank-up phonographs and radio were to the 1920s, small "portable" electric record players, transistor radios, and television were to the 1950s, only more so, because their deployment was built upon popular culture industries and infrastructure that had already been developing for thirty years and that were boosted to a new level by the advances refined in the technological pressure cooker of World War II.

And as it was in the 1920s, postwar African-America in the 1950s was energized for advancement on almost all fronts—social, political, and economic.

Swing America, like so many movies of the period and later, ended with
the image of the returning white GI doing the ecstatic lindy-hop boogie to
the music of Benny Goodman and Count Basie, out *On the Town* with his best
girl. That was the summer and fall of 1945. By the early 1950s the ex-GI had
decamped to the suburbs with the kids, was holding down a mortgage and a
car loan, and knew the truth captured in the 1955 novel *The Man in the Gray
Flannel Suit*. Calling it "one of the most influential novels of the 1950's,"
David Halberstam said:

> Its theme was the struggle of young Americans against the pres-
> sures of conformity and imprisonment in suburban life. . . . [The
> protagonists] lived in a community of people very much like them-
> selves; their neighbors, though pleasant and friendly, were, truth to
> tell, strangers, bonded by status and ambition rather than true
> friendship.[1]

Or perhaps that returning GI went back to a small town in semirural
America, especially in the South, where the line to the postwar gravy bowl
seemed a lot longer, but where those willing to get along by going along with
a shifting combination of what had always been—unremitting segregation
and black subjugation, dependence on a semiagrarian social economy in
resentful isolation from the North—and what was becoming were no less
hopeful.

The children and grandchildren of the Ellis Island immigrants returned
from the war seemingly transformed, not just from growing up in swing culture but from experiencing the reality of that romanticized multiethnic—
but not multiracial—foxhole. Whatever they were before—be it part Irish or
Italian or Polish—Americans after the war were on their way to the suburbs
as white and as American as swing. It was as though the color that had
reached such a high-water mark of visibility before and during the war, as
jazz resolved itself into swing, went into a kind of postwar recession and
decline, not unlike or unrelated to the decline of the old central city (soon to
be called "inner city") neighborhoods that the "white ethnics" were leaving
behind. Interestingly, big band/orchestra–based swing itself also went into

decline as America's defining music, though nobody really noticed until it was run flat over by rock and roll. The modal pop culture figure in the lull before the rock-and-roll storm was Frank Sinatra, as he and other young, mostly Italian-American crooners like Perry Como and Dean Martin as well as Bing Crosby became nearly the sole inheritors of the pop musical center. To be sure, black pop acts like the Ink Spots, Ella Fitzgerald, and the by-then-legendary Louis Armstrong held their own corners of the pop spotlight. But all the jazz that resisted the commercial pull of swing was taking the first steps down a one-way road toward the "art" music status that it's held ever since.

In that black space between the diverging streams of jazz, as commercial pop culture migrated from its roots in black communities, and seminal black creators—from Duke Ellington to Charlie Parker and Dizzy Gillespie—moved away from commercial pop, commercial rhythm and blues was born. It occupied the same largely segregated niche that the blues of Ma Rainey, Bessie Smith, and their progeny had been holding down since the early days of the recording industry, the niche the industry had christened "race records." They were largely made by smaller, white-owned and -run record labels and were almost exclusively distributed in record shops catering to black consumers or heard on jukeboxes in black bars and nightclubs. The name "race records" stuck until 1949, when the industry bible, *Billboard* magazine, officially changed the classification to "rhythm and blues." As legendary industry leader Jerry Wexler, then a young *Billboard* staff writer, put it, "race" sounded too much like "racist" in what he felt was the dawn of a more enlightened postwar era. In his history of the first thirty years of rock and roll, James Miller notes that the new label represented the first acknowledgment that blues music had a value and appeal that reached beyond the highly segregated black community. But at the same time, the industry could not entirely abandon the concept that a musical form dominated by black artists and primarily, though not exclusively, consumed by blacks must be marginalized, any more than the society could abandon the logic of segregation itself. As Miller writes:

> So the names changed. But the use of racially-coded labels remained intact. These labels reflected real musical—and racial—divisions. But they also artificially reinforced the divisions by making certain

genres of music, by definition, marginal to a mainstream that could scarcely have existed without all the tributaries feeding into it. In these years, it often happened that a country or rhythm and blues recording would sell hundreds of thousands of copies, and yet barely register in *Billboard*'s weekly pop chart, which was simply labeled "Best Sellers in Stores." At the same time, a handful of race and folk recordings, even in the mid-1940's, were simply too popular to ignore.[2]

The *Billboard* move had its early-1990s counterpart in the advent of the Soundscan system of capturing record sales in a greatly expanded range of retail outlets by using bar code scanners. The market demand for accurate measurement overcame the status quo inertia of tracking sales through indirect and somewhat arbitrary methods that tended to undercount sales of rap/hip-hop music. Then as now the old management axiom held true: Whatever you measure, you get more of—that is to say, you discover.

Histories of rock and roll are full of accounts of how entrepreneurs, especially record store owners and small-time record distributors, began to notice the demand from *white* teenagers for black rhythm-and-blues music. Statistics show that the postwar economic boom had created the first truly economically empowered teen consumer market in American history "with a total income of $7 billion a year and an average income of $10.55 a week—a figure close to the average disposable income available to the average American *family* just fifteen years before."[3] This condition also tracks with the market of the 1980s, not so much in the growth of disposable youth income but in the sharp rise in discretion over the spending of total household income that began to be ceded to teens and even preteens. As working mothers became the rule instead of the exception, teenagers gained more control over spending for a wider range of household consumption by default as parents had little time to shop for back-to-school clothing or even food and even less time to scrutinize what kind of music their children were bringing home.

Musically, early rhythm and blues was derived from the blues-based arrangements of hard-driving swing bands like Count Basie's and from the vocal style of legendary blues shouter Joe "Big Joe" Turner. First known as "jump," as in "jumping the blues," rhythm and blues emerged as "a simplified and superheated version of old-fashioned swing, often boogie-woogie based, usually played by a small combo of piano, bass and drums with saxo-phone and trumpet."[4] In 1944 "G.I. Jive," one of the biggest hits by the first master of the jump blues, singer and saxophonist Louis Jordan, became the first recording to ever top all three *Billboard* charts—pop, "race," and what we now know as country western—at the same time. Nevertheless, the main-stream record labels had little to no interest in the new style, or its commer-cial potential, for several years, leaving the field to upstart minor labels, usually owned by relative outsiders like King Records' Syd Nathan, a rough-hewn Jew, or Atlantic's Ahmet Ertegun, the immigrant son of Turkish diplo-mats. Soon the Nathans and Erteguns were joined in the emerging commercial culture by another kind of outsider, the small-town Deep South white man who wouldn't flinch at the term *redneck*, like Sam Phillips, the founder of Sun Records who "discovered" Elvis Presley, and Dewey Phillips (no relation), the renegade white Memphis deejay who in 1949 began burn-ing up the airwaves with the newly commercialized (but only slightly) sound of blues played and sung by natives of the nearby Mississippi Delta.

The big bang years of rock and roll can be neatly bracketed by two events. The first is Wynonie Harris's seminal 1947 recording "Good Rockin' Tonight," which dominated the race charts but was not distributed directly to whites because the words *rock* and *rockin* were understood to be black slang for the sex act. The second was New York deejay Alan Freed's racially integrated 1955 coming-out party (in Harlem's St. Nicholas Arena) for the now-mainstream craze, under the banner he literally attempted to trade-mark: "rock and roll." Those first eight years, from the first hit commercial expression, almost entirely confined to the black community, to the precise point of appropriation by the dominant commercial media institutions, bear some remarkable parallels with the emergent years of rap/hip-hop in the 1980s. One common feature is the role played by new technologies that inex-orably widened the aggregate bandwidth available for programming enter-tainment or other information. Just as the expansion of cable in the 1980s sharply increased the demand for new, distinctive programming to attract viewers, the early-1950s dawn of television shifted the attention of national broadcast network programmers to the new medium, creating a void in local radio that would soon be filled by pioneering rock-and-roll deejays like Phillips and Freed. Before long, of course, television would not only jump a good piece of radio's claim to the new trend, it would seize on the opening acts of the southern civil rights struggle as the "must see" programming that put television news on the map, much as tabloid TV programming saturation coverage of the O.J. Simpson trial put cable-TV news on the map.

There is also a broader historical parallel between the eras. The early 1950s and 1980s both have their pop cultural roots near the bottom of a cyclical trough in the state of integration of tastes in music, style, and expression across the races. Let me explain what I mean: Think of the heyday of Benny Goodman and Fletcher Henderson in 1943, or the high point in popularity of soulful pop-rock groups like Earth, Wind and Fire or especially Sly and the Family Stone about 1973, as peaks in transracial cultural time, high-water marks for periods of mutual discovery, acceptance, and recognition of a common cultural skin, notwithstanding the political status quo. From those peaks and through the remainder of the 1940s and 1970s, a combination of social, artistic, political, and commercial forces began once again pushing or pulling the market into racially divergent paths, resulting in a more or less voluntary reisolation of the black community. In the 1970s, beneath the pop cultural smokescreen of the disco floor (which was never as integrated as the audiences for the most popular exponents of soul that rocked, like Sly and the Family Stone), African-Americans burrowed deeper into funk, weaning a new generation on the teat of James Brown and funk disciples like George Clinton, music that initially resisted the prevailing notions of crossover. Meanwhile, "rock" became, from the black point of view, an unambiguously "white" thing; by the beginning of the 1980s, the patrimony of black rockers from Little Richard to Sly Stone was substantially disowned by most black consumers of a certain age. Looping back to the early 1950s again, once Charlie Parker's bebop took over the jazz imagination, jazz was doomed as black America's dance music and therefore was no longer white America's dance music, simply because the mercurial "Bird's" innovations tended to disconnect the music from a steady danceable beat. In sum, in the late 1970s the black audience walked away from rock and its black roots; in the late 1940s the black roots of jazz began walking away from the black audience. Either way the effect was the same: Jazz and rock became commercially white.

Culturally, the most significant connection between the rock-and-roll and hip-hop revolutions is the swift, surprising ascendance of "the real," a more frank and raw real than the Jazz Age ever suggested, as the paramount measure of cultural relevance. From its foundation in the more ribald and frankly libidinous aspects of the blues tradition, rock and roll sprang forth as "real" sex for its otherwise frustrated and repressed beat/silent-generation and early baby-boomer fans. It soon broadened to include "real" teenage anxiety about growing up under unprecedented pressures to perform as well as conform and under the shadow of the very first atomic mushroom clouds. The rock-and-roll ethos also developed around a strange new amalgam of materialism and self-absorbed nihilism best captured by the teenager who insists he has to have a new Chevy so he can hang out and do nothing in particular but do it in style. It's the same teenager, just a bit older, who flaunts utter indifference to everyone around him except as concerns messing with his blue suede shoes. Of course, placed side by side, what was thought to be "real" in early rock-and-roll culture looks to have been force-fed steroids as it's manifested in rap/hip-hop culture, the latter being at once so much more material, violent in its selfish nihilism, predatory in its sexuality, and absolutely preening in devotion to brand-name materialism. Yet in the end most of the discrepancies between the 1950s and the 1980s regarding the text of what was "real" can be explained away by adjusting for thirty years of a particular economic and social history that was unique, even for America. What cannot be canceled out of the two equations, however, is the subtext of the "real," the common denominator: the Negro. It was in the 1950s that the idea that the black experience was the most authentic and existentially vital American experience first went deep into the thinking of the intellectual elite. From there it slowly began (or rather resumed) its long, slow seep into mainstream consumer cultural identity.

Louis Jordan found early success "singing songs filled with images from ghetto life ('Saturday Night Fish Fry,' for example, recounts a police raid on a block party)."[5] Little Richard was a fly on a very different wall from most of Eisenhower-era America in "Havin' Some Fun Tonight," when he sang:

> I saw Uncle John with Long Tall Sally
> He saw Aunt Mary comin'
> And he jump'd back in the alley
> Oh, baby . . . havin' me some fun tonight

The white small businessmen who pioneered the rhythm-and-blues business that turned into the rock music industry were almost obsessive in their demand to record what they thought was the "real" in the musical culture.

Atlantic Records' Ertegun describes in *Flowers in the Dustbin* how he pushed legendary R&B singer Ruth Brown away from her aspiration to emulate the white pop sound of the day and toward singing more like a "real" Negro, and why:

> "When I first met Ruth Brown, her main number, the song she liked best," as he recalled, was by a white songbird, Doris Day, "or Jo Stafford, or one of those. . . . And there's nothing wrong with the urban black man getting into the general taste of the world, you know, except that that taste is never as good as what he had to begin with."[6]

Sam Phillips, who first recorded B. B. King when he was still shy around white people and couldn't play guitar and sing at the same time, says one of his biggest problems was getting the early black artists he was recording to keep it "real":

> I knew what I wanted. I wanted something ugly. Ugly and honest. I knew that these people were disenfranchised. They were politically disenfranchised and economically disenfranchised, and to tell the truth they were musically disenfranchised. . . . The big trouble in those days, if you were recording black musicians, was that they would start changing what they were doing for you because you were white. They'd look up in the recording booth and see a white man, and they'd start trying to be like Billy Eckstine and Nat King Cole. I didn't want that. The things that RCA and Capitol winced at, I loved.[7]

Phillips's feeling is very similar to that of the early "indie" recorders of rap/hip-hop—except that much of the latter was recorded not in a studio, destined to be sold on wax in stores, but on cassette tapes, to be traded in the streets. And of course, both groups were producing the sound of their own black peers, strictly for the benefit of their black peers.

In the early 1950s, for a complex set of reasons, certain genes of color that had been long dormant in the chromosomes of American identity seemed to be seeking madly a way to express themselves in ways beyond all that the Jazz Age had wrought. The recent scholarship on the period details the impact of shifting technology, unprecedented economic prosperity, the start of cold war and its politics, suburbanization, and the civil rights movement on the 1950s Zeitgeist. More than anything in the sociohistorical record, I am struck by the sense of *anticipation* that runs through the narratives. Something more than Hitler's armies and Japan's imperial aspirations were destroyed in World War II. Though the society was still effectively segregated, Americans had a profound awareness that they all had been through a life-or-death struggle together and had been delivered together. And for the duration of that worldwide conflagration, we knew who *we* were, different from our German foes and even our English allies, by dint of our participation in the "real" American culture. The thread of anticipation that stitched the 1950s together was sewn by the sense that we had fought for the absolute freedom to be ourselves, especially as individuals. The war brought a new focus and greater, though by no means complete, clarity to the sense of a distinct, emergent, and *insurgent* American identity. The anticipation was rooted in the gut knowledge that just as Hitler would no longer threaten that flowering, economic, technological, and—most important—social limitations would no longer stand in the way of what was to become. Somehow Americans just knew that even a dirt-poor redneck might become a rock star, before anybody had any idea what such a thing might be.

Going in, to be sure, America was seriously divided about the war's real purpose, reflecting the very real divisions of prewar society. Nevertheless, Americans came out knowing that the future would be driven by a flight from what they had clearly fought against: the tyranny of racial imperialism represented by Hitler and Hirohito. Freedom lay in some direction away from the racial and ethnic determinism central to Nazism, and nothing was farther from the Aryan than the black American. Freedom, in the American preconsciousness of the early 1950s, had something to do with the Negro. By far the most divided region in America, the Deep South, knew that best, despite its vociferous denials. The Deep South knew the "real" black culture best because, black and white, it was their culture, derived mostly from a few hundred years of interaction and no small amount of interbreeding. Everyone knows the story of how Sam Phillips set up his record business just in time for the coming of a white boy whose sound was genuinely black, almost like John the Baptist anticipating Christ. It's easy to stop at the first obvious lesson from that story: Racism dictated that "real" southern culture would never be commercially acceptable packaged in its natural brown skin. But the Phillips parable offers another, equally important lesson: Sam Phillips *knew* that that "black" white boy was coming. From what scripture, what old testament, could Phillips have drawn this great faith, given that the region universally anathematized the merest hint of race mixing? My guess is that he knew Elvis, Jerry Lee Lewis, et al. were coming, in spite of the political-whiteness status quo, because they were already there. The power of black music, Halberstam writes, was already premixed in Phillips's own white identity; he was certain he couldn't be alone.

> He had grown up poor in northern Alabama, aware of the tensions between blacks and whites. Every Sunday Sam Phillips went to a white Baptist church in town. About a block and a half away was a black Methodist church. "There was something there I had never heard before or since," he said years later. "Those men and women singing . . . the Amen and the rhythm. They never missed a downbeat." There was, he thought, so much more power in their music than his own, so much more feeling and so much more love. He felt pulled toward it, and he would leave his own church and linger outside the black church to listen.[8]

Phillips was no northern intellectual, and the contemporaneous task of articulating and imposing meaning on the browning of the American cultural phenotype fell to Norman Mailer. Mailer's 1957 essay that introduced the term *white Negro* to the world could have aptly been used to explain Phillips himself. In it Mailer described

> a new breed of youthful hipster, modeled after those found in urban locales like Greenwich Village where "the bohemian and the juvenile delinquent came face to face with the Negro." Race played a special role in the psychic economy [of the new white hipster]. As an object of endless fantasy in the mind of the youthful white hipster, the Negro came to symbolize a universe of forbidden plea-

sures: a creature of "Saturday night kicks," the hipster's Negro had relinquished "the pleasures of the mind for the more obligatory pleasures of the body," pleasures he conveyed to others through the mode of music, which gave voice to the character and quality of his existence, to his rage and the infinite variations of joy, lust, languor, growl, cramp, pinch, scream and despair of his orgasm.[9]

The South is where the new feeling was born, but few southerners would recognize anything of themselves in Mailer's white Negroes, which says as much about Elvis and Jerry Lee Lewis's authenticity as their native region's collective denial.

The most important gene that rock and roll turned on in the American identity genome was rage. Though commercial rock and roll could never really tolerate rage with a black face, and though it only inconsistently allied itself with the nonwhite political cause, black, blues-based rage, alienation, and the premonition of doom underwrote rock and roll's commercial cultural power from early Elvis to heavy metal to punk and beyond. To bend the gospel of John (the Apostle, not Lennon): In the beginning was the real—the rage, the fear, the will to live, love, and lust in the now because tomorrow is not promised. And the real was with the Negro; the Negro was with America from the start. In the 1950s, when America produced roughly half the world's economic output, an American commercial culture was destined to infiltrate and dominate the world, replicating this sometimes raging, sometimes just outrageous Negro DNA wherever it went. What was first transferred in the 1950s was not just the songs of the black creators but something of the spirit that would more fully express itself over time as it transformed those who were drawn to it. In his classic volume on rock and Euro-American identity, Greil Marcus, discussing the impact of the mythic black bluesman Robert Johnson on guitarist Eric Clapton, suggests that the "real," mature "white Negro" emerged as neither white nor Negro but as something more than the sum of the parts:

> The music that is animated by Robert Johnson today is not really found in new rock 'n' roll versions of his songs; Johnson's spirit is not so easy to capture. All of Eric Clapton's love for Johnson's music came to bear not when Clapton sang Johnson's songs, but

when, once Johnson's music became part of who Clapton was, Clapton came closest to himself: in the passion of "Layla" . . . after years of practice and imitation, Johnson's sound was Clapton's sound . . . there was no way to separate the two men, nor any need to.[10]

As the white Negro emerged and attempted to culturally separate from the mainstream white, the black Negro emerged from the social and political shadows and from his prewar self. As he came out, he found that a new aggressiveness and resolve to advance with dignity was more likely to be rewarded with economic and social opportunity than he had dreamed possible as few as ten years earlier. African-Americans were taking the first of a long series of steps toward self-recognition as creators of value and as consumers. The war had laid much of the basic groundwork for a relative boom in the postwar black economy. The war effort had pulled vast numbers of blacks into parts of the industrial economy that did not previously exist or were entirely unavailable to black labor. Even in the Deep South, black economic clout was rising, and everybody, black consumers and white capitalists alike, knew it.

After the war, the income of African-Americans, historically depressed, grew even more quickly than that of whites. In a city like Memphis, certain commodities were disproportionately bought by blacks. A pioneering survey of Negro consumers in Memphis, conducted in 1952, revealed that black Memphians consumed 80 percent of the city's packaged rice, 70 percent of its canned milk, and 65 percent of its all-purpose flour. The same survey showed that radios, once beyond the means of the average black family, had become a standard appliance—in Memphis alone, 93 percent of black households owned a radio, and 30 percent owned two. Advertisers eager to reach this newly affluent audience naturally turned to radio shows that featured [rhythm-and-blues] music.[11]

Again, there are striking parallels with the 1980s and early 1990s, up to a point. In both periods the fast-growing incomes of black consumers, lifting off from a smaller base, drew special attention from local, national, and soon-to-be multinational marketers. What we've come to call ethnic target marketing got its first real growth spurt in the 1950s, ebbed and flowed in the 1960s and early-affirmative-action 1970s, only to explode in the 1980s. Rising black affluence provided the sustaining consumer base for both early rhythm and blues/rock and roll and, to a different extent, for early rap/hip-hop, before they "crossed over." Black demand, in the economic sense and increasingly in the literal sense, created the conditions for the first crossover to be born. Doug Alligood, a senior vice president for special markets with BBDO, the New York advertising firm, recalls the near total indifference of mainstream radio stations and record stores to rhythm-and-blues music in the St. Louis of his boyhood. Alligood, a rare black veteran of the mainstream advertising business, remembers the first time a record by a black artist, Arthur Prysock, made the playlist of the leading "first five" (a playlist with heavy repetition of the top five songs on its pop chart) format station.

> You couldn't hear [black bluesman] John Lee Hooker on the "first five station" ... KXOW in St. Louis. ... They wouldn't play "those kinds" of records. They were reluctant to even play Nat Cole or Arthur Prysock. I remember the first time [Prysock] was on "first five." The disk jockey came on, Gill Newsome, very famous disk jockey, and he says, "Here's number 5, boy this really comes out of left field ... I never heard of this guy before." And every black person in St. Louis knew who Arthur Prysock was ... maybe every black person in America. And yet he'd never heard of him. That struck me very hard as a kid.

Undaunted, Alligood went to St. Louis's Famous Bar record store and asked for a Nat "King" Cole record.

> The woman put her nose up in the air and said, "We don't sell those kinds of records in Famous Bar." And I looked at her—I was just a kid—and I said, "One day, you will." That's all I said, and I walked out.

Alligood went on to make a career out of his belief in the power of markets over the ultimate course of marketing and advertising. Meanwhile, not five hundred miles *south* down the Mississippi River, Dewey Phillips was tearing up the Memphis airwaves with undiluted Mississippi Delta rhythm and blues, and Sam Phillips was discovering the most seminal white Negro of the decade, Elvis Presley. Elvis wore loud clothes from Lansky's, "a store more likely to be visited by flashy black men about town,"[12] like a pop cultural siren. The difference between St. Louis and Memphis in this regard was the critical mass of black economic demand. Memphis, Miller writes, was an early national leader in black radio programming. In 1948 WDIA-Memphis became the first station in America to play an all-black music schedule, hosted by all-black disk jockeys. The core black market made it possible for the otherwise all-white WHBQ to program a "race record" format at night, picking up where WDIA, which broadcast only from dawn to dusk, left off. The core black market validated, if not outright created, the commercial personas of pioneering "white Negro" disk jockeys like Zenas "Daddy" Sears in Atlanta, "John R." Richbourg in Nashville, and Hunter Hancock in Los Angeles. The late rhythm-and-blues legend Rufus Thomas, who was also the WDIA disk jockey nicknamed "Hound Dog," said of Phillips, his competitor, that "Dewey was not white . . . Dewey had no color."[13]

Perhaps, but color still had the ultimate power to affect the unfolding of commercial culture. This is where the 1950s and the 1980s cease to be in historical parallel; this is what distinguishes the mid-1980s and beyond from all that went before. In the 1980s the black face of rage and a new kind of outrageousness were not only acceptable but essential to commercial viability. In the 1950s the commercialization of color meant watering down, whitening. As control of the market for the new cool moved from fringe independents to major record companies, from local radio stations to national television networks, and as it spread from the music industry to film, fashion, and beyond; conventional business wisdom insisted that a product's acceptance, and hence its profitability, was inversely proportionate to the prominence of its connection to black communities and America's sociohistorical legacy of race. Slavery, after all, was still only ninety years or three generations dead in 1955. The high point of lynchings in the South was no more than still in recent memory. The civil rights movement, and the massive resistance to it in the Deep South, had only just begun in 1954. If the 1950s were the 1980s, then when Little Richard's "Tutti Frutti" began selling out of record stores all over the South, driven by demand from the white teenage majority, some enterprising entertainment conglomerate would quickly have developed and delivered a business plan to put his image on posters in every teenage bedroom in America. In the 1980s, after all, entertainment marketers were able to execute a similar strategy for the much less talented (though no less flamboyant) black transvestite RuPaul.

But the 1950s were in fact the 1950s. The record executive who tried to make Little Richard a fixture in suburban teen bedrooms would have found himself summoned before Senator Joseph "Tailgunner Joe" McCarthy's anti-Communist inquisition so fast, his head would spin. No entertainment conglomerate moved to make a direct connection between the new black "real" and the widest possible audience—that is, anyone with ears, disposable income, and the free will to choose; rather, a highly fragmented, infant segment of a much smaller record industry responded to "Tutti Frutti." In the most telling response, Randy Wood, the proprietor of a Tennessee mail-order record store and the Dot independent record label, hurried Pat Boone into the studio to do a white version of the song, deliberately draining the original of its gospel shouting power. Little Richard did, of course, manage to achieve considerable fame in the 1950s before giving up rock and roll for gospel music in 1960. His version of "Tutti Frutti" was captured in the seminal 1956 teen flick *Don't Knock the Rock*. As Miller describes it:

> Wearing a baggy suit, Richard stood silently after being introduced . . . and then tore into "Tutti Frutti." As the camera zoomed in for a close-up, Richard pounded the piano, tossed his head, rolled his eyes, and waved his arms, an image of jubilant anarchy. The song finished, he took an ironically exaggerated bow. Then he tore into "Long Tall Sally." . . . Arms flailing, he leaned back, kicked his leg onto the piano and shimmied while saxophonist Grady Gaines soloed, blowing his horn fron the top of Richard's grand piano.[14]

Little Richard even played ABC's *American Bandstand,* the epitome of the corporate mainstreaming of rock and roll. But the critical point is that in the 1950s only Little Richard could have gotten away with being as black and raw as he was. The same year he vamped all over *Don't Knock the Rock,* Nat

"King" Cole became the first African-American to get his own TV show. In addition to being musically brilliant, he was smooth, handsome, and urbane, "willing to smile and clown, but unwilling to suppress his native intelligence."[15] But even that persona was still too threatening, especially for southern markets; after the first season the show was canceled for lack of advertisers. Little Richard went on to be the only true rock-and-roll pioneer to last long enough personally install himself into America's cultural archives as a national treasure. The key to his longevity is the persona he created to navigate what he correctly perceived to be the new boundaries of opportunity for a black man in American pop culture. America was ready for something new in the sound of the genuine Negro, but it was still a long way from dealing with the old questions regarding the place of the Negro. In the early 1980s, when the fledgling MTV refused to play videos from Michael Jackson's *Thriller* album (because they were supposed to be airing "rock videos" and, ironically, were still wedded to the late-1970s idea that rock was by definition "white"), Jackson's multinational record label, CBS (soon to be Sony), put the considerable weight of its corporate foot down on MTV's neck, and it quickly relented. But that kind of backing didn't exist for Little Richard in the 1950s. To successfully play the hand he was dealt, Little Richard had to come up with a persona that was true to the "real" but somehow inoffensive to the core American fear of black male power, especially sexuality. He invented the bulletproof male diva.

> Richard intuitively grasped the issues at play: being black and being gay, he was an outsider twice over. But by exaggerating his own freakishness, he could get across: he could evade the question of gender and hurdle the racial divide. "We decided that my image should be crazy and way out," Richard recalls in his memoir, "so that the adults would think I was harmless. I'd appear in one show dressed as the Queen of England and in the next as the Pope."[16]

(For extra credit, compare and contrast Little Richard's *benign* outrageous, sexually ambiguous persona with the almost malign outrageous, gender-bending persona of the artist known in the 1980s as Prince. Hint: Little Richard threatened to scream "Whoooooooo" in your ear; Prince, in songs like "Let's Pretend We're Married," left no doubt about his intent to have his way with more intimate orifices.)

The 1950s were about meeting a new level of demand for commercialized black culture while appearing not to cede white control of the product or alienating more than an acceptably small minority of white adults, especially economically unimportant white adults. They were about giving the core teen market no more than it asked for, then diluting it as much as possible without ruining the sound or the show. The difference between rock and hip-hop is that while rock was also born black, its commercialization put it almost immediately on the road to becoming white. The fashion look that set the early Elvis Presley far apart from his white contemporaries might have been called "black pimp roll," if it been given an honest name. By the time he was fully "Elvis," the look was called "greaser," and it would forever evoke a period in the culture during which any blacks who participated were always kept in the background. *American Bandstand* featured otherwise wholesome "white ethnic" proto-greaser teens who learned most of their dance steps from black classmates in an integrated high school in Philadelphia, where the show was produced. But the show's standard practice was never to focus the camera on the handful of black teens present during the broadcast.

The Jazz Age had proven the commercial viability of the Negro's joy. As the 1950s became the 1960s, America developed a bankable taste for the sound and feel of black yearning, that combination of sexual and spiritual longing that runs from Sam Cooke through Smokey Robinson and most of the Motown sound, Aretha Franklin, Teddy Pendergrass, Luther Vandross, et al., right though the soul diva of the moment. From this platform a steady stream of black entertainers found increasing opportunity to jump into pop by the late 1970s. But 1950s-into-1960s popular culture also appropriated black rage, alienation, and potential for nihilism—and reserved it for white artists and performers. Even as black male athletes like Bill Russell, Willie Mays, "Sugar Ray" Robinson, and Wilt Chamberlain were bringing acceptance of color into professional sports in the post–Jackie Robinson era, they had to come off as noble warriors, not as renegade, arrogant, or boastful bluesmen. Muhammad Ali and Jim Brown, of course, were far off the scale in this regard, but so were their absolute athletic talents. They survived all that their mouths got them into—Jim Brown even made a few mainstream movies toward the anything-goes end of the 1960s. But neither really became a legitimate commercial pop icon until the 1980s, when rap and hip-hop vindicated all of Ali's arrogance and Brown's combination of nationalism, misogyny, and gangsterism, in general and by name.

With its appropriated black rage and all its creative potential in tow, rock and roll broadened as it blew into the 1960s whirlwind of cultural, social, and political ferment. Soul, the part of the culture that the white mainstream did not or could not own, also flourished, and for a time the two halves of the one cultural heart beat together. A brief golden age of music-based transracial youth culture flourished for a time, during which the lines between rock, soul, and rhythm and blues were willfully blurred. The celebrated Memphis sound, for example, was a genuine collaboration between black artists like Otis Redding, Wilson Pickett, and white southern studio musicians cut from the same race-bending cloth as Elvis and Jerry Lee Lewis. At the same time, popular culture rooted in (and largely produced for) nonwhite consumers in urban centers like Detroit, New York, and Chicago gained sufficient exposure to compete for mainstream attention, in a commercial culture market that was increasingly international.

Most observers date the end of this period at April 4, 1968, the day Martin Luther King Jr. was assassinated. The politics of racial unrest and the conservative backlash against integration temporarily dammed the rising interracial tide at the 1960s' end, much as it killed the black-white collaboration of the Memphis sound. But a new paradigm had been established. Association with black or brown skin was no longer an absolute bar to selling popular culture to whites, even in the South. The legacy of the 1950s in the late 1970s was the kind of commercial culture smorgasbord that we now call "diverse" or "multicultural." By then nonwhite creative talents had increased their penetration of previously closed areas of popular and high culture. Boomer-generation whites could *respectfully* pick and choose from a much wider variety of other-than-white-bread cultural tropes—from pop soul to hard rock, to blaxploitation movies and "youth" movies and to karate flicks and the remnants of hippie culture—without worrying about the racial implications.

❑   ❑   ❑

Disco was quickly discredited and denied after its hasty crucifixion around 1980, but it was undeniably *"urban"* (in the sense of "made by blacks but not just for blacks"), and it unquestionably ruled for over five years before suddenly being declared dead upon Ronald Reagan's first inauguration. Disco was the culmination of a long history of combining black, white, and more and more international cultural raw material in an increasingly powerful commercial blender. Its musical form was almost superfluous, in contrast to the truly transracial energies being released beneath all those glittering balls. The fundamental power that disco expressed did not disappear overnight. Disco, in fact, marked the dividing line between what became of the 1950s and what was still to come. Under that dry ice fog, in addition to the founding funk of hip-hop, the hands of technicians could be seen at work, mixing every kind of music in the world with a beat (and inserting beats where they pleased) and serving it up *without cultural value judgments* while traditional rock mostly vegetated on the sidelines. Like it or not, disco nurtured the embryo of every new pop music form that has come along since.

Disco, with its electronically programmed, cable-ready presentation, also coincided with the infancy of high-powered, multimedia-driven identity and lifestyle marketing. As narcissistic boomers entered their prime buying years, marketers discovered their nearly infinite willingness to pay to be something more than what their parents were: plain white Americans. When they were in high school in the 1960s, the leaders of their parents' generation had tried to block their right to rock, and explosive cultural anarchy resulted. By the mid-1970s marketers began to see how that energy could be channeled and, as we say today, more efficiently monetized. The World War II generation was nearing retirement age, and the boomers, fresh off the dance floor, were taking the levers of an emerging media-information industrial complex whose scope and centrality to the new American way of life could not have been imagined just a few years earlier. The Vietnam War and the civil rights movement were over; the moral weight of their protests were no longer an obstacle to commercial exploitation. Lifestyle choices that had been personal, political, and decidedly noncommercial in the 1960s were now fair game for packaging, refinement, and extension into the service of building brand loyalties on a global scale. Disco wasn't just records—it was the first global information economy. Hundreds of millions of behinds and chests worldwide were emblazoned with the same trademarks while moving to the same beat, sharing an unprecedented self-awareness of commercial cultural identity.

Soon you didn't just watch television, you channel-surfed in an endless quest to catch the next big wave in pop infotainment. The more channels they had to choose from, the less people cared about where any particular wave began: South Bronx or Beverly Hills, it was all just part of the mix on MTV or CNN or *Entertainment Tonight*. Even before disco died, you didn't just drink Pepsi, you were part of the "Pepsi Generation." The branding of American identity, with marks that said everything about cool and less and less about color, was just around the corner.

The competition to sell Americans expanded identities was on, forcing creators and marketers, aided by new communications technologies, to draw even more on nonwhite, non-European sources of culture. Culture itself would increasingly be called by a new, more coolly commercial and politically neutral name: *content*. The racial politics of the World War II leadership generation were finally no obstacle to the rising multinational marketing powers. If anything, Ronald Reagan and his fellow travelers were perfect foils for a commercial counterculture counterattack.

4

Marketing in Color: New Niches Flow into the Mainstream

In the spring of 1999, shortly after securing the freedom of three American soldiers captured by the Yugoslavian Army during the NATO miniwar on Yugoslavia over Kosovo, the Reverend Jesse Jackson paid a call on the headquarters of PepsiCo in the bucolic New York suburb of Purchase. Still basking in the glow of his latest freelance foreign policy coup, Jackson's mission was to press top executives to throw more corporate-securities-underwriting work toward certain black- and minority-owned firms. With a small entourage in tow, Jackson's very presence in the mostly empty halls of the secluded corporate campus caused a bigger stir than most anybody in the well-starched head office of the perennial number-two cola maker could remember. It remained for one older employee, a black maintenance man, to put the pagentry of the sales call into context.

"'This is the most excitement since the day Don King came up here,'" said Pepsi marketing executive Maurice Cox, quoting the maintenance man's words. Indeed, everyone involved with selling Pepsi seemed to remember the fall 1983 day when the already-legendary, if not infamous, boxing promoter's humongous white stretch limosine, "big—like the kind they have today, only it was back then," parked on the cobblestone path before Pepsi's executive suite. The day Don King brought Pepsi the then-outrageous proposal of a $5 million sponsorship deal for the twenty-three-year-old "soul

93

singer" Michael Jackson and his brothers was memorable enough to merit a chapter, just two years later, in Pepsi president Roger Enrico's 1986 book on the 1980s cola wars.

> Many important personages have come to Pepsico headquarters . . . none of them made the entrance King did. A land yacht of a limo pulled up, and out stepped this man in a white fur coat that had to cost as much as the car. King's pearly gray hair had been freshly electrocuted and was reaching the sky. Around King's neck was a blindingly shiny necklace, on which hung his logo, a crown with "DON" on top, just in case you might forget he is the king.
>   Such a man did not come quickly through the halls.
>   "Hi, everybody, I'm Don King," he told one and all.[1]

Enshrining the moment was the least Enrico could do, because his decision to take a deal that only Don King would think of proposing to a *Fortune* 100 firm back then fixed the word *legendary* before the former PepsiCo chairman's name and secured his place in marketing history. It was a meeting that no one doing marketing at Coke's Atlanta headquarters would forget, either. For decades Pepsi had been desperate to gain a marketing edge over Coke. Enrico, who had just become president of the Pepsi-Cola division, was determined to do whatever it took to pull Coke, still the most hallowed American brand name, down to earth. Beyond the theatrics of the messenger, Don King's message was that Michael Jackson was about to shatter previously shatterproof barriers between black entertainers and mainstream popular culture. But even King's bombast failed to anticipate the financial records Jackson would also break along the way on the strength of the *Thriller* album. Released early in 1983, it had already topped the charts with nearly 10 million copies sold by the time King came to Pepsi. *Thriller* went on to quadruple that number and became the biggest-selling album in history. Guinness actually held the presses on the 1984 edition of the *World's Records* book (a first in itself) to include *Thriller* as the top seller of all time, passing Carole King's 1970 *Tapestry*, when the industry-shaking album had still hit only 25 million in sales. The $5 million sponsorship deal Pepsi announced in December 1983 was also a Guinness record; it lasted until Jackson signed a $15 million personal endorsement deal with Pepsi two years later.

The awards, concert attendance, television ratings, and the like connected with Jackson during the mid-1980s, summed up by the term *Michaelmania*, could make up a book by themselves. So could the impact of the "Jackson phenomenon," as it was also called, on the very foundations of media-driven commercial culture. It spawned an orgy of "who is he and who are we as a society" journalistic navel-gazing not seen over a performing act since the Beatles landed in the States in 1964. In one week in March 1984, culture critics at both *Time* magazine and the *Washington Post* vainly exhausted more than six thousand words trying to plumb the connection between the Jackson persona and our collective psyche. Writing right after Jackson took eight out of a possible ten awards at the 1984 Grammys (another record) and searching for meaning, the authors seemed to be drowning in the sea of statistics (1 million albums sold per week for over twenty-four weeks and still counting), in the flood of celebrity swells (Jane Fonda, Elizabeth Taylor, Katharine Hepburn, Brooke Shields, Steven Spielberg) attached to the Jackson tide, and in the wave of historical icon comparisons (Babe Ruth, Al Jolson, Elvis, Howard Hughes, the Beatles).

All they really knew for sure was what the *Post*'s Richard Harrington asserted:

> The combined evidence of the bottom line, the hard listen and the long view is difficult to resist: Jackson is the biggest thing since the Beatles. He is the hottest single phenomenon since Elvis Presley. He just may be the most popular black singer ever.[2]

And still they missed it.

Harrington was to the point in noting that the breathtakingly styled music of *Thriller* wasn't a breakthrough in itself, and that "Michael Jackson is far more popular than influential (again more like Elvis, rather than the Beatles)." But *Time*'s Jay Cocks came closer to the pith of the moment in observing that:

> *Thriller* brought black music back to mainstream radio, from which it had been effectively banished after restrictive "special-format programming" was introduced in the mid-'70s. Listeners could put more carbonation in their pop and cut their heavy-metal diet with

a dose of the fleetest soul around. "No doubt about it," says composer-arranger Quincy Jones, who produced *Off the Wall* and *Thriller* with Jackson. "He's taken us right up there where we belong. Black music has to play second fiddle for a long time, but its spirit is the whole motor of pop. Michael has connected with every soul in the world."[3]

But neither analysis detected the fault lines deep in the crust of popular culture that happened to intersect with the frail black performer's mercurial rise. Michael Jackson the earthquake struck where the emerging entertainment-information economy met the mother-seam of color at the core of American popular culture. At the epicenter, on the surface, was the thing called pop.

Pop, as a music-industry (as opposed to musical) category, had always been a euphemism for *white* until Michael unleashed "the power of *Thriller.*" For example, Chuck Berry, for all his classic hit songs and unimpeachable claim to rock and roll's paternity, landed only one number-one pop single in his career, and that was at the end, with the novelty tune "My Dingaling" in 1972. In the 1960s and 1970s, the biggest Motown acts, the Bacharach-David-produced Dionne Warwick hits, and a few black bands like Earth, Wind and Fire garnered black performers their first significant "crossover" spots on the pop charts, but most black acts could aspire only to *Billboard*'s rhythm-and-blues chart.[4] As part of the Jackson Five, Michael Jackson had been one of the exceptions to the industry practices that limited black access to the pop charts. Between 1970 and 1976, the group had landed seven singles in the pop top ten.

Yet for nonwhite performers, even holding precious slots on the pop charts did not a pop star make. Until *Thriller* the unofficial "King" or "Queen of Pop" had always been white, no matter how many records a black artist sold or how much airplay it got.

American pop, as it turned out, is more than an industry chart. True pop icon status, at the very top, is a state of grace that approaches divine right over one's consumer-subjects in the marketplace. It's a cross between being royalty and being in the top management of mainstream affinity, complete with rituals of respect, ceremonies of adoration, and titles. Pop is what Elvis was after he stopped his initial blues shouting and let Colonel Parker make him the perfect (but not too perfect) heartthrob for white teenage girls as the 1950s became the 1960s. He was the "King." Pop is the firm Sinatra controlled before Elvis, and for many Americans over a certain age, he remained the "Chairman" until the day he died. By the time your parents could be seen nodding in agreement with their peers that "I Want to Hold Your Hand" was really classically inspired, it was the Beatles, one of whom (Paul McCartney) was actually knighted by the queen. Pop is the universal white blue-collar factory that Bruce Springsteen ran in the late 1970s and into the 1980s. He was "the Boss."

To be sure, there were titles enough to go around in the marginal kingdoms of R&B and soul and gospel and Latin music: Aretha Franklin—Queen, James Brown—Godfather, Celia Cruz—Queen of Salsa, and so on. Still, no nonwhites needed to apply for mainstream pop music honorifics as the 1970s became the 1980s. Ditto, with a few notable exceptions, pop positions in television, movies, and (significantly) fashion and style. Bill Cosby, Coke's primary general-market pitchman in the 1970s, also sold well for Jell-O and Ford. O. J. Simpson broke entirely new ground for retired black professional athletes with his ubiquitous Hertz commercials. But neither man would be recognized or recognizable as a pop icon until the early 1990s, and not just because they had yet to star in their respective hit televison shows. Until Michael Jackson and *Thriller*, marketers simply assumed that no matter how successful a nonwhite performer might be, whiteness was an indispensable requirement for the exaggerated state of mass identification that constitutes "pop stardom."

Then Roger Enrico bet the farm on Michael Jackson and *Thriller*—and won.

As the 1980s began, the business of whiteness-centered pop was, as usual, lurching between cyclical feast and famine. But by the decade's end, the same forces that brought *Thriller*'s eruption would move whiteness from indispensable to merely useful in the business of pop, *permanently*, while raising the influence, the reach, and most important, the aggregate profitablility of pop entertainment to unimagined heights. By 1990 America's collective pop culture, bonded to the cutting edge of a revolution in telecommunications and information technology, had assumed the lead role in the world's most powerful global economy. Think about it: In 1980 the business of pop could not have imagined the multidimensional marketing star power of Michael Jackson, Michael Jordan, Whitney Houston, or Eddie Murphy. It hadn't seen the platinum branding of predominantly nonwhite professional basketball, football, and baseball or the "Nike-ization" of marketing that attended it. It hadn't even seen a hint of the multibillion-dollar music-fashion-style-literature industry called hip-hop. In other words, in 1980 American commercial popular culture hadn't seen nothing yet.

❐   ❐   ❐

The National Basketball Association was widely reported to be close to foundering in 1981 and 1982, as weak attendance and anemic ratings imperiled it in the years after it merged with the upstart American Basketball Association. In 1980 eighteen of its twenty-three franchises were running red ink, and four were said to be close to folding.[5] It's hard to even imagine today, but in 1982 the big pro basketball business news was that CBS would actually air the championship series *live* in prime time, for the first time since 1978! Midway through the 1982–83 season, NHL hockey was actually drawing 35 percent more fans to the arenas than NBA games. The NBA was the first major sport to be tainted by association with the problem of cocaine and other drug abuse. Well before the grand jury of public opinion returned the larger indictment of pro athletes as selfish, money-grubbing, team-hopping, coke-sniffing malingerers, NBA players were acquiring an image as overpaid, lazy, and morally suspect druggies. It was significant, and no coincidence, that these stereotypes initially came to rest on the first major team sport whose rosters had become overwhemingly black. Sports journalists, though much more reluctant to raise racial issues directly in their columns than they are today, privately expressed the opinion that professional basketball could only go downhill as a predominantly black league.

When David Stern took over as NBA commissioner in February 1984, the league itself had just sixteen employees and was little more than the entity that hired referees, made up season schedules, and periodically negotiated contracts with the players' union and with CBS for the games it felt like televising. Promotion was mostly limited to the local efforts of franchise owners, who focused on their own teams as a whole, not on individual players. The NBA relied on history, as reported and interpreted by the middle-aged white

that time, and the NBA was smart enough to take advantage of that. He had . . . personality, an aura about him, a sense of confidence, and a smile that is very addictive. The people on ad street, they love that. A lot has to do with his attitude and personality. That's a gift that God has given him. Even though he doesn't speak well . . . he still gets opportunities because he's still Magic. And there's something magic about him.

Magic and Bird did the running and rebounding. But Stern's indispensable contribution, beyond the legal agreements he struck early on, was that he saw so much possibility in what the NBA players had to offer, and how it could be marketed, when so many other white male experts, like the doubters at the *Boston Globe*, couldn't.

What did David Stern see? First, it must be remembered *how* he saw, which was mainly through the eyes of a fan—David Stern. A long interview revealed Stern as an information age savant as conversant in the language of rating points, homes passed, and direct satellite distribution as any cable network operator and as intuitive about brand managment, image building, and media presence as a marketing executive from Procter and Gamble. A lawyer by training, he picked up all these capacities as he went along. But in the end, he says, it was his gut feeling that "these are our guys"—that is, some of the most uniquely talented individuals in the world—"and the fact that these are people that you would like to know" that guided him. All "his guys" needed, he said, was exposure to the target audience, especially to young adult and teenage males. Familiarity with their faces and personal story lines, he maintained, would quickly overcome racial barriers and breed affection, not contempt. No major professional sports league had ever previously worried about nurturing familiarity with its stars as individuals. None had had to. In basketball, for example, from the day he entered the league, it was a given that Jerry West was a rookie named Jerry West, not some new "white guy." It was a given, because other white guys were writing the sports columns. Stern realized that as the NBA player census crossed into the 70 percent black range and beyond, the assumption that even a bright young star like Michael Jordan would be seen first as an individual and not just as another preternaturally athletic (read, softly: subhuman) black kid couldn't be taken for granted. Bob Williams, president of Burns Sports, an Evanston, Illinois, sports marketing firm that advises marketers on signing athlete endorsers, credits Stern as the first sports executive to figure out how to turn an image liability into a most valuable asset. Professional football under then-commissioner Pete Rozelle, said Williams, quickly took note.

> I think David Stern and Pete Rozelle realized that they needed to promote the individuals in the game. One reason baseball is behind in popularity is they promote the game . . . wonderful, pastoral—America's pastime. And it is—[but] the NBA and NFL were able to put faces people could identify with. . . . At the same time America's view on race had evolved enough that people wouldn't care. They wanted to see great basketball more than they wanted to see a bunch of white guys playing basketball. Stern saw that the individual could be the rocket fuel . . . to take the game to greater heights on an international basis, which both those leagues have done better than baseball.

To be sure, when Stern began, many advertisers couldn't be convinced that the mostly black teams they were being asked to sponsor were really seen as individual clubs composed of individual players.

> I do [remember] early on . . . in the early 1980s, when we couldn't sell ad time, and people would say privately that their clients didn't want to buy into a "black" sport. And we said, "But that's not an enlightened view" and asked, "Does your client know who's watching this 'black' sport?" Because if you looked at the numbers, the audience was predominantly white. They said it didn't matter; the sense was that it was just a black sport. I think that was the same attitude of an older white male [audience] that came to be dissipated by coming to realize that this was in fact very good sport.

To get those ratings, Stern first focused on seeing the NBA for what it was, then looked for opportunities to market against it. One striking case in point is the embrace of the slam dunk. The modern dunk shot, the conclusive, crowd-pleasing end of a successful drive to the basket, was first popularized by Julius "Dr. J" Erving when he entered the old American Basketball Association in 1975. Erving, of course, didn't invent the dunk, but he was the first to do it with such seeming ease as to replace the basic layup shot in his game. But to the contemporary astonishment of even the most casual basketball fan born since 1975, basketball purists turned up their noses to the dunk for almost the first ten years of Dr. J's career. The dunk was tainted by its association with the wilder, woolier, and yes, blacker upstart ABA, which was so desparate for attention it used a three-point shot (which the NBA later adopted) and balls painted red, white, and blue. Dunking was an ABA sideshow, practiced primarily by big-Afro-ed blacks like Erving and the amazing David "Sky" Walker of the Denver Nuggets, a guard with the temerity to make a career out of jumping over centers to put the ball directly through the hoop. While the ABA thrived (to the extent that the money-plagued league could be said to thrive) on such ostentatious theatrics and even featured a slam-dunk contest before its annual All-Star game, the NBA refused even to acknowledge a place for the dunk in its league, except perhaps from the rare seven-foot-plus center standing close to the basket. Promoting the flying dunk as an exciting part of the game was out of the question, seemingly because few if any white players held up as icons of the game ever dunked. On television commentators windily opined it to be poor form for a player to dunk when a layup would do. They reacted to the increasing number of dunks in a game the way Presbyterians respond to the aberrant shriek of "Yes, Jesus!" during a sermon.

Thus, when the ABA limped into the NBA in 1976, the All-Star slam-dunk contest was cast into purgatory. One of the first things Stern did as commissioner was bring it back as a feature of the NBA All-Star weekend in 1984. It instantly became the most talked about event besides the All-Star game itself, each year drawing forests of coverage in the days leading up to the game, especially after five-foot-three Spud Webb of the Houston Rockets won in 1986. The dunk contest made the All-Star game into an entire week-end event. And in the hands of a new generation of players entering the league in the 1980s and since the dunk quickly became a legitimate weapon in winning the game on the floor. Having players who routinely finshed plays with dunks became a competitive necessity. But even if the dunk were merely entertaining, David Stern realized its great value in sparking the interest of a much wider fan base. Ever more spectacular dunks, he understood, could be expected to lead the sports highlights on the local news shows. Purists may have seen the NBA fast becoming a black circus, more appealing to small children, urban dwellers, and the soon-to-be-dubbed "slacker" teens than to white men over thirty-five. But the dunk, along with the style and attitude that came with the new dunkers, was the next big thing. Stern saw it. It was generational change, he said, and if that meant breaching some historical dams holding the place of black men in popular culture in check, so be it. Yes, there was race-related resistance to change, Stern told me. The grumbling has been periodically quelled by league success, like Michael Jordan's incredible run, but never completely silenced.

> Having been here long enough to see that people thought the three-point shot was a joke, that Afros were bad, and slam dunks weren't part of the game, I can tell you that . . . times change. What one generation grows up on, they think is the norm. They may not exactly be receptive to the next generation's iteration or derivation or variation. Then all of a sudden you get the next generation— that's just life.
>
> Take our success as a tribute to obduracy. The fundamental proposition we deal with is that our league is our league. Its components, its [racial] makeup is whatever it is, and it's our job to market it and make it succeed for the benefit of the players, the owners, and ourselves. If yesterday is Afros and tomorrow is cornrows, so what?

The managed resurrection of the NBA was the most powerful engine driving a larger revolution, now taken for granted: the rise of the nonwhite all-American sports icon. Some of it could be seen as just plain luck, a series of seemingly unrelated developments in sports, marketing, entertainment, and popular culture that could be linked only in hindsight to the eventual revolution of race in pop culture. In the summer of 1984, a year after Stern took over the NBA, a new generation of black Olympians, led by Carl Lewis, Jackie Joyner-Kersee, Edwin Moses, Michael Jordan, Patrick Ewing, Mark Breland, and Pernell Whittaker took center stage at the Los Angeles games. Later that year Debi Thomas grabbed the first of hundreds of headlines when she became the first African-American figure skater to represent the

United States in world competition. She did it by coming in second to Asian-American Tiffany Chin. The 1984 games were the first in history to be mostly paid for by big business. American firms donated $180 million to the U.S. Olympic Committee and to the Los Angeles Olympic organizing committee. Major marketers then sank $500 million into promoting their association with the games, wrapping everything and everyone connected to them in a special red-white-and-blue media blitz edged with Olympic gold. The marriage of corporate brand names to the patriotic embrace of "America's Team" allowed its stars to shine brighter than any in Olympic history, regardless of race. The Olympics in Magic Johnson's Los Angeles gave birth to the now-familiar quadrennial deluge of "official Olympic sponsor" marketing campaigns. At the time it was seen as the biggest sports-marketing gamble in history. But it paid off, in a formula that for the first time featured nonwhite athletes as avatars for the mass audience's embrace of American identity through the consumption of sports entertainment, along with every other good or service being hawked in the commercials.

A sprained ankle here, a missed shot there, and much of this history would have to be rewritten. And reasonable skeptics might still dismiss the connection between changes in sports marketing and changes in popular culture as mere coincidence. But the fact is that all these developments are bound together by two clear noncoincidences: the new realization on the part of major sports institutions like the NBA and the U.S. Olympic Committee that they were in the entertainment-marketing business, and their willingness to see nonwhite athletes as mainstream stars who, with proper management and promotion, could carry the show. All commercial sports, including big-time collegiate sport programs, would follow suit to some degree before the decade was over. The nonwhite all-American sports icon, an oxymoron at birth, was a special case of the larger browning of mainstream pop culture that was taking place simultaneously in other forms of entertainment. By the end of the 1980s, roles for these new athlete-entertainers would include everything from "good ol' boys" like basketball player Karl Malone, to all-American hotdogs like Deion Sanders, to "America's sweethearts" like skaters Debi Thomas and Kristi Yamaguchi.

"They all fit the image, the . . . good guy all-American," says Kellen Winslow, who admits to having a bit of that recognition himself. "But it's the colorization of the all-American image." Burns Sports president Bob

Williams says that before the early 1980s, when an advertiser used the phrase *all-American type*, it could reliably be taken as a euphemism for *white, nonethnic*. "Now that label encompasses athletes of all colors," he says. The all-American boy now, at the core, is the boy or girl next door that we can all relate to—like a Magic Johnson. It's a clean image—an image that is not going to be a detriment to a company."

Even for consumers who never lived next door to anyone like Magic Johnson, who grew up in a poor black part of Lansing, Michigan?

"Well, if you live in New York or Chicago, there's definitely a different perception of *all-American* today than if you live in Salt Lake City," Williams answers.

And even in Salt Lake, where nonwhites are the fastest-growing segment of a fast-growing population, the definition of *all-American* is also being rewritten.

❑   ❑   ❑

Imposing a time frame on such a retrospective analysis is always arbitrary, but I place the first moment during a time-out for a Coke commercial in Super Bowl XIV in January 1980. Today the expense, production, and entertainment values of Super Bowl ads rival those of the game itself, but that Sunday in 1980 marked the unintended debut of the first blockbuster Super Bowl commercial. The unlikely star was a big, fierce black man stooping to kindness toward a little white boy. The one-minute ad, which was immediately acclaimed by media and marketing critics, went on to win numerous awards and remains a fixture on "top commercials of all time" lists to this day. Jack Rooney, a former account executive with Foote, Cone and Belding who later headed marketing for Miller Brewing, echoed the response of every advertising or marketing professional I interviewed when I mentioned the commercial. He said he remembered it "like it happened yesterday." "The big joke in the industry was that something like seventy people claimed responsibility for it," he said.

> (Scene: Down the tunnel leading from the football field, Pittsburgh Steeler linebacker Joe "Mean Joe" Greene, battered and bruised, fairly limps toward the locker room. A small white boy with a bottle of Coke follows.)

Boy: Mr. Greene—Mr. Greene . . . do you—do you need any help?

Greene: Unh-Unh.

Boy: I just want you to know—I think—I think—you're the best ever!

Greene: Yeah, sure.

Boy: You want my Coke? It's okay—you can have it.

Greene: No, no.

Boy: Really—you can have it.

Greene: (sighs) Okay—thanks.

(Music swells: "A Coke and a smile . . . makes me feel good. . . .")

(Greene downs the Coke in a ten-second-long gulp, then turns toward the locker room. The boy, dejected, starts walking back to the stands.)

Boy: See ya around.

(Greene turns back.)

Greene: Hey, kid . . . (tosses his soiled jersey to the boy)

Boy: Wow! Thanks, Mean Joe!

True, O. J. Simpson had already been the star of a long-running (no pun intended) Hertz campaign for some time when the Joe Greene Coke commercial made its debut. But unlike Simpson's smiling, clean-shaven re-creation of his evasive gridiron maneuvers—in a business suit—"Hey, Kid," as the spot was dubbed by the ad agency that created it, was the first major commercial to harness, if not confront, the fearful stereotypes of black maleness that American political culture had built for centuries and that mass culture had always emasculated or avoided altogether, to make a positive selling point. Here's Joe Greene, a big (six foot four, 260 pounds), belligerent, bearded black warrior-athlete featured in an unguarded (i.e., out of sight of authority) moment of pain and frustration when, presumably, his animal instincts could lash out against an unspecting white innocent. No levity or dancing was employed to divert the viewer from the almost primal tension building in each moment until Greene accepts the offering of the Coke. When he throws his head back and opens his throat, and the feel-good music swells, all the power in the scene is focused on the magic in the act of sharing this all-American beverage. As the energy of racial tension in the one-minute drama was gathered and then dispelled, the desired main effect was to move the viewer toward having a Coke. But the more powerful side effects flowed from the momentary cathartic relief of race-related tension. Among them is a benign repression of awareness that the tension had anything to do with Joe Greene's racial persona. Any initial consciousness of the source of the tension is washed away in the wave of joy that follows Greene's jersey into the arms of "the Kid."

Repeated exposure to the ad compounds this repression effect into a long-term deracialization (not the same as deracination) of Joe Greene himself. Perhaps a better term is *humanization*. As the psychological dynamic of cognitive dissonance comes into play over time, the mind finds it uncomfortable to simultaneously hold the specter of Greene as an undifferentiated black brute and the image of the man who shares this special bond of trust and adoration with "the Kid." To reconcile the dissonance, the viewer must embrace one understanding of Greene and abandon the other. Former Coke executive Chuck Morrison joined Coca-Cola's marketing team in 1981, when the Joe Greene ad was still fresh in the beverage industry's mind. As he explained to me when I interviewed him:

> What's interesting about it is it also changed the image of "Mean Joe" Greene. What most people forget is that prior to the commercial Joe Greene was [seen as] one of the dirtiest players in the NFL. Vicious, mean . . . I mean, he wasn't called Mean Joe Greene because his college team was called the Mean Greenes. He was a mean sucker! After the commercial Joe Greene became this curmudgeonly, accepted character—which shows you the power of the Coca-Cola brand.

Or rather, it shows the power of archetypes in popular culture, skillfully manipulated by advertising professionals and massively propagated with the resources of a major multinational marketer. Association with the Coke brand made Greene into a new kind of all-American icon, but only through the exploitation of his images—of the man himself and of his racial persona. Greene, now a coach with the NFL's Arizona Cardinals, says the net effect of the exchange was "liberating." Where once he was seen as unapproachable and depicted in posters in opposing-team cities as "grotesque," the commercial "softened the image and made me more approachable, not just to people who might like football but to young kids, grandmothers, grandfathers, and mothers. To talk not about football but about the commercial, or just to say hello—I enjoyed that very much."

The dynamic elements of "Hey, Kid" the commercial set a pattern that, with ever-evolving variations, could also describe the later mainstreaming of athletes and entertainers of color into commercial pop culture. But at the time, the team at McCann Erickson Worldwide that created the ad were thinking only about selling soda. At first, when interviewed, the commercial's writer, Penny Hawkey, told me the role of race in marketing was the furthest thing from their minds as they set about casting the spot. All they wanted in the athlete was a contrast with "the Kid," and in theory any large, tough, star football player would have done. White quarterbacks naturally headed the list of candidates at the time. The only rules they sought to break were those of then-current soda-jingle conventions; their ambition was to create a one-minute drama. But after thinking it through in hindsight, Hawkey said she realized they ended up casting Greene because they needed the power of race to boost a creative leap.

> The rules we were breaking weren't race but the dull wallpaper jingles. It wasn't that he was black, it was that it was a Coke commercial that had never been done before with dialogue. We said, "Hey, what about dialogue, people's real relationship with this drink," recapturing the moment when a Coke is a normal part of the day.
>
> Race wasn't a factor . . . it was juxtaposition. The first candidate [we] had in mind was Terry Bradshaw. But he wasn't big enough. . . . I guess, well now that I think about it—*he wasn't black enough.*

Greene, inducted into the NFL Hall of Fame in 1987 for his on-field prowess, has enjoyed his "liberation" from the precommercial "Mean Joe" image for twenty years. But he told me he never thought much about exactly what prison he was liberated from, or the mechanism by which his freedom was wrought.

I always said "a large black man and the small white kid—it was the contrast." But I didn't delve into the social ramifications. If you start to dissect them, there's probably some truth [to the notion of racial alchemy in the power of the ad], in that this imposing black man, with a reputation to go along with the size, look, and color, became a person. That's how it affected me personally.

Hawkey, who is now executive creative director with Medicus Communications in New York, said, "We didn't realize we were breaking into new racial territory or opening doors. We didn't realize it would have the impact it did." But the conscious, semiconscious, and unconscious use of racial and ethnic notes to achieve creative and commercial breakthroughs would become a repeated theme as marketers navigated the American dreamscape of color in the 1980s.

❑　　❑　　❑

Coca-Cola did not create Joe Greene's Hall of Fame success or his style on the football field. And Coke had nothing to do with the racial archetypes that fueled the drama; indeed, its creators were barely conscious of the chemicals they were mixing. But what Coke did do, with its investment of marketing resources, was validate a deeper social trend by giving it expression in commercial popular culture. Baby boomers who came of age during the civil rights movement had been cheering black athletes like Joe Greene on the plantations of our national pastimes for over a decade, without being given permission to idolize them in that most American way: to buy products associated with their names. Coke, however unintentionally, sucessfully exploited that unvalidated desire to embrace nonwhite hero athletes *in all their nonwhiteness* to sell soda. Four years later, as the NBA was figuring out how to position its product to satisfy and stoke a similar unmet, ineffable desire for something new and exciting, the same unvalidated potential brimmed in popular culture at large.

Maybe it was coincidence, but 1984 just *happened* to be the year that Vanessa Williams broke the color line at the Miss America pageant; that Eddie Murphy starring in *Beverly Hills Cop* virtually tied *Ghostbusters* for the number-one grossing movie ($234 million worldwide, back when a million dollars was a million dollars); and Bill Cosby's *The Cosby Show* debuted as the number-one-rated show on television. And maybe it was a fluke that the artist who was known in 1984 as Prince grossed $58 million that summer playing a black rock star in an interracial romance in *Purple Rain*, while selling out dozens of big-city arena concert dates within hours after the tickets went on sale.

Roger Enrico and Pepsi didn't create Michael Jackson's talent or music, and they certainly didn't create the central place that African-Americans occupy in American pop culture. All Pepsi did, by leading the procession to crown the first black "King of Pop," was to validate what the mass market had already decided. It simply associated brand Pepsi with a fact on the ground that even the music industry hadn't yet recognized, to sell soda. Enrico's moves were all the more radical because, by all accounts, they were unhesitating and virtually unimpeded by deliberation over Michael Jackson's color, which at the time was still unambiguously brown. One result: Pepsi was one of the first major marketers to catch the pop wave beneath a black artist well before it crested, maximizing the return on its investment. It would not be the last.

Enrico acted on his intuition about where the culture was going without regard to race. It hardly seems revolutionary, in retrospect, but it was way-out-of-the-box thinking at the time.

Coke, the Joe Greene commercial notwithstanding, certainly didn't see it. The preeminent soda marketer had three opportunities to get in on the Michael Jackson *Thriller* phenomenon, and it passed each time. The first chance came in the studio in December 1982, right before the album was shipped. Chuck Morrison, then head of Coke's "ethnic" marketing, met with Michael Jackson, Jackson's father and then manager Joe Jackson, and album producer Quincy Jones. Michael really wanted to represent Coke, Morrison told me, and assumed that a preview of the *Thriller* album would seal the deal.

> I'll never forget, Michael looked at me and said, "What can I do for you?"' ... And I said, "Nothing: The question is what can I do for you? Because I'm gonna sell Coke whether you do it or not." Joe [Jackson] asked for a million dollars, which was unprecedented at the time. I took it back to management at Coke, and they flat said no. They weren't interested in being tied into a personality like Michael. It wasn't that he was black; he just wasn't Cosby to them.

Six months later Jackson electrified a worldwide audience with a now-legendary performance of "Billie Jean" during the television special saluting Motown Records' twenty-fifth anniversary. "Michael gives that performance of a lifetime . . . but they still say no," Morrison recalled. Coke's last chance was the day before Jackson signed with Pepsi. Don King called Morrison "and says, 'Chuck, Michael has said to us take another run at Coke'—but now the price is five million. I go back up, and Coke says no again. The next day he signs the deal with Pepsi."

Coke bottlers "went nuts" the day after it was announced. Marketing chief Sergio Zyman tracked Morrison down in a Los Angeles restaurant, ordered him back to Atlanta, and authorized a $7 million counteroffer, Morrison said, "but the deal was done."

> And the rest was history. That summer of '84 Michael Jackson takes $2.4 billion to the bottom line of Pepsi-Cola. Six share points, just like that, gone. He was absolutely that hot. It was a whole phenomenon; I'd never seen anything like it. It was absolutely brilliant, because it killed two or three birds with one stone. Obviously it was a boon for them with African-Americans, but Michael Jackson was *everybody*. White teenagers loved this boy. Latinos. It was brilliant stroke, as a brilliant as Joe Greene had been for Coke five years before.

Pepsi's success with Jackson opened Coke's eyes to the idea of the browning mainstream. Indeed, in the spring of 1984, singer-songwriter Lionel Ritchie's single "Hello" topped the pop charts. It was no fluke: six other Ritchie-penned songs, most sung by Ritchie (he also gave Kenny Rogers and Diana Ross their biggest hits with "Lady" and "Endless Love," respectively) had reached number one in the previous three years. Suddenly, after Pepsi signed the Jackson deal, Coke could see Lionel Ritchie as a pop star. It pursued the former Commodores lead singer and was about to sign a deal with Ritchie's manager, Ken Kragen, Morrison recalled. Then Pepsi found out.

> We were supposed to fly to Las Vegas on a Friday to sign the deal. Kragen says Roger Enrico found out, flew to Las Vegas, and put a contract on the table for $8.3 million. But the deal was he had to

sign it now, or it's off the table. What do you think Kragen did? Called us and said, "Love you guys—'bye."

The bidding war coincided with *Washington Post* critic Richard Harrington's insightful observation that Ritchie's success, like Jackson's, represented a quality of crossover for black performers that hadn't been seen before.

> In any other year but this one belonging to Michael Jackson, Ritchie would be the biggest story in the business. At 10 million copies and counting, his *Can't Slow Down* album is living up to its name. He's just begun a forty-city tour expected to gross $12 million.... He was the first black entertainer to host a major awards show alone— the recent American Music Awards. Ritchie's concerts now attract predominantly white audiences, reflecting the appeal he developed in his last few years with the Commodores.... Richie is also more popular with white record buyers than black.[7]

Again, it's not that black acts hadn't overcome the record industry barriers to the top of the pop charts before. In fact, as Harrington went on to point out, where some thirty-five songs performed by black acts crossed over to reach number one in the early 1970s, only thirteen had done so in a similar period in the early 1980s. But the categorical difference with Ritchie, as it would continue to be with Jackson, was that no major marketers competed hammer and tongs to project those black 1970s acts, performers like Stevie Wonder and Barry White, as genuine pop stars. After Ritchie, Coke went after Tina Turner the same way, for Diet Coke, but lost her to Diet Pepsi. "Pepsi took Lionel *and* Tina; Enrico wanted to keep his foot on Coke's neck," Morrison told me. "That's how we ended up with Whitney Houston."

Houston, in Morrison's recollection, was a "dowdy looking" newcomer with a "mediocre hit" in "Saving All My Lovin' for You" and considerable record industry hype about her musical family pedigree.

> We signed her for Diet Coke, and Lintas Advertising glamorized her, put her in this black dress, bought her some hair, and put $22 million worth of general market media behind her. Two months later Whitney Houston was the darling of this country.

Morrison may be overstating the power of Coke's sponsorship at the expense of Houston's considerable talent. Dowdy or not, she had already been featured as a fashion model in the mainstream magazines *Glamour*, *Seventeen*, and French *Vogue*. But Morrison's larger point rings true. In the age or rather the moment of *Thriller*, major corporate marketers were now willing to do for Whitney Houston what they would not have considered doing for her cousin, the once-incomparable Dionne Warwick, in the 1960s. Early in her run as "Queen of Pop," Whitney Houston was actually packaged as America's sweetheart. She played the role well enough to carry a major movie with it. In *The Bodyguard*, opposite no less a white romantic leading man than the then-red-hot Kevin Costner, Houston played an international pop diva whose appeal far transcends race. It's hard to say whether it was art finally imitating a life like that of Diana Ross or Donna Summer or Tina Turner in the 1970s or merely an extension of the new Houston icon from music videos to feature film. Audiences apparently had little trouble suspending disbelief. Powered in part by her top-selling sound track, the 1992 film took in $411 million worldwide.

❑   ❑   ❑

By the late 1980s, what began with the specific case of Michael Jackson's crossover from the *Billboard* rhythm-and-blues chart to the pop chart had become a much broader and yet diffuse phenomenon whose substance was hard to pin down and whose political authority was negligible. Color was weaving through music, sports, television, movies, news media, and literature in a bold band that never been seen before. It was the sixty-three-year-old Miss America color line broken four times in one decade. (Okay, Suzette Charles was only runner-up to Vanessa Williams until Williams was forced to abdicate, but she still wore the crown.) It was double takes on top of double takes at what people of color could almost routinely be seen doing or be heard saying on television. It was that megawatt moment at the 1990 MTV awards when Madonna, flanked by her black backup singers, snapped her fingers three times while describing the letter Z in the air with that just-so flick of the wrist, and the dismissive gesture crossed over from sisters in "the hood" to the world at the speed of light, without a word uttered in any language but soul.

But most of all it was selling. By the end of the 1980s a potent new distillation of commercial popular culture was everywhere on the rise: modern brand marketing. At the same time that nonwhite singers, athletes, writers, actors, and others crossed racial lines into the mainstream culture, the lines separating sport, singing, dance, drama, writing, fashion, journalism, and comedy began to blur into a larger phenomenon called "infotainment." Every once-discrete form of popular entertainment and information culture, and much high culture too, began boiling down to the common denominator of logos, labels, icons, and celebrities, four plural nouns that in turn boil down to just one thing: brands. By something more than coincidence, non-white individuals in general and urban- (read: black-, Hispanic-, or Asian-) identified cultural forms in particular became basic, and sometimes indispensable, elements in establishing or building brands.

One unappreciated thread tying race to the rise of brand marketing is the special fondness that the working poor were found to have for status-labeled merchandise. In the 1970s jeans makers discovered a seemingly limitless demand among the masses to bear a quality brand on their behinds, like cattle. The hunger for self-esteem, instantly gratified by bearing the right name next to your skin, would spread logo mania to all manner of sportswear in the 1980s but especially to sneakers. "Shoe companies were just starting to see athletes as a way of reaching the masses, especially in the inner city," says football Hall of Famer Kellen Winslow, who hails from the gritty black town of East St. Louis, Illinois, "because a pair of shoes [was] a major event in our lives."

The browning of the American mainstream combined with the ascent of branding could be called the "Nike-ization" of commercial culture, because the Beaverton, Oregon, shoemaker invented itself from that union. Nike was first among unequals to seize the imagination of the baby-boomer mainstream that was once characterized as joggers and, despite some serious slippage in recent years, has never let go. But brand Nike's incredible value with its core market—white middle-class males of a certain age—was first derived from the loyalty of urban youth and then the suburban youth who emulated them. That loyalty was fed by heavy investments in advertising that made urban culture, especially playground basketball and the style of its mostly black adepts, into an iconic national pastime. Nike boiled urban music, sport, style, and folk culture into a little checkmark logo that's now globally better known than even the dollar sign. Long before Tiger Woods, this ghetto-fueled brand value helped Nike rule even on golf courses, where older, lily-white and upper-class brand names had always reigned. Think about it: Nike-ization, extended into the form of a cable network, established the creative and commercial foundation for ESPN, where it's often hard to tell where a Nike commercial ends and the Nike-fied programming (especially including ESPN's own branding spots) begins. Today's ESPN is not your older brother's all-sports network; it runs on a formula that is much evolved from the days when Nike-ization was new and is based almost entirely on the deification of mostly black athlete endorsers. But the marks of paternity, as the brand images of the players are commodified into "news" delivered just like a commercial several times a day, are clear.

The branding of the black athlete-as-entertainer may have reached its 1980s peak not with Michael Jordan but with former football and baseball star Bo Jackson. It's hard to think of another athlete of any color whose prodigious achievements were as highly leveraged in so short a time. In 1989, his third year in pro sports, the Kansas City Royals outfielder and Oakland Raiders running back's brand had become instantly known by just two letters: *Bo*. That year Nike created an insanely successful campaign just by adding the word *knows*: "Bo knows" became a kind of pop mantra form of the moment, inspiring variations in both commercial and noncommercial culture. Most telling is that writers like Mark Heisler of the *Los Angeles Times* could compare Bo-mania only to the hype surrounding the still-ascendant Michael Jordan and the still-reigning "King of Pop" himself.

> The entourage winds through the back halls of the Astrodome. The high-pitched screaming of young girls bounces off the concrete walls. What manner of teen heart-throb comes this way? Michael Jordan? Michael Jackson? He has a policeman for an escort. . . . He wears a Raider uniform, huge shoulder pads . . . a diamond in his left ear. He smiles at the hubbub . . . the one, the only.
>
> Bo.
>
> Banners bedeck the stadium, 75% with his name on them . . . in another team's town: "Bo Don't Know Pain . . . Bo's Not Going to Do Diddly." In Philadelphia, there was, "Bo Doesn't Know Whitney," a reference to the fact that Eagle quarterback Randall Cunningham has been seen with Whitney Houston.

How big is Bo?

How big is there?

His importance to Nike . . . is rated second only to Jordan's. "Whether a [John] McEnroe or an [Andre] Agassi is in the same league is questionable," says Fred Schreyer, Nike director of promotions. "Right at this particular point in time, Bo's as big as anyone in the world of sports endorsements."[8]

Still, despite the utter lack of precedent for such a flood of mass-market adulation for any black individuals *in history,* the commercial browning trend flew mostly below the radar of serious sociopolitical discussion. The phenomenon, defying accurate measurement and eluding clear labels—beyond the politically correct and culturally inert concepts of diversity and multiculturalism—was a trend that could not speak its name. Yet while the sum went generally unrecognized, the parts were everywhere on display as brands, especially in the form of individuals who by some stroke of talent, design, or circumstance had been elevated to celebrity. One proxy measure of this effect is its visibility on the cover of the magazine that the icon-obsessed 1980s made the most profitable and mainstream standard-setting book in America: *People.*

Only 12.5 people of color appeared on the cover of *People* from its debut in 1974 through its first seven years.[9] But in the seven years from 1984 through 1990, *People averaged* nine covers a year featuring nonwhites. To be sure it was hardly a broad or cutting-edge representation of the color; the editors' weekly decisions now look almost quaintly narrow-minded, if not bizarre. Yoko Ono, for example, was 95 percent of all the Asians seen on *People* through 1990. Michael Jackson, of course, was on ten times between 1984 and 1990, including four whole covers in 1984. Mr. T (remember *The A-Team?*) actually graced the cover of *People* twice in the early 1980s. In a sign that the adage "what was old will be new" applies to the first generation of mainstream black "celebricons," Mr. T is the current spokes-icon for AT&T's collect calling service, long after all but die-hard fans have forgotten *The A-Team.*

But even by the late 1980s *People* had no real claim to represent the avant-garde. *People* is the third-generation reflection of what the mainstream has already digested through an ever-expanding array of media inputs. By the time celebrities have made it to *People*, their fetish is so strong with the general market, and their face and personal opera is so well known to the broad public, that they could have their own talk show, as indeed many of them have. There aren't that many *People* of color, but that's the point: Only Princess Di got more covers than O. J. Simpson or Michael Jackson or Prince in their hottest years. In the not-so-long run, no one on earth will *ever* be on the cover of *People* more than Oprah Winfrey, who showed up more than fifteen times between 1987 and 1998. There is no broader confirmation of individual celebrity brand value than being a *People* cover perennial. Something is radically changed in America when a black woman who neither sings, dances, runs, or jumps has only to gain or lose ten pounds to make the cover of any major magazine she chooses to grace!

◻   ◻   ◻

Recall for a moment the theorem of classical economics known as Say's Law. Expressed simply, it says: Supply creates its own demand. When an entrepreneur decides for whatever reason to add to the supply of widgets by opening a new factory, the supply, when priced right, will elicit from the market an increased demand for widgets. The 1980s proliferation of cable networks, satellite broadcasting, and new mini–broadcast networks like Fox represented a sharp increase in the supply of outlets for advertising goods and services. The increase in supply created unprecedented demand for recognized, brand-name infotainment programming. At the same time, the new supply of available advertising time set off a furious competition on the part of new and existing national marketers, including the networks themselves, to create, develop, and maintain brand images as a store of value. The smart campaign endorsed by the right celebrity can increase the intangible value of the brand name, and the financial value of the stock, far more than it can increase the current year's bottom line.

Suddenly, the marketer of an upstart brand of soda or Asian-made car was no longer limited to the big three television networks' available ad time or confined to the narrow range of what ABC, NBC, and CBS thought the "mainstream" audience wanted to see.

When MTV debuted, it was clearly a case of a supply of bandwidth looking to create demand just because it was there. But the business lesson that the market quickly taught MTV was revolutionary: Reject the racially segregated programming model that still dominated radio. MTV learned that its product, the thing that creates and maintains the value of its brand worldwide, is short filmed performances and other programming that reflects what's most relevant to its target youthful audience without regard to race or racially defined musical categories. Once MTV saw the light in the reflected glow of the ratings Michael Jackson's videos brought it, brand MTV, which started out as a venue for "rock" (read: white) videos, could never be seen as "white" again.

MTV took off and has yet to look back. The supply of bandwidth facilitated, even forced, the discovery of demand for racially and to a lesser culturally diverse musical entertainment product appropriate to a new market: consumers who want to hear and see music first and see race second if at all. It's no coincidence that this market is disproportionately young and non-white, because that's where the greatest unmet demand for a break with the racial status quo is.

As a marketer, one of the first things David Stern did as NBA commissioner was respond to the new supply of distribution outlets for pro basketball games—ESPN and the expanding number of superstations like Atlanta's TBS. Exposure on cable, Stern realized, would actually increase the size of the regular broadcast audience and thus the demand for advertising on CBS, his primary venue until 1989. But to satisfy that increase in demand and to build his business, Stern explained to me, he realized he also had to reinvent the NBA, not as an athletic competition but as a brand.

> What we were doing was trying to figure out what our game was. The reality is that our game was in the here and now. What the brand was, brand NBA—it was young, it was today, it was hip. We did analyses like "What do people who want video games and MTV clips want?" . . . Well, they're gonna want baskets scored in two-point increments in twenty-four seconds over something that was slower. We thought that the advent of the MTV generation was something that we could relate to—our players. We thought they could be to the sports culture and kids everything that the stars of MTV were to their audiences. It happens that music and video in an NBA context are pretty good—it's more fun to watch a

variety of things going on around the court in sync to music than in other sports. For us—and you can talk to Wynton Marsalis about it—basketball was jazz. It was the ultimate improvisation within a team concept. It allowed that kind of expression.

In other words, like MTV, Stern repositioned the NBA brand to channel the fundamental transracial energy of American culture. He invoked jazz as a metaphor, with all the echoes of the Roaring Twenties, when a new music had set white America to dancing for the first but not the last time. Indeed, the young jazz traditionalist Marsalis, on his way to becoming a uniquely 1980s black high culture icon himself at that time, was a prominent endorser of Stern's NBA brand, turning up with his horn in promotional ads to declare, "I love this game." But Stern could just have easily compared his new brand image to rock and roll in the 1950s and invoked the same insurrectionary transracial energy embodied in the appeal of Little Richard, who, interestingly enough, also showed up in NBA "It's faaaaaan-tastic" commercials.

❑   ❑   ❑

In the 1980s new cable and broadcast networks, like new widget makers grabbing raw materials, sharply bid up the price of sports entertainment packages like NCAA basketball and the Olympics. After each deal raised the advertising stakes, the sports bodies and television producers were compelled to invest ever-greater sums in the value of the brand, in a bid for the knockout ratings they had to get to make a profit. In that environment the market demanded more stories and a greater diversity of stories, and nonwhite athletes/entertainers were hot and hungry to meet that demand. Thus we learned all about the late Florence Griffith "Flo Jo" Joyner's many-hued fingernails and saw enough of one of her legs in her self-designed running suits in 1988 to redirect young men's fancies thighward. The 1992 U.S. Olympic basketball "dream team," the cream of the NBA's crop including Michael Jordan, Charles Barkley, Magic Johnson, David Robinson, and Patrick Ewing, carried with it enough commercial hype to overshadow the rest of the U.S. Olympic team, if not the games entirely. It had to, because NBC, which *The Cosby Show* led into dominance by the end of the 1980s, had bet the farm on both the Olympics and the NBA.

In 1989 NBC made then-forty-one-year-old Dick Ebersol, known primarily as the 1970s wunderkind who had created its hippest show, *Saturday Night Live*, president of its sports division. One of his first acts was to grab the rights to broadcast the NBA from CBS, by tripling the licensing fee to $150 million per year. NBC had already committed a record $401 million for the 1992 summer games. The dream team was making news and drawing ratings for six months before the Barcelona games ever opened. Wherever one turned, there was Nike, or the NBA, or NBC, or any number of Olympic sponsors pushing the all-too-familiar personas into America's consciousness. The dream team, NBC hoped, would be the main attraction for the first-ever Olympic pay-per-view offering, called the TripleCast, to which they committed a $100 million marketing and promotion budget. Even NBC was shocked when the dream team's routs of international opponents in the pre-Olympics qualifying games drew NBA playoff–like ratings. But considering the aggregate billions of dollars of now-worldwide exposure accorded these black superstars during the 1980s, it shouldn't have been. Just seeing them all together, taking the hippest of American games to the world stage, was a spectacle beyond the final score.

No wonder, then, that in interviews Stern always points to Barcelona as the highest realization of his vision as a brand manager.

> It all came together by the gold medal ceremony at the Barcelona Olympics. Because by 1992 a predominantly black team had gone to represent the United States, to bring home the gold—in a sport that people were saying a dozen years before was too black. The world got to see them, and what they appreciated was that it was as though you were bringing the New York Philharmonic to town. These were the maestros; that was a level of acceptance that was extraordinary.

By Barcelona, Stern told me, the NBA had become "a self-activating brand." To explain what he meant, he drew a road map of overlapping circles—hubs and spokes and boxes—and intersecting lines representing a new media machinery that he didn't create but learned to exploit. The oversize gymnasiums that housed the franchises in the 1970s became multimedia entertainment centers. The explosion of media competition led to the afore-mentioned competition to broadcast games. Media proliferation also am-plified news coverage, not just by sports journalists but in entertainment, lifestyle, and society sections and segments. "Then we discovered that not only would they cover us, but they would pay us to put us on TV," said Stern. "Then all the sponsors came in who were willing to pay [us] to adver-tise their brand in [our] places. Then we discovered that the licensing busi-ness might actually be a business, going from $40 million of T-shirts to $2 billion" in a full sportswear line and more. Finally, said Stern, the pattern of supply creating demand began replicating itself on a global basis.

> It sounds silly, but with the march of [global economy] capitalism, there was more television distribution, as state-owned TV net-works gave way to privatization. Now there was a great need for advertisers to associate themselves with enterprises that seemed to capture people's attention: the players and the NBA.

❐   ❐   ❐

A decade after he breached the fortress and became the "King of Pop," Michael Jackson pretty much had his way with the kingdom. With the pro-ceeds from *Thriller,* he bought, among many other things, the rights to the entire Beatles musical catalog. He affected Sinatra's trademark rakish pose on an album cover, right down to the snap-brim hat and sport jacket slung over the shoulder on a finger. He married, for a short time, Elvis's only daughter. If there is still such a thing as a "King of Pop," being black or white now has little or nothing to do with it. Michael may also have even made the world safe for a looser definition of *male* and *human* in the icon business.

The Cosby Show, from its debut in 1984 through its eight-year run, was widely credited with not only establishing NBC's still-invincible Thursday-night lineup but with rescuing the sitcom form itself from the grave.

Just two years after giving up her crown in scandal, ex–first black Miss America Vanessa Williams sank an even deeper stake into the heart of the mainstream with the first of a series of successful pop soul recordings so middle-of-the-road they were more likely to be heard in a Nebraska Wal-Mart than in a big-city black radio station. Williams, who has also acquitted herself well in major movies, television specials, and cosmetics advertising, has yet to top out as a mainstream entertainer and beauty icon. In Christmas 2001 she showed up on the PBS network singing next to Placido Domingo—and holding her own.

George Foreman, who made his seemingly incongruous debut as an affable pitchman in 1987, signed over the rights to his likeness to the appliance maker Salton in a December 1999 deal worth $137 million, including shares amounting to a 7 percent stake in the fast-growing appliance-marketing company. Before the deal the value of Foreman's overall icon-driven marketing business was estimated at over $200 million.

To be sure, however, not every run at the browning mainstream begun in the 1980s struck pay dirt.

Sprinter Valerie Briscoe-Hooks never did cash in on her gold medal performances at the 1984 games, and while Carl Lewis and Jackie Joyner-Kersee laid the foundations of pop semistardom in Los Angeles, by far the big endorsement winner of the games was white gymnast Mary Lou Retton. The late Florence Griffith Joyner also failed to capitalize on her three-gold-medal triumph at the 1988 Olympics. She retired within a year of her Seoul triumphs, unable to escape the shadow of the performance drug scandal that cost black Canadian sprinter Ben Johnson his hundred-meter-dash gold medal that year. The taint of that scandal, and more recent drug accusations, has crimped the earnings of mostly black elite sprinters from around the world ever since.

The NBA's ascent to the pinnacle of marketing prowess leveled out with the retirement of Michael Jordan and the public relations nightmare of the 1998–99 lockout season. The business of selling sneakers led the boom in celebrity icon marketing, but it also was first to greet the end-of-century bust in the athletic shoe industry. Only Jordan himself, it seems, can still reliably coax consumers into buying $140 sneakers. Even Laker center Shaquille O'Neal lost his deal with Reebok in 1998; Reebok has since cut its roster of athlete endorsers in half. More broadly, almost twenty years after eating and digesting their words of skepticism about the prospects of a mostly black league, some sportswriters are not-so-quietly intimating that the current hip-hop generation of players, with their "inner city" values so prominently on display in lurid headlines about irresponsible and sometimes violent behavior, are threatening to choke the NBA golden goose to death.

The selling of the game is not just about hand-checking and jump shooting, and hasn't been since David Stern took over the corner office at Olympic tower. There is a challenge for the new crop of NBA sneaker pitchmen. Commissioner Stern's marketing miracle is clearly at a junction, if not the crossroads. The sport may be in danger of returning to the third-class status behind football and baseball that it previously held, before Stern forged a scratch-my-back partnership with the networks and shoe companies, helping his players become endorsement and promotional tycoons.[10]

Washington Post sports columnist Michael Wilbon, who is black, says the problem is that the NBA's reach in marketing players as pop stars now far exceeds the players' grasp of what it takes to be winners.

Look, the marketing thing has boomeranged on the NBA, in that you can have a commercial, like Penny Hardaway, with Tyra Banks in it and your own shoe named after you in the third year in the NBA—and not be any damn good—not having won anything. Now he's not even an All-Star; he's just another guy in the league who [by dint of talent] should be a god.

But Commisioner Stern remains sanguine; he's heard it before. He's much more focused on building the brand abroad. He went to Japan to open the 1999 regular season with two games featuring the teams of the future. One of them, the Sacramento Kings, featured a white point guard, Jason Williams, whose style is so consistent with the current hip-hop athletic Zeitgeist, according to Wilbon, that he might be the "great white hope" of young *black* America, and second only to Philadelphia 76'er guard Allen Iverson in public identification with street sensibility. Williams's (since dealt to the Memphis Grizzlies) nickname, early in the 1999–2000 season, was "White Chocolate." Chicago sports marketing consultant Bob Williams shares *New York Times* columnist Harvey Araton's view that, as things stood in 1999, the Iversons of the league, with their tattoos and braids and dreadlocks and rebel-without-a-cause attitudes, will never become the mainstream icons that black all-Americans Magic Johnson and Michael Jordan were. But on the other hand, he told me,

I could see Allen Iverson, if his team wins a championship or two, and he's the NBA MVP and top scorer—all of a sudden he's got a lot of Michael Jordan attributes. Then maybe that type of urban image will take a seat at the marketing table with the Michael Jordan image—and we'll have both images instead of one.

I interviewed Bob Williams before Iverson came within two wins of satisfying his "what if" conditions, with his heroic leadership of the 76'ers in the 2001 NBA championship series. Williams also spoke prior to Jordan's heroic/quixotic return to the game in the uniform of the lowly Washington Wizards. The Wizards were actually in the playoff hunt until Jordan withdrew for the season due to injury. But if he keeps his vow to return in 2002–2003, marketers may yet get the clash of old school/new school icons that makes them drool.

Meanwhile Stern is sticking behind his latest crop of "guys" while also growing the Women's National Basketball Association (WNBA) brand extension. Building on everything he learned in the 1980s, he's been able to position the first women's pro league for a core audience of teenage girls and their soccer moms without any of the historical racial baggage he inherited with the NBA in 1984. While only slightly more racially and ethnically mixed than big brother NBA, the image of the league is about sharing the triumph of women in pursuit of excellence, period. Stern's WNBA metaphor and sound track are even more soulful than jazz, while less threatening than rap. "I'm not sure if it's hip-hop—but it's rhythmic," Stern said. "In some cases it's really more like gospel; it's more subliminally about the sisters." Always betting in the direction of the future, in 1999 Nike signed WNBA rookie phenomenon Chamique Holdsclaw, who was a toddler in a Queens, New York, housing project when Stern took over the league, to the largest shoe deal ever struck for a female athlete.

NBC scored a ratings coup in Barcelona in 1992 but reportedly lost $100 million on the complicated deal anyway. Still, the network was undeterred and bet even more money on the 1996 Atlanta games, where it finally made its Olympic killing. In so many ways, the Atlanta success—for Team USA, multinational corporate sponsors, and broadcast and cable television networks—represented a landmark on the road to the browning American pop culture millennium. It began with no less a new (or newly rehabilitated) black all-American world figure than Muhammad Ali lighting the Olympic flame, and it ended with Jackie Joyner-Kersee enshrined in pop sport culture as the greatest female athlete in history, as an injury ended her Olympic career just short of another gold medal. The black-majority city of Atlanta had labored for two years to present itself to the world as the epitome of multiracial, multicultural America. Throughout the games NBC wielded a sound track to match, featuring seventeen hundred songs from dozens of artists including Boyz II Men, TLC, Coolio, James Brown, and Gladys Knight. Cuban-American singer Gloria Estefan's "Reach" was one of two semiofficial theme songs. Everywhere, it seemed, NBC's cameras were focused on black runners in Nike-American uniforms. Even the U.S. gymnastic team was seen to be racially integrated.

But of all the big-bucks mainstreaming of color on display, nothing captured the essence of the Atlanta games like the presence of Ray Charles. NBC started setting the tone weeks in advance, with saturation advertising promotions featuring Charles's signature, soulful renditions of "Georgia" (which the state later adopted as the official interpretation of its state song) and "America the Beautiful." After the fear and pain of the bombing at the Olympic Plaza, it was Ray Charles who rocked tens of thousand of visitors, and the world, with his classic "What'd I Say." For Charles, whose original recording of "What'd I Say" in 1959 was a seminal moment in the history of rock and roll, the 1990s must have truly seemed like another century. His 1991 Diet Pepsi commercial with the chorus of "Uh-huh, uh-huh—you got the right one, baby!" became such an instant pop culture hit that it beat out the venerable Energizer Bunny in audience popularity, according to the 1991 survey by Video Storyboard. Writers observed in amazement that, as with Bo Jackson mania two years before, the presence of nonwhite icons in high-powered ads was shifting America's cultural center of gravity, especially in language. As *New York Times* advertising columnist Stuart Elliott wrote in 1992:

> The language of the streets is becoming the language of Madison Avenue, as advertising slogans veer toward the vernacular. A growing number of broadcast commercials and print advertisements are

affecting a breezy informality by borrowing colloquial expressions and slang terms from everyday speech. Words like "gotta," "yo," "gonna," "hey" and "uh-huh" are becoming as important an ingredient in ads as catchy jingles or celebrity endorsers. Of course, advertising has never rigidly adhered to the King's English. . . . But the latest trend is far broader. . . . [O]ne reason for adopting the vernacular [is that it] enables advertisers to co-opt popular phrases that are already part of the language rather than attempt to sear some slogan into the public consciousness.[11]

Ray Charles had been an American musical treasure for more than forty years, but it took the Diet Pepsi campaign to make him the mainstream commercial icon that seemed to almost be the face of America at the Atlanta games. Still, advertising didn't put the resonance of Charles's musical persona, with his synthesis of gospel, jazz, country, and rhythm and blues (i.e., every musical form developed here since Columbus) into the heart of mainstream America. Advertising, by Pepsi and then by NBC, merely exploited the Ray Charles that had lain sleeping in our collective pop culture unconscious. And when the marketers awakened it, it wasn't a black minstrel show character nor an exotic, untouchable outsider like Nat "King" Cole or Lena Horne. No, the marketers invoked a Ray Charles for the 1990s, a persona more urbane than urban, and more consistent with the truth about our culture than ever before thought possible. More than respected, the Ray Charles in the Olympic advertising was a venerated elder, the beloved uncle with the hip sense of humor, style, and confidence. Patting a near-life-size cardboard mock-up of Charles and the Uh-huh Girls backup singers (who almost had fifteen minutes of fame all by themselves in 1989) for emphasis, Bill Katz, president of BBDO New York, the powerful advertising agency (part of Omnicom) whose roster of clients includes Pepsi, FedEx, and Visa International, insisted to me that the browning of mainstream culture was already apparent in society when his firm made the ads; all BBDO did was channel it into the service of selling product.

This is fashion. This is our commercial. That's fashion. That's not black, not white. That's not a conscious effort by Pepsi to appeal to

African-American or Asian users. This is the agencies' depiction of what influenced style in America at the time, maybe 1990 or 1991. It comes through the pores; you can sense it and smell it, and feel it in everything. As you sense it, smell it and feel it, you reflect it in your work. A coolness, a hipness, an urbanity, an attitude, a self-assuredness that is graphically portrayed in that picture right there. It's not because these women are African-American or not African-American. It's because the times have given us that as its portrayal of what is cool and self-assured and stylish and fashionable. *It was defined for us; we didn't define it.*

According to Katz, the flow of color into the 1980s cultural mix was so natural, so obviously right and normal that it penetrated beneath the public consciousness of the politics of race. Consciousness is focused on the entertainment experience and then, hopefully, on the product, not on race, which is exactly where marketers want it.

Take when Michael Jackson had his hair burned up. People will say, "I remember this moment in life when the Jackson brothers were dancing for Pepsi-Cola—and Pepsi burned his hair up by mistake." They won't say, "I remember when for the first time ever a black group was in the most popular commercials in America, frontlining for one of the most popular soft drinks." It was secondary that there were five black entertainers. People don't say, "Did you see that commercial with five black people?" What they remember is the commercial, not the phenomenon of a black person in the commercial. That's the beauty of advertising. Because it only works if it entertains you. You remember the "Mean Joe Greene" commercial because it entertained. It had a compelling emotion attached to it.

The peculiar dynamic by which racial identification is almost magically stripped from nonwhite performers and cultural forms as they pass into the mainstream presents an obstacle to finding the larger meaning of all these developments for race and commercial culture. The measure of that obstacle will be taken at length in the conclusion of this book. But there is another nagging question to be raised here and, I hope, to be put to rest. If Ray Charles had already been a living legend for forty years, why did it take so long for marketers and their ad agencies to recognize and exploit it? Why didn't Ray Charles have a national commercial like that in the 1970s? When I asked Katz, he recalled my hypothetical anecdote about what would have happened to the ambitious record executive who, in 1954, set out to put a Little Richard poster on the bedroom wall of every teenage girl in America.

Why no "Uh-huh" in the 1970s?

> Because that guy who was gonna haul the record executive of the 1950s in front of Joe McCarthy still influenced society more than he does today. Because society was not prepared to embrace that. It wasn't until society at large was prepared . . . that advertising could take its cue from that [readiness] and portray it.

The first part of Katz's answer is straightforward enough. Corporate American mass media and marketing had been gaining the power and autonomy to ignore the values and biases of the American social and political establishment since the day the first radio station went on the air. If that power and autonomy could be plotted on a graph, said Katz, it would be an upward curve that finally crossed the social and political color line in the 1980s, not the 1970s. If Katz's argument is consistent, the triumph of Madison Avenue over Capitol Hill was primarily enabled by what was real in the culture, not by the size of Pepsi's checkbook or the power of the new technologies it employed. But Katz, and most other observers I interviewed, was utterly at a loss to explain how we as a culture suddenly became ready to accept what we did, when we did. The difference between advertising and the cultural environment in which it operates, said Katz, is that the culture "just happens—you can't pick out a moment in life where you say, 'I remember when I decided it was okay to be multiculural or multiracial.' In the end the *how* and the *when* is for the sociologists and historians to ponder. All marketers focus on is the fact that 'it' happened, and that 'it' superseded or obliterated any issue of race.

Pepsi said, "I want an entertainer to represent my product. I want to be part of the biggest thing in entertainment since the Beatles. I want . . . the imagery Michael Jackson represents to a new generation of constituents out there. I want the fashion associated with Michael Jackson and his brothers. I want *THAT*. I don't want black; I want that." *At some point, it was no longer that cool was represented by black. It was that cool was cool. And I want cool.*

5

Transracial
America Sells

On November 2, 1997, Disney revived its *Wonderful World of Disney* Sunday-night variety show franchise with a $12 million remake of an even older Disney legacy, the musical story of Cinderella. The media hype leading up the broadcast could have launched a new network or two. Disney's new Cinderella was the subject, in part or whole, of more than three hundred newspaper and magazine articles between September 1996 (when the deal was announced) and the night it aired. More than three hundred more were published in the eighteen months that followed.

Why all the fuss about the reroasting of this seventeenth-century chestnut? Because Disney cast in the title role not another blond ingenue whose previous credit might have been playing Heidi. This Cinderella's last and only well-known role was playing a "round the way" girl named Moesha, and the rest of the cast was so racially mixed up that it looked, as one reporter saw it, "as though they were recruited from a United Nations mixer." The description, deep in an unusually generous early story based on a visit to the set, was facetious. But the headline in the *St. Petersburg Times* said it all: "The New Face of TV."

The Rodgers and Hammerstein musical was made by the production company of pop superstar Whitney Houston, who by then was becoming as bankable an actor as a singer. Houston had wanted to play Cinderella herself some years before, but by the time Hollywood was ready for a black Cinderella, the "Queen of Pop" had outgrown the part, so she settled for Fairy Godmother (not to mention co–executive producer) and passed the torch on to then-eighteen-year-old Brandy Norwood. Brandy, as she is known, was already a pop princess in her own right; her 1994 debut album sold 4 million copies. Veteran musical diva Bernadette Peters, whom one writer felt pained to describe as "milk-skinned" to make the point, played the wicked stepmother, while one of her "natural" daughters was played by a black actress and the other by a white actress. Filipino-American actor Paolo Montalban had the role of the lovestruck prince. Whoopi Goldberg was cast as his mother, the queen, while the king was played by actor Victor Garber, who is white.

The novelty factor alone made the casting news. Cinderella has always been the epitome of white fairy-tale heroines. The first filmed version of the musical starred Julie Andrews in 1957, and the second, starring Disney movie icon Lesley Ann Warren in 1965, was considered definitive and eternal. Interest in the new production deepened as the adjective *multicultural* (as in "the multicultural *Cinderella*") was attached to the TV movie musical. But the term was inaccurate. No African or Filipino songs were added to the score. The slipper was still made of woman-torturing Western glass, not an Asian sandal or a comfortable feminist running shoe. No ethnic Filipino dances were inserted into the ballroom scene. The ballroom was traditional Baroque, not the salon of a Latin-American hacienda or Louisiana juke joint. The only thing about this *Cinderella* that wasn't straight out of the seventeenth-century European fairy tale set to 1950s show tunes was that a considerable dose of 1990s American pop sensibility had been added to the dialogue and the rhythmic structure of the original Rodgers and Hammerstein score. As the broadcast date moved closer, previewers started focusing on the real news: the decentering of whiteness in a well-known work of popular culture and the high commercial and cultural stakes at risk.

At $12 million, the budget was at least triple that of the average TV movie. Musicals had been declared a dead form on television years before, but Disney was looking for something to make the relaunch of *The Wonderful World of Disney* a stand-out in family entertainment, as it was in the 1960s and 1970s. Disney upped the stakes by scheduling *Cinderella* on a very competitive night during the first week of the November ratings sweeps, where a big failure could taint the whole first half of its year. In for a penny, in for a pound, ABC–Disney scheduled in the slot after the fairy tale a made-for-TV film *Before Women Had Wings,* with Oprah Winfrey and Ellen Barkin.

Success, on the other hand, would produce multiple dividends because the Disney of the 1990s owned a wide array of outlets for distributing the product worldwide. And Disney had unprecedented promotional clout to back up its play. But why place such high stakes on a black Cinderella? A cynical headline in the *Buffalo (New York) News* called it "stunt casting" in a desperate bid for ratings. A sarcastic piece in the *Times* of London dismissed the casting and other elements as keeping up with the "modern American fad" of political correctness. In retrospect, one wonders why they were so interested in a show that would not be airing in England anytime soon.

> [T]he cast is, as one critic suggested, "not just rainbow, it's over the rainbow." The queen is played by black actress Whoopi Goldberg while her king is white actor Victor Garber. Stretching the rules of verisimilitude to a degree unprecedented even in fairy tales, their offspring, the prince—and object of Cinderella 's affections—is played by a Filipino. Intriguingly, one of the heroine's stepsisters is black while the other is white. They will no doubt be referred to as "beauty challenged" rather than plain old ugly. Similarly, under the politically correct jargon of the 1990s, their "wicked" mother will no doubt have to be renamed "abusive."[1]

But most critics had nothing but nice, albeit superficial, things to say in advance. "Disney's newest *Cinderella* passes multicultural muster with flying colors," read the first sentence in the *Raleigh (North Carolina) News and Observer.* "It cost $12 million . . . but Disney's production of *Cinderella* would still be a deal at twice the price," said the *Baltimore Sun.* As the Disney public relations machine kicked into high gear, the stories, many written by enthusiastic, motivated minority journalists like Claire Blickley of the *Toronto Sun,* began to focus on the unique value added by the so-called multicultural casting.

> And so, the beautiful white girl grew up, married the handsome white prince and they lived happily ever after in their creamy white world.

Or so the story went.

Tonight, Cinderella gets not only a TV revival but also a major makeover, literally changing the complexion of the classic fairy-tale.[2]

On the day of the broadcast, *New York Daily News* culture writer Denene Milner, who is black, led her column with:

> This time around, Cinderella's got braids, and her fairy godmother is so sassy, sexy and beautiful that even the ill-treated orphan-turned-princess does an immediate double take. "You got a problem with that?" the fairy godmother, portrayed by Whitney Houston, snaps at her charge, hands on hips, attitude apparent. "If you'd rather have an old lady in a tutu . . ." Yup, you got it. Tonight at 7 p.m. on ABC's $12 million television musical production of Rodgers and Hammerstein's *Cinderella*, a black girl's going to the ball, and it's a sister who's sending her there.

So Disney took black Cinderella to the ball. And the next day, just as in the fairy tale, it found that Brandy's size nines fit their glass slipper perfectly. Nielsen estimated 60 million Americans tuned in, almost 30 percent of all American's watching TV that night, giving ABC its best rating for the time period in thirteen years. *Cinderella*, pulling its audience into the Oprah Winfrey movie that followed, actually won the key ratings week for the Disney network. Most interesting, and significant for the ultimate bottom line, Nielsen estimated that a whopping 70 percent of girls aged two to eleven watching TV were tuned to Brandy's Cinderella. That meant that Disney now had a property that could be remined with videos and reruns well into the new century. In fifteen years, less than half a generation, only Americans over fifty will have any tender memories of a Cinderella who wasn't Brandy. I myself can't remember what Lesley Ann Warren looked like in the 1965 version. Brandy, I'm thrilled to say, is the only Cinderella my four-year-old daughter will ever know, and she knows it from the same people who bring her *The Lion King* and *Winnie the Pooh*.

Thus the story of Disney's new Cinderella could itself be likened to a fairy tale, but it was no fluke. It was another accurate forecast in the new marketing climate called Transracial America. Forget politics: America was ready to buy a doe-eyed, chocolate-brown girl with braids at the emotional center of one of the deeper myths of female identity. Disney, hoping to capitalize on Brandy and Houston's already-established pop stardom, made an astute bet that nonblack viewers, particularly girls, could now see themselves in a black Cinderella and Fairy Godmother the way black audiences had always been forced to see themselves in white ones. Similar bets are paying off across the landscape of American commercial culture today.

Ask yourself a few questions about race and marketing in America. Why is Muhammad Ali, once typecast as an overbearing, anti-American, draft-dodging acolyte of the Nation of Islam, now a national treasure and gold-plated name that major marketers would kill to rent? Why has his onetime nemesis George Foreman, once the embodiment of a crude bone-crushing black man, been reinvented as the guy everyone trusts for everything from auto repair to home appliance choices? How is it that in commercials for Chevrolet cars, the wheels with the most red-white-and-blue product image in the industry, you're almost guaranteed to see nonwhites included behind the wheel? Why have most successful action movies since the early 1990s relied on a black-white buddy relationship (or two) near the center of the plot? Why are nonwhite performers like actress Halle Berry, singer/actress Jennifer Lopez, singer Beyoncé Knowles, and Brandy fronting cosmetics commercials that until recently featured only "natural" (read: white) blonds? Why do more openly multiracial performers and athletes—from Mariah Carey to Tiger Woods to Yankee Derek Jeter to Halle Berry to Jimmy Smits—seem to be on fast tracks to a kind of superstardom once reserved only for "pure" whites? And how on earth do you explain Dennis Rodman and RuPaul getting away with their race- *and* gender-bending commercial success?

The simplest answer is that Transracial America[3] sells. Transracial America, in the marketplace, is a vision of the American dream in which we are liberated from the politics of race to openly embrace any style, cultural trope, or image of beauty that attracts us regardless of its origin. Executing the Transracial American vision requires retrofitting and reinventing the mythologies of what Lind calls Euro-America[4] to reflect a new reality. Or rather, Transracial American marketing revises the myths of American identity to reflect what was always real. So, for example, the Übermensch, blue-collar man delivering the new half-ton Chevy pickup truck to some industrial site in a shower of welding sparks and testosterone, in the 2000 season of that commercial series, is a strapping African-American who stirs the collective-unconscious memory of John Henry, the original steel-driving black man of nineteenth-century American legend.

The selling of Transracial America is really the result of thousands of discrete and seemingly unconnected creative decisions in casting, marketing, and advertising. Individually they include mixing races in casting; using blues, gospel, salsa, or merengue as an aural bed; depicting a nonwhite as the prototypical consumer or "star" of a commercial; and expanding the use of nonwhite celebrity icons. But taken together, these individual decisions represent more than a fashion or even a trend. They add up to a paradigm shift in mainstream marketing based on a new principle in global marketing: Blackness (or nonwhiteness) now suffers less and less of a discount in the marketplace, while whiteness commands less and less of a premium.

In more and more commercial media, from print ads to movies to television shows and especially television ads, the stigma attached to people and cultures of color that once kept nonwhites out of the commercial mainstream is in permanent decline. The new transracial marketing principle rests in part on demographic necessities. The incomes and rates of consumption in most categories of goods and services are growing much faster for racial minorities than for whites, and marketers now routinely respond to that fact. Demographic reality has created a direct economic incentive to broaden the racial and ethnic appeal of mainstream product advertising and entertainment. (The impact of higher marginal growth rates among nonwhite consumers will be discussed in more detail in Chapter 7.) But the imperative pushing transracial marketing also flows from deeper truths about the place of race in American identity that are now bubbling to the surface. There's a little bit of a black Cinderella in all of us, because the story of innocence abused and faith rewarded is both the quintessential minority experience in America and an archetype of American identity. As a culture, we've been searching for a way to embrace our inner John Henrys for more than a hundred years. Nonwhiteness, especially blackness, bears a historical-cultural taboo, but as with all forbidden fruit, the taboo has always been alloyed with allure. As this taboo melts in the marketplace, whether as a reflection of social reality or in spite of it, the underlying energy of desire associated with racial prohibition is being liberated for exploitation by commercial marketers.

As the impediment of color declines, so does the premium on whiteness. To be sure, whites in general and blonds in particular still "have more fun" in these commercial spaces, and they still tend to predominate. But they no longer rule by divine right, as they did as recently as the early 1980s; their undisputed hegemony is over. For example, a hair-color campaign with the tag line "Is it true blonds have more fun?" would be inconceivable today, unless perhaps it took care to include black, Latina, and Asian "blonds," too. In today's market whites share more and more foreground space with non-white others. Their very whiteness is subtly being redefined. Their lips are fuller (see Calista Flockhart in *Ally McBeal*) and so are their behinds (see singer Britney Spears and actress Jeri Ryan). The shapes of their eyes, noses, and cheekbones are expanding in range to reflect the genetic inheritances of models and icons of Hispanic and Middle Eastern descent who effectively "pass" for white, like supermodel Christy Turlington, singer Ricky Martin, and most unavoidably Jennifer Lopez. They channel Aretha Franklin, like the little white girl Hallie Eisenberg in the hot-selling 1999 Pepsi campaign. In the 2001 version, little white Hallie morphs into big black (or half-black) Halle Berry, all to the delight and amazement of a young black male. In the wake of her very public affair with Dennis Rodman, Madonna lost no whiteness premium, though many questioned her taste, because Madonna, the proto-typical race-bending pop icon of the 1980s, had very little whiteness to lose.

High-status fictional characters, real-life role models, and icons of the month, year, or decade don't have to be exclusively white anymore: among these newly colorful characters are police detectives, lawyers, judges, doctors, military officers, fashion models, and especially computer geeks. It's not about altruism, it's about television ratings and box-office take. My favorite daily read on the transracial marketing paradigm is what I call the Macy's-Bloomingdale's Index, an unofficial survey you can take every day in the *New York Times*. Now New York, our teachers always warned us, is not America. It's only the preeminent center of finance, fashion, publishing, print and broadcast news, and fine and performing arts. The city gets its spirit from a polyglot people whose distinct cultural, racial, and ethnic backgrounds are somehow ultimately subsumed by a larger identity, "New Yorker," that supersedes "American." New Yorkers, the mythology holds, are not real Americans in the cultural sense. We are individually too "ethnic," too yellow, brown, or black, to be average Americans. Even our hair comes in too many combinations of colors, textures, and lengths. Collectively we need too many spices in our food, too many beats per second in our music, and too many sources of stimulation in our lifestyles to be genuine "heartland" Americans.

But while New York may not seem to be America, America, it seems, is always becoming New York (when it's not becoming southern California). the *New York Times* is America's paper of record for news, for editorial copy, and for public notice through its advertising. It is far from infallible or comprehensive in either capacity, and television is still the primary source of news and information for most Americans. But the paper published in Times Square (the address itself is as good a proxy for ground zero in global pop culture as it gets) is agreed upon by people and institutions of influence as the single most important arbiter of mainstream culture. Most national and global media take the *Times* as a baseline for what is important, relevant, and agenda setting on a given day. And as the reporters, editors, producers, bankers, and brokers of the world turn its broadsheet pages, the display advertising in the *Times* becomes received wisdom in their minds.

As recently as the early 1980s, images of people of color were so few and far between in *Times* ads that none could be counted for months at a time.[5] Marketers, particularly fashion retailers whose ads were most likely to use pictures or illustrations of people, clearly saw no need to represent the real New York mixture of races and ethnicities to America, to the world, or even to the New Yorkers who were the core of the *Times*'s circulation.

In an admittedly unscientific marking of the transracial tide, let's skim the *Times*'s display ads during 1999. Leave aside the entertainment and arts sections for the moment, because nonwhites are already likely to appear in ads for movies, records, and live performances.[6] Entertainment and lifestyle sections of the paper are also skewed toward the preferences of younger readers, who are a special case when it comes to race. Skip too the (admittedly few) ads for packaged goods and electronic gadgets that show people with the products, because they are likely to deliberately reflect the demographics of the target consumer. (It should surprise no one when Pampers ads feature black or Hispanic babies and mothers.) And hold consideration of the business section ads until a little later in this chapter.

Let's just focus on what historically has been the "whitest only" category of advertising in America's most influential paper: the fashion ads that run on the high-priced pages near the front of the A section and on the expensive leaves of the Sunday magazine. They are key barometers for the mainstreaming of color because unlike ads for, say, motor oil, personal computers, or laundry detergent, ads for fashion apparel, accessories, and cosmetics represent objects of aspiration and desire for all segments of adult society. Women, whether they are file clerks, lawyers, restaurant servers, editors, or pampered suburban homemakers all dream themselves into the shifts and sweaters and scarves in a Saks Fifth Avenue ad. Men with dress-white shirtsleeves, grease under their nails, or sweat under their blue-collar uniforms will linger on the feminine forms—especially those modeling bathing suits or lingerie—for their own fantasy pleasures as well as for cues as to what is desirable in a high-status gift for a wife, daughter, or sweetheart.

Thumbing through twenty-five days of A and Sunday magazine sections of the *Times* selected at random during April, May, and June 1999, I found people of color prominently represented in classy fashion ads on eighteen days. Most were in full-page ads, mainly in the magazine; many used people of color as the sole image. They ranged from lifestyle-action photographs, the kind that look like stills from a television commercial, to classic fashion illustrations in which the racial characteristics themselves are part physiology and part aesthetic imagination. An example from the lifestyle genre is a double-truck (two consecutive full pages) Bloomingdale's spread for designer khaki shorts. On the left-hand page, four hunky "boy next door" white guys and one dark-brown-skinned African-American lean shoulder to shoulder on one another on a windswept deserted beach in knee-length shorts. The black model's shorts are from the Sean John sportswear line of rapper-mogul Sean "Puffy" Combs, but they look no less preppy than the Kenneth Cole, Nautica, and Tommy Hilfiger styles on either side. On the right-hand page, the clean-shaven, clean-cut studs bare their chests and chiseled stomachs. The full-color ad plays on the razor-sharp contrast among blue sky, white sand, tan shorts, and pink and brown skin. Like metal to a magnet, the viewer's eyes are drawn to the black body in the middle, which is just a bit more strapping and posed full front than the rest, as if he were the anchor keeping the entire scene from blowing away.

In another example, a Sunday magazine full-page ad for a Liz Claiborne sweater uses a black woman, also on a beach, on her belly as if she has just slid into second base headfirst. Her pretty, short-Afro-ed face is tilted up, laughing as if only the devil would care about the sand getting all over the expensive knit. "Get comfortable," it says below her chin. The look typifies the racial transformation of the "all-American" image in fashion marketing. Even cosmetics, long considered to be as racially personal and particular as skin itself, are now sold in general-market television ads using models of different races. "Cinderella" Brandy also represents Procter and Gamble's Cover Girl brand, one of the largest mass-market makeup lines in the United States. Many observers, including journalists who ought to know better, merely chalk the increasing number of black, Hispanic, and Asian women representing American beauty to demographics and target marketing; that is, they're there to sell products to the growing numbers of their own kind in the marketplace. Wrong. Nonwhite "Cover Girls," are very much on display in general market (read: predominantly white readership) magazines like *Glamour, Seventeen,* or *Cosmopolitan,* as well as in minority-targeted books like *Essence.* Even I was stunned to see Queen Latifah, a beautiful but somewhat plus-size black woman, back to back with white country superstar Faith Hill on the back page of the February 2002 *Cosmopolitan.* The Cover Girls were selling foundation, just different shades of beautiful skin.

"What is considered 'all-American' has changed," said Kimberly Stewart, a spokesperson for Cover Girl cosmetics in a 1996 interview. "All-American now means everybody; the most all-American brand is the most inclusive brand," not the whitest one anymore. What was socially unthinkable as recently as 1980 is now economically inescapable: "Black lips can sell lipstick to white women," Stewart said.

A 1997 study of race and marketing trends found minorities depicted in more than 25 percent of ads in the thirteen most popular mass-circulation magazines that had people in them at all.[7] The survey, based on a one-month sampling, found that automobile ads had the highest use, with minorities depicted in 19 percent of *all* the car ads. (Bear in mind that some 45 percent of the ads do not depict people at all.)

What goes for print fashion ads goes double for general-market television advertising, because unlike niche-targeted magazines like *Vogue, Essence,* and *Vanity Fair,* network television spots generally aim for a broad cross-section of the entire market. It's hard to name a category of product pushed on television today that doesn't prominently include minority actors or celebrity endorsers. From the high-profile Michael Jordan multiproduct marketing machine that was at its height before his second retirement (Gatorade, Nike, MCI), to the pushy black woman in the Phillips' Milk of Magnesia commercials, to the hot salsa-dancing Latinos in a popular 1999 Visa card campaign, to that incongruously mixed group of apparently black, Hispanic, Asian, and white folks whooping it up on some country porch with Garth Brooks for Dr Pepper, people of color are now a fixture in commercials selling most goods and services. According to the Screen Actors Guild, nonwhite actors doubled their share of jobs in TV commercials between 1985 and 1994.[8] Black, Hispanic, and Asian actors got 21 percent of all commercial jobs in 1995, compared with 10.8 percent in 1985. Of these jobs, African-Americans filled more than half the roles in 1995, or 12 percent of all roles. Twenty-one percent is not quite parity—the three groups constituted about 26 percent of the population in 1995—but it's close, and the direction of the trend is unambiguous.

"It's not that the mainstream is being replaced by multiracialism. The mainstream is becoming multiracial," says Bill Katz.

❐   ❐   ❐

For all the complaints about the programming content that fills the spaces between television commercials, the transracial principle is nevertheless clearly at work and gaining momentum in the shows that deliver consumers to advertisers as well. According to data from the Screen Actors Guild, in 1985 whites received 86 percent of all acting jobs in television and movie productions covered by union contracts. In 1997 the white share was down to 78 percent, just four points higher than the actual non-Hispanic white share of the population. The television program data for that year reveals a sharply uneven distribution of color between race groups and genders. What race/gender group, with respect to its share of the U.S. population, is the most represented on television? African-American males appeared in prime-time shows at 171 percent of their actual proportion of the population in 1997, beating out even white males at 122 percent. Black females, at 85 percent, were underrepresented in prime-time roles, but proportionately they were still more common than white females, who appeared at just 70 percent of their share of the population.[9]

Incorporating research on the cultural content of television portrayals with the SAG data, George Gerbner, Bell Atlantic Professor of Telecommunication at Temple University in Philadelphia, compared the proportion of good/successful to bad/unsuccessful characters by race in 1982 to 1992 versus 1995 to 1997 and observed:

> The pattern reported in the prior study . . . has changed from casting non-white characters disproportionately in roles of villains and failures. While Latino/Hispanic and Asian/Pacific characters formerly had higher ratios of failures per success, now the only characters that fail more than white males are those with foreign national origin and those with mental disability. The ratios of failures per success are 1.22 (mental disability), 0.72 (non-U.S. origin), 0.56 (white males), 0.56 (Asian/Pacific), 0.55 (Latino/Hispanic) 0.35 (all women), and 0.33 (African American).[10]

Similarly, despite the often-repeated charge that African-Americans are primarily depicted as thugs and criminals on television, Gerbner found that black characters were slightly less likely to be dangerous than the television average; white men were slightly more likely. Meaning? The persistent belief that blacks suffer consistent and overwhelming negative stereotyping in television entertainment is just not true. And while local television news is still rightly faulted for giving disproportionate coverage to crime and other social conflicts in poor communities of color, typified by a surfeit of shots featuring blacks and Hispanics being led away in handcuffs, even that injustice is strangely offset by weekend national news broadcasts. While broadcast journalism is still struggling to meet its own modest racial diversity goals, the weekend anchors of two and sometimes all three of the big network shows are minorities, usually blacks, and it seems the majority of correspondents working weekends are black, Hispanic, or Asian. The effect, after a Saturday or Sunday in which most sports programming features minority athletes on the field, minority commentators on the sidelines, and increasingly a minority anchor in the studio, is the impression that the news of America at leisure is dominated by Americans of color.

In movies, six of the fifteen top-grossing movies for the summer of 1998 featured minority lead characters or creative talent. As more black actors get movie vehicles that transcend limitations that were firmly in place as recently as 1980, "the stigma has been lifted," said a senior Paramount movie executive in 1996 who did not want to be identified, after a summer in which African-Americans starred or costarred in five of the ten top-grossing movies.[11] "The market says these guys are stars," the executive added.

❐   ❐   ❐

The shrinking status discount associated with minorities in pop culture coincides with the reinvention of New York in particular and urban centers in general as the locus of American pop culture life. The city that was metaphorically given up for dead by President Gerald Ford in 1975, the city whose essential character Ronald Reagan successfully ran against in 1980, emerged phoenixlike from the cultural and fiscal onslaught of Reaganism in a place nearer to the heart of American pop than it was when Nixon was first elected. The new New York of pop imagination was resurrected as—surprise, surprise—the bustling immigrant mecca and melting pot that was still the number-one destination for "real" white Americans looking to make their fortune. Only in today's New York myth of self-creation, the immigrants are overwhelmingly nonwhite, and the music, fashion, and style are dominated by hip-hop. Somehow what was too black, brown, and pathological about the city is now the perfect backdrop for the kind of gallows optimism that passes for 1990s-style happy endings (think of the movie *As Good As It Gets*). It's no coincidence, in transracial marketing America, that so many lenses are focused on the major cities in which WASP America, the ostensible dominant culture, is far from dominant and is often downright invisible.

New York, right up to the terrorist attacks of September 11, 2001, had been in such demand as a backdrop for movies, television, and commercials[12] that Hollywood was increasing its investment in bricks and mortar here—at a time when more and more U.S. film production was actually leaving the United States. Preliminary data suggest that the force driving production offshore—high costs—will likely have a much bigger impact on filming in the city than the destruction of the World Trade Center. The trend toward setting stories in New York will continue, even if, as is increasingly the case, most of the locations are shot in Toronto. Most sitcoms and police dramas on television are set in a New York (or Chicago or L.A.), where it is understood (if not always faithfully depicted) that whiteness is not the norm, even when the lead characters themselves are mostly white. Television dramas are filled with stories of "cool" white people who know how to thrive in multiracial urban environments. (Compare and contrast the white characters of *ER*, *NYPD Blue*, and *Homicide* with the white people of 1970s hit prime-time soaps like *Dallas* and *Dynasty*.)

Color is rising and whiteness is receding in filmed entertainment in concert with a shift of imagination within the creative nation whose twin capitals are New York and Los Angeles. It began in the legitimate theater of the 1970s with the nontraditional casting movement. Today in filmed dramas minorities are routinely cast in high-status roles—detectives, lawyers, doctors, military officers, corporate executives, computer jocks, judges—playing characters that weren't necessarily written either as black *or as white,* in positions that were not seen as credible for people of color twenty years ago.

Hamilton Cloud, a film and television executive who was executive producer of the NAACP Image Awards show from 1987 to 2000, has seen growth in the number, quality, and range of performances by black actors nominated for the Image Awards during those years. In 1986 the awards competition had just one category for top female actors, "outstanding actress in a television movie, drama series, or special," "and Cicely Tyson would win it every year," Cloud joked to me. "Now there are three categories covering the same universe of performances, because it's grown that much."

> I think what we're seeing is that the drama producers have figured out that black characters are inherently interesting. You have all the basic human stuff going on, and then there is the racial tension to play with. Say you have a cop who is a cynic—that's interesting, but we've seen it before. But if he's a black cynic, it's more. And if he's a serious Catholic—well, that's something, too. But if he's a black Catholic and a cynic, it's a wow. Because we've never seen it before.

Cloud was talking about the role of Detective Frank Pembleton, created by actor Andre Braugher on the critically acclaimed NBC drama *Homicide.*[13] Published interviews with a number of most-demanded African-American actors, including Wesley Snipes, Denzel Washington, and Angela Bassett, suggest that they place a premium on roles that were not necessarily written as black, because they often offer a greater range of artistic possibilities than the typically conceived "black" role. It's no coincidence that Braugher was recognized by critics as the best actor on television for most of *Homicide*'s four-year run.

The arc of actor James Earl Jones's film roles also tracks the larger trend. In his 1970 big-screen breakthrough, he re-created the role of Jack Johnson in *The Great White Hope,* about a black man at the turn of the century who stood almost entirely out of his time as heavyweight champion of the world. Jones's 1972 film *The Man* was about his character's struggle being the first black president of the United States. The improbability of a black man in the White House was so central to the film that it played more like science fiction than political drama. Fast-forward to 1990, and we find Jones in a major supporting role in *The Hunt for Red October* running Naval Intelligence with an admiral's rank, and race has nothing to do with it. He repeated the role in two more hit films based on Tom Clancy spy novels; his character's death in the last one provided the emotional catalyst for the drama's resolution. In *Field of Dreams* (1989), another critical and commercial success, Jones's character is central to the plot as the embodiment of what is pure and noble about the American spirit, as enshrined in the game of baseball. He's a reclusive writer, not an athlete, and race once again has nothing to do with it.[14] Today it's hard even for boomer audiences to imagine a white actor packing the same transcendent gravity into the role that Jones did, even though we were raised with nothing but great white father figure actors in such parts. For Gen-X and Gen-Y, who grew up with Jones in those roles, imagining it otherwise it is probably as impossible as, say, imagining Darth Vader from *Star Wars* speaking with some other voice than Jones's unmistakable baritone.

For most of the decades since World War II, there was usually only one black actor at a time—Diana Ross, Richard Pryor, Sidney Poitier, Harry Belafonte, Diahann Carroll—in lead or supporting lead roles in films intended for a broad audience, and their films were few and far between. But since 1986 the roster of African-Americans starring and costarring in mainstream (i.e., not primarily targeted to black audiences) films has swelled in a way that's categorically different from anything that's gone before. At the

moment it seems that Denzel Washington, Angela Bassett, Laurence Fishburne, Whoopi Goldberg, Morgan Freeman, Samuel Jackson, Charles Dut-
ton, Eddie Murphy, Whitney Houston, Will Smith, Wesley Snipes, Martin
Lawrence, Forest Whittaker, Ice Cube, Chris Rock, Chris Tucker, Cuba
Gooding Jr., Ving Rhames, Delroy Lindo, and Danny Glover can at least co-
star in as many movies a year as they are willing to undertake, *all at the same
time*. Note that this list does not include a rising cadre of younger actors, like
Taye Diggs, Omar Epps, Sanaa Lathan, Tisha Campbell, Nia Long, and a
widening group of rappers who are getting film debuts in more and more
major theatrical releases. In the mid-1980s their movies, usually with all-
black casts and grounded in African-American or urban cultural idioms,
could be locked into the category of black film, as isolated from the mainstream as so-called foreign films used to be. But today movies like *The Best
Man* (1999) and *How Stella Got Her Groove Back* (2000) are widely reviewed
and advertised in mainstream print media and are mentioned heavily in
celebrity-driven tabloid television like *Entertainment Tonight*. Though the
core first-run audience for these films are black, it crosses over into younger,
hip-hop-acculturated whites. Finally, these movies receive huge secondary
distribution from major pay cable (like HBO), regular cable, and DVD-
video release.

Meanwhile, Hispanic actors Jimmy Smits, Jon Seda, Antonio Banderas,[15]
Jennifer Lopez, Cameron Diaz, Benjamin Bratt, and John Leguizamo have
also broken through in a big way in the late 1990s, a way that predicts an
even greater Latino penetration of mainstream movies in the very near
future, because the mainstream audience does not see relationships between
lighter-skinned Hispanics (unlike blacks), and Anglo-whites as interracial.
This transracial perception gives Hollywood free rein with romantic pairings
predicated on the one thing that matters, sensual heat, and widens the menu
available to serve audiences' romantic/erotic appetites, particularly those of
the male audience. Thus the hot "funk in the trunk" pairing of Jennifer Lopez
and George Clooney in the critically lauded *Out of Sight* was the most-talked-
about love scene of 1998. I mention the Hispanic penetration of mainstream
films here to compare and contrast it with the situation for African-Americans.
The point is that while the acceptance of Hispanics, with or without Latino
cultural cues attached, is an important part of the larger story of the brown-

ing mainstream, blacks come to Hollywood carrying much heavier racial and social baggage. (I'll discuss the special case of Hispanics and Asians in the emerging transracial American identity in detail in Chapter 7.)

Sex, of course, is second only to violence as the most potent and enduring active ingredient in popular culture. Nonwhite and interracial sexuality, with its historical-political baggage, has always been an even more potent spice and thus is used exceedingly sparingly, even today. But everything indicates that the wrappers are coming off and will be entirely discarded in the not-too-distant future. Acknowledged interracial relationships, usually black-white, have been a staple of daytime soap operas since the 1970s.[16] Interracial black-white romances figured in the plots of several successful prime-time shows in 1999, including *Ally McBeal, ER,* and *Spin City,* with little or no public comment. Again, it's now hard to tell whether affairs involving Hispanics and Anglo-whites, like those on NBC's late-'90s sitcoms *Jesse* and *Suddenly Susan,* even count as such. And don't even try to factor the interracial sexual equations created by of the growing number of Latino actors playing non-Latino characters and vice versa.

Meanwhile, syndicated trash TV, from crass talkers like Jerry Springer and Rikki Lake to late-night dating tease games like *Change of Heart,* has opened a window on sensationalized sexuality across racial lines, as a disproportionate number of the guests baring their shameful desires and guilty pleasures are nonwhite. This syndicated universe is particularly significant because it brings primarily working- and lower-middle-class Americans together across racial lines, in the studio as well as at home, around the intimate stories of barrio, ghetto, and trailer-trash life, or of people one step removed. It cuts deeper than higher-brow racially integrated or "multicultural" fare because trash talk hits where most people really live—their genitals, their jealousies, their sense of victimhood, and their quest for redemption—rather than their black, white, or Latino political identities. Growing up in America and coming of age with the term *white flight,* I never thought I'd see the day when whites and nonwhites would air so much sexual or otherwise personal and intimate dirty laundry on national TV as freely as if we all were really next-door neighbors sharing over the clothesline in an integrated neighborhood.

To be sure, black-white romantic pairings are still not very marketable in movies. It's hard to say who is less ready—Hollywood or black actors—for movies to permanently dismantle the last and most significant barrier between the races in popular culture. Denzel Washington has made a political point of not taking roles that might disappoint black audiences; chief among them is that his love interests will be black or at least nonwhite. In the wake of a slew of box-office-busting black-white buddy flicks (*Lethal Weapon, Beverly Hills Cop, Die Hard with a Vengeance, Men in Black, 48 Hours, Fled, White Men Can't Jump*, and the almost identically cast *Money Train*), Hollywood routinely pairs the races in certain action-dramas, but when it comes to romantic comedies and dramas, the reigning black and white stars never meet.

"I'm not going to pretend that America is ready for interracial love stories," the Paramount executive said. "I don't think you can put an Angela Bassett in a movie with Tom Hanks or someone like that and just have it be a romantic story."

"Nevertheless," he added, "One day soon somebody's gonna do it, and it's gonna be great."

That was 1996, and while we still haven't had yet the black-white Bogie and Bacall flick, we are closer than anyone thinks. The fact that the artistically woeful but commercially successful *Swordfish* (2001) will be best remembered for exposing Halle Berry's breasts in the girlfriend-of-the-antihero role was yet another straw in the wind. I was especially impressed by how much attention Berry's role in the film received from worldwide media. "Sexy Seductress Steams Suspense Screen," from the headline of a press release by China Southern Airlines announcing *Swordfish* addition to the inflight movie fare, was my favorite. *Swordfish* was quickly followed by Berry's costarring role in the critically hailed *Monster's Ball* (2001). The performance earned Berry a best actress Oscar, the first for a black woman. The film centers on her romantic relationship with a white prison guard played by Billy Bob Thornton. Berry's work in the passionate love scene—one that appeared to shatter the very barrier to Hollywood's readiness the Paramount executive perceived—was mentioned prominently in every important review.

Actually, black-white and other interracial romantic pairing has been a frequent if not everyday element in one category of filmed entertainment: science fiction. Bassett, in fact, was paired with white actor Ralph Fiennes in a crypto-romantic plot in the science fiction film *Strange Days* (1995) . Science fiction has long been fertile ground for the transracial literary imagination.

The first interracial kiss on television, for example, was not on a soap opera but on *Star Trek* in 1968. In our digital-information-driven culture, so much of today's science fiction is blending into science fact that that the genre itself bleeds into present-tense action, drama, and even comedy films. Within these true and pseudo-science-fiction films, blacks, Hispanics, and Asian-Americans have acquired a special place and a new, affirmative stereotype: the supercompetent minority soldier or computer geek. It's as though every minority kid who passes through the "Be All You Can Be" volunteer military comes out an engineering, electronic, or aerospace whiz. (Think of the black radar guy played by Courtney Vance in *The Hunt for Red October*, Will Smith's fighter jock in *Independence Day*, Joe Morton as the computer engineer who develops the doomsday computer chip in *Terminator II*, Morton again as the high-tech bomb squad coordinating guy in *Speed*, and Morton yet again in a similar, more heroic role, disarming a nuke, in *Executive Decision*.)

Science fiction, it seems, allows writers, producers, and directors to diversify the cast, potentially widening the film's appeal without sacrificing credibility or disturbing the suspension of disbelief. In today's market nobody is going to shun a sci-fi thriller like *The Matrix* (the number-two-grossing film of 1999) just because a black man, Laurence Fishburne, is one of its stars, but it instantly broadens the film's appeal to domestic minorities and in global markets. Having nonwhites as successful, integral parts of an American civilization that, in the not-too-distant future, leads the world by dint of its brilliance and goodness (a American tenet of faith) adds great value for the core audience, because it's consistent with the genre's core assumption that in the future scientific rationalism and technology must eventually make race distinctions as we know them irrelevant.

Suffice it to say that the market demands a significant minority presence in every science-fiction film made these days. Beneath all the reasons I've already mentioned lies a more fundamental dynamic driving transracialism in high-tech literature: it matches the audience's aspirations for a society in which whites (much less human beings) are no longer the undisputed majority. Or rather, it supports a vision of whites continuing as first among equals in a multiracial if not multispecies universe. I call it the *Star Trek Future*. It is comforting to all Americans to know that when we challenge the unknown voids of future dimensions, galaxies, technologies, and alien civilizations, or when they challenge us, we will standing shoulder to shoulder, black, white, brown, and yellow, for an American vision of what is right and good—just as we did in *Independence Day*. Transracial American culture requires the reinvention of the World War II foxhole as a space capsule in which soldiers of every race and ethnicity combine their unique talents and sacrifice for the common good. Today there is no limit to the endowments of leadership, heroism, and especially technical skill of the nonwhites in space. One of them could be president, as in *The Fifth Element* or *Deep Impact*, or the officer in charge of the mission, like Lawrence Fishburne in *Event Horizon*.

◻   ◻   ◻

The special case of science fiction is the general case in more and more categories of advertising, when it comes to transracial appeal. But while advertising is also a fictive medium, its vision must flow not from literary imagination but from a meaningful social reality. The value of transracial imagery in advertising flows from what marketing experts see as a long-range shift in American social attitudes and lifestyles as well as demographic trends. The blurring of race and ethnic lines in advertising is a marketplace reflection of a new equilibrium in the post–civil rights politics of race. As people of color are no longer entirely discounted in the sociopolitical mainstream, they are no longer marginalized in the mainstream of advertising. It's as if, at the end of the 1970s, a new set of social values was licensed by society and then was bankrolled by big media businesses.

Offscreen, the real New York that, going into the 1980s, survived white flight, near fiscal collapse, and a perpetual economic roller-coaster ride now takes inspiration from its salvation: the flood tide of predominantly Asian, Caribbean, Mexican, Middle Eastern, and African immigrants whose energy and industry make the city hum. The climate of fear and suspicion that has followed the attack of September 11, 2001, I think, will eventually resolve itself in a reaffirmation of this view, if only because if recovery is to succeed we have no choice but to dance with the one who brought us. It was no coincidence that one of the first commandments on September 11 from then-mayor Rudolph Giuliani (and for that matter from President Bush) was to hold New York's Muslim and Arab communities harmless: "They" are part of "us." In a way that cannot easily be undone, diversity, *or at least the image of diversity,* has been established as an unalloyed good—good for marketing, good for managing, and good for society—in the corporate canyons of Manhattan that still dominate the major media industries, especially on Madison Avenue.

BBDO's Katz, who runs the number-four advertising agency in the world, lives in the ethnically diverse New York suburb of West Orange, New Jersey.

> My kids go to school with Chinese, with black people, with Muslims, with Indians, with Jews, with everybody. My son's best friend is from a mixed marriage. His father, one of my best friends, tells me how [the mixed-race son] came home one day after somebody asked him about his race. He had answered, "I'm a blend." Then he turned to his mom and said, "Isn't everybody a blend?" My son figured that's probably true—that he's a blend of some kind, too.

How great is the impact of Katz's experience of transracial reality in the New York suburbs on his perception of the browning mainstream in his business?

> Immense. Immense. Because as soon as it becomes real, we portray it. And it is now real. And you will see it, too. If you go home and watch MTV or Nickelodeon, where advertising is specifically geared [to twelve-to-twenty-one-year-old consumers], you'll begin to see it. And it's getting exponential now—it's there. It's reality.

At one level, products that aspire to be seen as "all-American" are almost compelled to depict a racially diverse image. Thus the traditional Chevrolet commercial montage of scenes from the American good life always includes black or urban families in the mix. Another technique of "all-American" brands is to deliberately blur and bend notes of race and culture. Hence the Pepsi commercials in which the cute little white girl variously channels Aretha Franklin or Isaac Hayes to pump up "the joy of Pepsi." Another approach casts nonwhite icons in brand-new general-market pitchman roles. Former heavyweight champion George Foreman's remarkable postring career is the most prominent example; soon more Americans will know him as a spokesman for Midas mufflers and indoor grills than as a boxer. Soft drink and other goods makers have been joined recently by a host of financial and personal service firms like life and heath insurers, telecom providers, banks, and stockbrokers. These spots invariably feature a range of adorable infants and children in a backdrop that looks like a UN school. My favorites in the "all Americans together" category are the sports-related products that feature regular people using everything from Nike sneakers to Foot Locker shoe stores to Gatorade, because they tend to focus on visceral human common denominators: sweating, panting, thirsting, and straining.

Advertising is created in a decidedly nonpolitical process, experts say. The transracial vision has acquired an aspirational value in the broad market not because it's politically correct but because it's how America wants to see itself: as a unified multiracial culture. That's why blues music, for example, in all its variations, is now so ubiquitous in commercials as a sound track for the American dream. B. B. King and his talking blues guitar Lucille have plugged McDonald's hamburgers. In 1996 Reebok teamed bluesman Buddy Guy with Chicago White Sox slugger Frank "The Big Hurt" Thomas to confess the hitter's career heartbreaks along the way to stardom. The punch line: "If the blues don't kill you, brother, it'll make you mighty mighty mad." A Pepsi campaign that same year featured John Lee Hooker.

Now in the real world between 1989 and 1996, the number of blues festivals and clubs actually doubled and *Billboard* established a separate blues chart to track booming sales. Yet Reebok insisted its move had nothing to do with hitching its mainstream product to the up-trend in blues consumption. Reebok may have come to the conclusion honestly, said Bill Ferris, former chairman of the National Endowment for the Humanities under President Clinton and longtime director of the Center for the Study of Southern Culture at the University of Mississippi, because the rise of the blues in marketing is more a case of the trend overtaking the mainstream than the other way around.

Quite simply, Ferris told me, the blues sells products to the mass of consumers who will never buy a blues album or go to a blues club, because it unifies Americans at a gut cultural level.

In a way, it's a quest by America to discover its own roots, to find meaning in their lives at a time when such meaning is hard to locate. It goes back to Huck and Jim on the raft, the attempt by white America to try to bridge the eternal divide on race. For many whites the division is a tragedy, something we seek to reach out and touch to change. Blues is one way that happens.

Transracial sells in advertising because, with the triumph of big-box retail chains coast to coast, that's how people buy. The arrival of a "Big K" Kmart or Home Depot or Wal-Mart in an area instantly offsets, to some degree, decades of local residential racial segregation, at least on weekend afternoons, because the patronage area of the typical gigantic store crosses most neighborhood boundaries, drawing clientele from a range of races and income groups. Older chains have increased their size and retrofitted their images where necessary to compete. Brand-new chains like Old Navy have successfully burst onto the market with a quirky kind of transracial populism built in. As writer Cynthia Joyce discovered:

> Old Navy store displays announce that it's the '50s all over again— but this time around, both American patriots and their one-time proletarian adversaries are united in a populist rhetoric of low-cost fashion. Big old American cars are incorporated into merchandise displays; star-spangled nail polish comes in red white and blue. . . .
>
> Old Navy brand allegiance is classic case study in what historians call an invented tradition. The print ads . . . suggest that the three-year-old chain is actually an old American institution in the midst of a renaissance. But however confusing the messages of the chain's ad campaigns may be, Old Navy does fill a genuine market niche.
>
> The populist rhetoric, it turns out, isn't just rhetoric—Old Navy is where the locals shop. It seems like the only time you are likely to encounter a socioeconomically diverse group of people is either at the Department of Motor Vehicles or in the self-consciously prole precincts of Old Navy. The last time I tried on a pair of jeans in Old Navy's co-ed dressing room, I emerged to find a heated button-fly vs. zipper debate taking place among the young Asian salesgirl, a middle-aged black man, and a Mexican mother of

three. And as I examined my prospective purchase in the three-panel mirror, each of them freely offered their opinion of the fit. These aren't the most momentous breakthroughs in democratic culture, to be sure. But Old Navy's success has reversed a long-standing disdain for anything Middle American.[17]

Or, rather, Old Navy and the rest of the big-box retailers have given "middle American" a long overdue redefinition to reflect transracial reality.

No matter how many times or ways I asked experts to explain exactly how and why Transracial America sells, the answer always boiled down to the belief that Transracial America is real. As BBDO's Katz put it:

> There may be this sociopolitical division [between races and ethnic groups]. They may have these thoughts [of racism, alienation, ethnic chauvinism]. But they are still living the way they are living. Their environment is as it is. The images they see are the images they see, and the malls they go to are the malls they go to.
>
> The reality is that this is the gestalt of society. Advertising is not interested in recognizing the sociopolitical issues. It is only interested in realizing [consumer] reality, the gestalt. It can't affect sociopolitics, it doesn't want to go near it; it avoids it like the plague.

Color in advertising is especially reflective of reality for younger consumers, the so-called Gen-X (born between about 1965 and 1978) and Gen-Next or Echo Boomers (the late children of the baby boomers, born since 1978), because, as with science fiction devotees, it meets their expectation of what's next. One of the most salient psychographic markers of under-thirty-five consumers is their expectation that as they mature they will be immersed in an increasingly multiracial world. Remember those striking ads for Schick razors in which the faces of the shavers magically "morphed" from white to Asian to black and back to white? The goal was to capture the attention of eighteen-to-thirty-five-year-old shavers by combining what were then cutting-edge special effects with the leading edge of the Gen-X worldview, according to Dave McSpadden, who created the long-running ads for the J. Walter Thompson agency in 1993.

We decided to tap into the mind-set of younger people—how they see the world. . . . In all the casting we had people who were realistic looking, not necessarily the perfect upscale ideal. We wanted to have a range of ethnicities; we thought it was truer to the marketplace and truer to younger people's perception that they are living in a multicultural world. We saw immediate sales growth when we introduced it. There are two things consumers like about it. One is the morphing technique—and as a group the characters seem approachable and likable.

The depth of this transracial perception for younger consumers was brought home for me by a full-page Jordache Jeans ad in 1995 in *Vibe* magazine. A chiseled, chest-naked, blue-black man hoists a very blond bra-clad model off her feet up to his shoulder and peels her prominently labeled jeans from her behind like a banana. She gazes toward the ceiling in near rapture. Flaunting taboo and provoking stereotypes, the ad seemed to break every rule of mass marketing. But Jordache's advertising director, Kaaryn Denig, told me that when it comes to consumers of a certain age, the rules are being changed.

We've always done sexy images—but it's the first time we've brought a black person into the imagery. With the youth of today, I think the walls between the races are breaking down. They've grown up in atmosphere where everyone is considered equal and interracial dating is no big deal.

Denig said she did get some calls complaining about the image, but not from people in her target age group. *Their* calls were enthusiastic. "I got a call from a girl in Utah in her early twenties. She loves the image—wanted to blow it up and put it on her wall," Denig said. (A fuller discussion of youth culture as a driving force in the browning of the American mainstream appears in Chapter 6.)

People of color, primarily blacks and Hispanics, sell well beyond expectations based on social status because of what I call the *heat factor*. Black and brown skin stands out and warms up any scene before the cameras, especially when it's reflecting the energy of a "down home" black or Latino cultural style. That's why black actor Cuba Gooding Jr. was seen pushing white men out of airplanes to launch the new one-calorie cola Pepsi-One in 1998. Or at least that's how it looked to me. "Actually he's not pushing white people out of an airplane," explained Katz of BBDO, which made the spot. "He takes the product, throws it out, and induces white people to go after it. It has nothing to do with race."

Which means that BBDO did not see either Gooding's race or the audience connection to his most recent film roles, which could generally be described as "over the top." But, Katz told me, they did feel Gooding's heat.

> He delivers the spirit, the intensity—he delivers the kind of entertainment value that you need when you're simply telling people there's a new product out there that tastes as good as any regular cola. We chose him as a person . . . [for] the energy that comes out. You want to watch him. You buy his act. You don't say he's going too far; there's an infectious quality to him.

Transracial sells because it is often more efficient to market and promote a unified brand image to consumers of all races than to ignore nonwhites in the general market, as many firms once did, or to create entirely separate campaigns confined to minority-targeted media. This principle can hold even for a product line that has been to some extent racially particular, like cosmetics and beauty products. Lipstick, makeup, eye-color, and hair-care products, categories once thought to be inherently segregated by race, are now commonly advertised using models of all races to reach all races. How it has become common is a parable of the inexorable triumph of transracial marketing over the "separate but equal" ethnic-targeting model that rose in the mid-1980s only to start falling by the early 1990s.

As recently as 1991, major industry players Cover Girl and Revlon offered few cosmetic items formulated with black or Hispanic women in mind, and they did even less to promote their lines to women of color. Black, Asian, and Hispanic women still used the products even though they rarely saw themselves in their marketing. That year, however, Maybelline scored an instant hit with the Shades of You line of face and eye makeup. Designed with black and Hispanic women in mind, Shades was marketed primarily through black- and Hispanic-targeted media and was promoted at "ethnic" community events. At retail Shades was displayed separately from the rest of the Maybelline line, usually in the separate aisle reserved for "ethnic" health and beauty aids. In 1993, after Shades, with 41 percent of a previously unrecognized "ethnic" market, showed there was money to be made, Cover Girl and Revlon joined the competition. But the two firms jumped in with very different strategies.

Revlon launched the ColorStyle line, featuring darker shades and formulations optimized to work on the skin types common to African-American and Hispanic women. It also mimicked Shades' separate advertising, promotion, and retail display strategy. ColorStyle had some initial success, but by 1996, said M. Katherine Dwyer, then president of Revlon Cosmetics, research showed unexpected responses to the line from both white and nonwhite women. For starters, even though white women generally didn't see the minority targeted ColorStyle advertising, they saw the widened range of shades available because, especially in urban areas, they shopped in the same stores.

> We found that 60 to 70 percent of buyers were Caucasians. . . . They liked the dark shades—particularly lip and nail coloring. We [also] found that [minority] women didn't want to be separated out from the main brand.

Cover Girl, meanwhile, took the transracial tack. It responded to Shades' success by adding seventy-two new hues to its existing line of foundations and lipsticks, hired its first black models, and slowly integrated them into its advertising. By 1996 Cover Girl had 29 percent of the market and Shades was down to just 22 percent. ColorStyle, which never got higher than about 20 percent, fell to 7.5 percent that year, prompting Revlon to fold the items back into its main lines while stepping up its use of nonwhite models in general-market advertising.

Shades might have still given Cover Girl a run for its money, but as Shades reached maximum distribution, Maybelline found it increasingly costly to support separate lines in thousands of retail stores in dozens of markets; it was forced to cut back Shades' marketing budgets. "When you do 'separate but equal,' you set up a smaller business within your bigger business; when resources become tight, the smaller business tends to take the brunt" of cuts, said Shades marketing manager Bridgett Chisholm. To regroup, Shades began advertising in mainstream magazines because research found that while black and Hispanic women trust their own ethnic magazines, "they also want to see ads in *Cosmopolitan* and *Vogue,* because they are still arbiters of fashion," Chisholm told me.

What happened? Once the firms discovered women of color as a market and attempted to address them, they found that, despite real physical and cultural distinctions, women were more alike as cosmetics consumers than they were different because of race. Concepts of beauty, or rather aspects of beauty, turned out to be a lot more fluid across racial lines than anyone suspected, especially from nonwhite to white. As Revlon's Dwyer pointed out to me:

Women like to look at beautiful women no matter what color they are. They want to look and capture a piece of her no matter what she's got, whether it's the shape of the eye or lip or the attitude. With the exception of certain foundation shades, if it's a truly beautiful color, a lot of women are going to want to try it to see if it works for them. Remember, a lot of Caucasian women buy slightly darker shades, because they want to have a look of a tan.

"One benefit of an integrated line is there's a lot of cross-purchasing," said Cover Girl spokesperson Kimberly Stewart. "With segmented marketing you might not get other women sampling the entire shade range, because someone has already made the decision that it's not for them."

How did racial lines that looked immutable less than a decade before blur so quickly? I asked. Stewart explained:

We've done a lot of research on this ourselves, because we were intrigued by it, too. If you look at who the heroines are—there are some barriers that got broken in the 1980s that, if you don't recognize them, you're not contemporary anymore. Aspirational images are no longer exclusively Caucasian. You think about who our sports heroes are—Bill Cosby on TV—they influenced what people thought, what people wanted to move towards. Kids today are as likely to look at Whitney [Houston] and Janet [Jackson] and Toni Braxton as role models for all colors. There's an acceptance of different kinds of beauty as beautiful.

New York Times culture critic Margo Jefferson offers a more subtle parsing of the dynamic of race and beauty images in the fashion marketplace. As a black woman, Jefferson recalls that living through decades with only white fashion models to contemplate forced upon her a "fine visual and imaginative training . . . learning to be at ease with something that on the surface seems quite removed from you. " But the fact is, Jefferson writes, that not only don't all white models look alike, but as they are selected and posed to reflect the aesthetic visions of particular designers at a given moment, they don't necessarily look like most white consumers, either. Now a selection of women of color have broadened the universe of fashion and beauty images, but they still don't add up to "some comfortably all-purpose African-American type." Still, now that they're here, Jefferson notes, women of all colors have quickly gotten used to sharply enriched daily lessons in visual reimagination:

> When we look at a fashion layout, all kinds of conscious and unconscious reactions roil around inside us. If the model is our ethnic or racial twin, we may find ourselves rooting for the home team. If the model is wildly exotic or "other," we may borrow the fantasy for an everyday costume or encounter. We may feel judgmental or condescending or intensely envious. But we have to feel curious and excited, eager to be (or play at being) something we hadn't yet dared to imagine.[18]

To further underscore the point, Revlon's Dwyer recalled a 1995 focus group session with an ethnically mixed group of women. "The women in the room were talking about what the various brands represent. . . . The women said that Revlon was them—three blacks of different shades, various Caucasians. And I said, 'Wow—we communicated what we really intended to communicate'—in other words they didn't associate Revlon with just one [kind of] woman."

Cover Girl's next 1996 campaign, called All Skins, focused on the fact that the line covered every shade of woman. Revlon countered with In the Flesh, showing eight women who spanned the racial spectrum, "the point being that In the Flesh colors are good for all skin types; you'll be seeing more of that kind of advertising in the future," Dwyer predicted.

How right she was. Maybelline, overtaken by its larger rivals, was acquired that year by L'Oréal. As it happens, the Paris-based global giant is emphatically bent on taking the transracial approach to women's hair and beauty products to another level. Under the heading "whiteness," Roget's International Thesaurus indexes fourteen synonyms for *blond*. But that didn't stop L'Oréal from putting a burnished-copper-colored African-American model on the box of the Nude Gold shade in its 1998 rollout for the Feria hair-color line. In fact, as seen in the matching television ad, model Janine Green's do isn't even straightened! The Feria ad featuring Green ran for two years. Sometime in 2001 Green was replaced in the "black blond" model role by pop singer Beyoncé Knowles of Destiny's Child.

"We made a very conscious decision, not only in the United States but in world, that we want to represent beauty in all cultures and races," said Joseph J. Campinell, president of L'Oréal's U.S. retail division. What L'Oréal thinks makes the entire industry think twice because, after a series of acquisitions including Maybelline, it is now the biggest U.S. beauty advertiser, spending $250 million in 1998. L'Oréal's aim, said Campinell, is to create one multiracial image of its brand for all consumers. Targeting specific groups with separate messages "is not the philosophy of the L'Oréal brand." Just one year after acquiring Maybelline, L'Oréal became the number-one U.S. cosmetics maker, with a 34 percent share, besting both Revlon and Cover Girl, with about 20 percent each. Remember that study of nonwhites in major magazine print ads? After cars, the sample found that health and beauty ads had the second-highest representation, at 18 percent of all ads in the category (including the nearly half that had no people depicted at all).[19]

It's hard to say just how much farther the race-blending trend can go in hair and beauty product marketing. Now that marketers have succeeded with hair-, lip-, and eye-color products, it seems hair-texture-related products are next. Hair marketing has always been segmented by the real genetic differences in hair texture that generally lead white, Asian, and most Hispanic women to wash and condition with greater frequency than women with predominantly African racial heritages. Shampoos and conditioners have mostly been separately marketed to black women, usually in tandem with the relaxer products to straighten otherwise tightly curled hair. But with the new century, more and more general market shampoo and conditioner ads are depicting women of all races as users. A recent Pantene-Pro V conditioner campaign took the unprecedented step of addressing racial hair differences directly and linking them to a product attribute. Over a montage of races and hair styles, it made the point that whether a woman's hair is long or short, straight or kinky, beautiful hair is healthy hair. In other words, the product's common benefit to women is more important than their genetic racial differences.

The only limit on nonwhite demand for products that actually alter inborn racial differences beyond hair texture seems to be the availability of effective technology. The most prominent example is the market for colored contact lenses. The $200 million worldwide business is primarily driven by brown-eyed people who want the option of hazel, green, blue, or gray eyes. Blacks and Hispanics buy about 40 percent of colored contacts sold in the United States, according to Tom Steiner, vice-president of marketing with Wesley Jessen Visioncare, maker of the market-leading Durasoft brand. Some 85 percent of wearers are female; 30 percent don't even need their vision corrected.

"A significant portion of the wearers are doing it even if they need no vision correction—they just like the effect," said Andrew Jay, an industry analyst with BT Alex. Brown. "And the lenses are improving. With better aesthetics even more people will move toward them. Think in terms of the number of people who dye their hair." Now, for the 60 percent of white American wearers, using race-bending cosmetic fashion is no big deal. Whites have always been free to view their superficial racial characteristics as fluid and entirely subject to their fashion choices. If a white man is thinking about dreadlocking his hair, or a white woman is considering a curly perm or filling out her lips with collagen or making her brown eyes blue, the primary concern is style or taste or safety, not racial politics. Interestingly, Jay sees "a lot of legs" to the boom in colored lens sales in Latin America and Asia because these populations too seem more inclined to view eye color as a cosmetic rather than a racial characteristic. But for nonwhites in America, particularly African-Americans, using technology to alter racial features for fashion has always been considered self-hating racial treason. The long history of chemically straightening black hair has always been told with a slight undercurrent of shame. Yet thirty years after natural blackness was declared absolutely beautiful and, for a hot minute, threatened to put straightened hair permanently out of fashion, straight hair styles are more prevalent than ever with black women. Improved technology for hair straightening and hair weaving might be seen as the primary culprits, but they exist only in response to demand.

So it is with colored contacts, which were first introduced in the late 1980s. Wesley Jessen Visioncare had no idea that blacks and Hispanics would provide the core of its sales, Tom Steiner told me. "Initially the audience found us—we didn't make it happen." Afterward, when he began advertising in black- and Hispanic-targeted magazines, Steiner said he did get some letters from people who didn't like the idea of marketing more Caucasian features to African-Americans. "What we always say is, it's not our intent to suggest that the natural eye isn't beautiful, but we're just providing change for people—because that's what they want," he said. Interestingly, he said, the only significant marketing criterion—for all races—is the perceived naturalness of the shade. The greater the likelihood that the hue could in fact occur naturally in a group, like hazel in African-Americans, the more popular it is. Clearly, the very concept of "natural" itself is subject to continuous redefinition, not by pronouncements of political or academic leaders but by developing technology applied to the passions of the marketplace. Think about it: In less than a decade the term *black blond* went from oxymoron to common noun.

To be sure, there is still a separate black beauty care industry, generally stressing racial pride as a marketing edge, and it will survive into the twenty-first century.[20] Race- and ethnic-affinity-based marketing in general will also grow in the new millennium, albeit from a small base. But as I will argue more fully in Chapter 8, the browning of the general market has been and will continue to be a permanent drain on the viability of ethnic target marketing.

❐   ❐   ❐

At the same time that big corporations are discovering that transracial marketing sells packaged goods, more leading firms are browning their corporate images in order to sell themselves to the broad public, to potential investors, employees, and voters. Blending new multiracial and multicultural imagery with an old name and logo helps new firms quickly seem some combination of progressive, visionary, and ready to compete in the global marketplace. Cisco Systems, which (for the few people who haven't heard by now) is the biggest supplier of key computer hardware used for Internet business applications, burned itself into the public eye with a long-running set of commercials in which a globally diverse cast of vaguely third-world everymen stare straight into the camera, recite statistics about the projected growth and global reach of the Internet, and then ask repeatedly, "Are you ready?" Cisco was, of course, and to represent the enormity of Cisco's vision and readiness, its ad agency found it effective to evoke a semistark image of the world as it really is—predominantly Asian, African, and Latin American. In style the ads echo the spare, almost logo-free impressionism of some Nike ads. The most riveting effect is the feeling that the so-called third world is in fact a very close second, close enough to be right in our faces speaking perfect, if just slightly accented English.

Some of the most prominent, if not infamous, established firms identify themselves with Transracial America to reposition their images, usually in the direction of cutting-edge technological prowess and social awareness. A campaign that shows that a firm knows what time it is when it comes to the multiracial future is an especially useful tool for getting the public's mind off a major embarrassment. Thus just over two years after Texaco was thrashed in the court of public opinion (and on Wall Street) for systematic discrimination against minority employees, it launched its first-ever corporate image campaign. In a typical spot in the campaign, a black petroleum explorer leads a team through a sandstorm, mounts a dune, whips out a pocket computer, and shouts with a chortle, "This is it—we are here!" Later, setting up camp, he leaves viewers with "Don't you just love this job?"

In November 1996 after one of its former executives released tape-recorded conversations of Texaco officials making disparaging remarks about blacks, Texaco settled a race-discrimination suit for a record $176 million. While the 1999 ad campaign was admittedly conceived to atone for the

specific image problem stemming from the 1996 incident, its larger goal was
to establish Texaco's fitness for a rapidly changing global industry environment. An image of diversity is "critically important" for recruitment, said corporate advertising director Mary Moran, "not just to say that we value it, but
that we will be perceived as a more agile, younger, and forward-thinking company." In other words, transracial and transcultural imagery has become the
shorthand for all that a company should be in the challenging new century.

The global imperative facing American companies looking to do business
abroad seems to require the same shorthand. That's the only explanation for
the June 1999 full-color, full-page ad in the *New York Times* business section
from German banking giant Deutsche Bank. Having just purchased New
York's Bankers Trust Company, the page was half-full with a dark-brown-
skinned man in a blue banker's suit with one arm folded across his waist and
the other bent upward at the elbow with the hand half-clenched before his
chin. He stares convincingly into the camera as if seized with the certainty of
an idea whose time has come. Above him, in quotes as if he were a real
banker speaking, he pronounces: "Deutsche Bank and Bankers Trust. That's
a combination of strength and innovation bound to produce results."

Why does a German bank need to send this message? While discussing
the role of corporate media in the browning of the mainstream, Jeff Bewkes,
chairman of HBO, told me he found the Deutsche Bank ads to be telling—
and aimed at "the entire world."

> Deutsche Bank—there's a real message there. It says, "We're
> sophisticated, we're open, and we're serving a market that we know
> isn't just a bunch of white guys." [It says,] "We need women to feel
> comfortable, minorities, etc., because we are hip. Because Deutsche
> Bank . . ." These are the Germans—and this is America. We had a
> war. There was the whole Jewish thing there. So they're saying,
> "We're not Deutsche Bank-stodgier-than-Citibank. We're multira-
> cial!" They're trying to say "We're multiracial" to prove they're not
> German. "Don't think of us as German; it's too limiting. The only
> way we can be not-Germans is to be multiracial Americans."

At the same time, in strikingly similar full-page layouts, IBM and investment banker J. P. Morgan were promoting a different variation on how trans-

racial sells corporate America. These ads dramatized nonwhite employees as critical human resources epitomizing their firms' core values. The IBM ad used an actual employee's face, along with a thumbnail résumé. Message: IBM is people. "People who think. People who do. People who get it." And people who are not necessarily white and male. The J. P. Morgan ad went even further in its first-person identification between the image of a black professional and the corporate creed. "I can help build companies . . . I can tolerate mistakes. But I cannot tolerate repeating them. . . . I can be confident in my answers because I've already asked the questions. . . . *I work for J. P. Morgan.*"

While all of the earlier-mentioned benefits of being seen as progressive, visionary, and up-to-the-minute accrue to firms using ads like these, the purpose of the message is somewhat skewed toward impressing their own current and potential employees more than investors or the public at large. More and more firms are coming to realize that a sincere commitment to "diversity" in employment and promotion practices requires (or inevitably leads to) a seamless correspondence between the way a company presents itself to itself and the way it presents itself and its products to the world. In other words, transracial sells as transracial does as transracial is. My favorite example is a legendary early 1990s FedEx commercial (it ran for over a year) that featured a black female executive using its then-new instant package-tracking software service to get the drop on her white male counterparts. (Punch line: "Oh, *that* package, Martha!")

The commercial was cast with a black female executive protagonist, in part with an eye toward reflecting an image of the product consistent with FedEx's image of itself. As it happened, the no-nonsense female executive in the spot was actually modeled after one of the company's own executives, Sybille Noble, who was managing director of contracts and business transactions for the Memphis-based leader in overnight package delivery. "I said, 'Just imagine a Sybille Noble type,'" said Bob Miller, then vice president for marketing, recalling his instructions to the advertising agency, BBDO New York. Miller told me that FedEx often previews its ads to its ninety thousand employees and solicits their responses before they are aired. For Miller, who is African-American, there was no inconsistency between the way he saw the company, whose employees were 35 percent minority, and the way he saw the reputation, quality, and benefits of the product.

The commercials [performed] better than any we've done in the last ten years. What I've said to the agency is that I want to see people like me, and the people I know in my life. [FedEx] does a particularly good job of including the wide range of people who not only live in America but who work here. It's not a big deal around here; it's expected. In today's business you have to toss out terms like *nontraditional*. Everything is changing, and fast. We have to keep up. We just think about the market. [Because] companies can't provide job security—only customers can. Those are our customers, real people in real situations. That's how they dress, and that's how they look.

Which is to say that in Transracial America successful companies are compelled to align their corporate cultures with the sensibilities of the broad public they serve. As they do so, being in touch with their customers and their employees becomes one and the same thing. The convergence as a matter of fact becomes reflected in advertising fiction.

❐   ❐   ❐

The final and perhaps ultimate manifestation of the transracial dynamic in the marketplace is the ascendant visibility of pop culture icons who acknowledge, if not boldly assert, a mixed-race identity. Once upon a time, and not very long ago at that, the literature regarding Americans of mixed race was confined to one form: tragedy. Indeed, only in America could the term *tragic mulatto* enter the literary glossary. The tragedy, of course, was that one metaphorical drop of African blood doomed an otherwise-worthy human being to the second-class social status accorded the mass of the black population that was presumed to possess a much greater volume of such "blood." While lighter-skinned blacks have always been accorded a measure of privilege denied darker-skinned blacks, people of direct black and nonblack parentage have never had room to claim an identity as being neither black nor white or equally both.[21] Attempting to do so was the ultimate proof of the adage about the folly of walking down the middle of a highway; you get hit from both sides at once. Hence the tragedy. So traditionally blacks who could "pass" for white either did so in great but undocumented numbers or went out of their way to declare their subjecthood, if not undying allegiance, to the condition of black race.

The rise of black consciousness during the civil rights movement and its subsequent "black power" phase made it even tougher for mixed-race people to occupy a theoretical middle ground. African-American cultural politics embraced a concept of blackness that was as absolute and unaccepting of divided racial identity as the Ku Klux Klan's understanding of whiteness. But somewhere during the late 1980s, like new land pushing up from the mouth of a submerged volcano, an island began growing in the mainstream on which mixed-race people could stand and plant an identity flag. (A fuller discussion of the challenge such people will eventually pose to the legitimacy of the one-drop rule itself will be taken up in Chapter 7. The largest group of mixed-race figures in popular culture, Hispanics, as well as people of Eurasian backgrounds merit separate treatment because, in American pop culture as well as history, the one-drop rule has never really applied to their "blood." In effect, they are already free to enter the mainstream if not as whites outright, then without the specific burden that the one-drop rule imposes on people of undeniable African descent. The critical role of Hispanics in this aspect of American racial identity will also be taken up in Chapter 8.)

The small group of part-black pop culture figures who refuse to pledge traditional racial allegiance is significant far beyond their numbers because their media-magnified images are like a wrecking ball aimed at the very wall that Transracial American marketing is bent on toppling: the wall between black and white. My baseline for the emergence of the multiracial pop star is the movie *Flashdance*. Everyone remembers the hit songs it spawned, but no one remembers that in the starring role the nominally black actress Jennifer Beals passed for white. Her racially mixed parentage wasn't widely reported until the movie was a runaway hit. Beals has granted very few interviews in the intervening eighteen years, and by all accounts she has tried hard to distance herself from the issue. She neither declares herself to be politically black, like biracial actress Halle Berry, nor stands up for being something else.[22] Nevertheless, she may be America's last big tragic mulatto. *Flashdance* was more than the number-three-grossing movie of 1983, behind only the phenomenally successful *Terms of Endearment* and the *Star Wars* sequel *Return of the Jedi*. *Flashdance* was hailed as the feature film that established the power of music videos in popular culture. The very name *Flashdance* became a fashion statement built around the ripped sweatshirts and dance leotards that

Beals's character wore so well. Launched from that platform, any white actress of similar talent (or even less) would have landed at least a half-dozen golden opportunities to establish herself playing romantic heroines. But the closest Beals came after *Flashdance* to a romantic lead in a major film was as the bride of Frankenstein (*The Bride*, 1985), opposite rock star Sting. In the cruelest irony, Beals's most prominent appearance in recent years was in the 1995 *Devil in a Blue Dress*, in which she played a mysterious femme fatale whose secret, central to the plot, was that she was a mulatto passing for white. *Devil* bombed despite being based on a best-selling Walter Mosley novel and having Denzel Washington in the starring role; critics roundly blamed Beals for an unconvincing portrayal of the pivotal character. Perhaps, through no fault of her own, it was easier for the public and critics to believe her playing what she was not in *Flashdance*, a white woman, than playing what she was in *Devil*: a mulatto.

Flashdance-forward to 1999. New York Yankee All-Star shortstop Derek Jeter is on his way to his second World Series in as many years in the majors. Thousands of young and not-so-young white women in the stands wear his name on their backs. Many also wear his name painted on their faces, arms, or legs. When he comes through with another key run batted in, there might be a shot of his parents in the crowd: his father is black and his mother is white. No Yankee in recent memory has been treated to such unconditionally effusive national press, and Jeter's career has only just begun. Of course, he has extraordinary talent and is reportedly a consummate professional and all-around nice guy. But the fact of his biracial heritage, and how he has handled it, adds an entirely new dimension to his iconic appeal and potential marketability. For starters, the camera loves his sharp but racially ambiguous features. Every time it lights on him, the eye wants to linger, not just on the total package of good looks, but on each of the parts, in a vain attempt to calculate the racial whole. Fans, especially women, never tire of watching Jeter because as much as they look, there is still something ineffably more to apprehend. After a home run, some might look with longing for a familiar white man with whom to identify, but they won't quite find him. And after a great double play, some others may want to see a familiar great black athlete in his face, but they won't quite find him, either.

It's not a question of features. It's the fact that Jeter insists on not being anyone but Derek Jeter. And as a pop icon in Transracial America, he can get his wish granted with pleasure, having firmly put the question of race identity behind him from the start. Would that Jennifer Beals had had the same resolution of character! By all rights, she should have been a contender for everything that Kim Basinger, Andie MacDowell, or any other white actress who bowed in the mid-1980s has gotten with no greater endowment of looks or acting skills.

In a similar but more complicated vein, Tiger Woods's prodigious talent has mounted him on a global stage, multiracial identity and all. His 1997 declaration of "Cablinasian" (some combination of black, white, and Asian) racial identity thoroughly rankled many African-American pundits, presumably reflecting significant similar sentiments in the black community. But frankly, by resisting the badge of the "Willie Mays of golf"—that is, the first true black superstar in a mostly all-white sport—Woods thwarts any attempt to confine his appeal, or his potential marketing clout, to identification with one race. Like Jeter, he is freely packaging his talents for a shelf labeled "class by himself." Indeed, while discussing with me the marketing potential of various nonwhite athletes, Bob Williams, the Chicago sports marketing consultant, placed Woods in an entirely different category from most star athletes of any color.

> Tiger Woods is the perfect international product endorser for a company. He will have appeal in many parts of the world that is far stronger than [marketers] can get if they hired individual athletes for the Asian appeal, black appeal, American appeal, etc. Tiger Woods can do all three for them, under one image, instead of breaking the image up over three people. He just embodies where business has gone. He's multicultural, multinational . . . his appeal is exactly where businesses are going, and there's going to be no turning back from that. The days of U.S. companies hiring U.S. athletes just because they appeal here in the U.S. and to heck with the rest of the world are over.

In Transracial America, being neither and both like Jeter, or none and all three like Woods, is more powerful than being just black or Hispanic or Asian-American or, most important, just white. It's not just because the mixed-race icon might command the combined loyalties of disparate ethnic audience segments. Mixed-race icons are powerful because their whole beings represent more than the sum of their racial parts; they are the embodiment of the new transracial ideal. They are walking, high-performing, high-status billboards for the natural and perhaps inevitable positive resolution of the tension imposed on the freedom to enjoy an individual identity in a multiracial society. Their success outside the racial and ethnic identity boxes in which most of us are trapped makes us all feel good and tempts us to indulge the latent desire to free our own personas from racial and ethnic restraints, at least when Jeter is at the plate or Woods is at the tee.

Most significant, from a marketing point of view, avowed mixed-race icons enable a transracial paradigm that goes above and beyond the basic racial crossover phenomenon that has driven the browning of the mainstream to date. Ever wonder exactly what it was that platinum-black icons like Bill Cosby, Michael Jordan, and Whoopi Goldberg actually *crossed over* on the way to the bank? Experts say the line they traversed was that of being thought of as "black" by the audience. That doesn't mean they became "white" in a political or cultural sense, as many African-American and other politically correct observers disdainfully and simplistically conclude whenever a black performer is embraced by whites. Is Bill Cosby a whitewashed "white man's Negro"? Ridiculous. Nobody with half a brain or one working eye would ever doubt Cosby's stewardship of black identity and black pride. Crossover doesn't necessarily mean that its avatars have rendered themselves utterly nonthreatening or passive, either: see garrulous athlete-warriors like Charles Barkley, Reggie White, and Dennis Rodman. In just one lockout-shortened 1999 pro basketball season, New York Knicks guard Latrell Sprewell went from infamy as the thuggish black street baller who choked his white coach to the heroic figure in an epic postseason quest that fell just short of a championship. Sprewell hadn't crossed all the way over at the season's end, but he was well on his way, as New York was covered with billboards echoing national television commercials for upstart Philadelphia-based sportswear maker And 1, in which Sprewell, aggressively braided hair and all, looked dead into the camera and said, "Some people say I'm America's nightmare. I say I'm the American dream." The company was started in 1993 when three young white ex–Wall Streeters decided that the sanitized "all-American" images of athlete icons like Michael Jordan weren't true enough to their identities as hard-core, bleeding-edge "street" basketball fans. One profile of its founders explained the essence of its approach:

> For decades, black athletes have been made over for the comfort of white America. Madison Avenue may have marketed Joe Namath, John McEnroe, and Andre Agassi as rebels in the tradition of James Dean, but only nonthreatening black athletes saw any real endorsement opportunities. Twenty years ago Julius Erving shaved his Afro when he wanted to become a pitchman. . . . Commercial opportunities were denied to those who wouldn't conform to advertisers' ideas of what a "safe" black athlete should be. . . . But now "And 1" is able to tap a vibrant cross-cultural youth market eager to embrace sports stars spouting antiestablishment mores. The sneakers of supposed [Michael] Jordan heirs like [Grant] Hill and Kobe Bryant haven't sold nearly as well as those promoted by players with more exciting and dangerous images, like Allen Iverson and Sprewell. [And 1 CEO Seth] Berger heard himself derided as a white guy who is peddling black culture for profit. He argues [that] playing to urban culture is not the same as playing to a strictly black clientele. You can be hip-hop, in other words, and not be black. "MTV helped create a youth culture that sees beyond race," Berger says. "As long as you're authentic. And 'And 1' is all about ball."[23]

America's collective heart raced as Muhammad Ali lit the Olympic flame at the 1996 Atlanta games, but it was not as if time or the symptoms of Parkinson's disease had erased white America's awareness of Ali's place in history as a black man. Everyone by now has digested all that indelibly makes Ali politically black, and for many those things will always remain distasteful. But everyone still was thrilled because it was *him*, Muhammad Ali, the greatest: a one-of-a-kind American. The political differences, over time, have become just that, political, like whether you voted for Nixon or Humphrey in 1968. Ali's politics have become separated from Ali the man, and in comparison with what America sees in Ali the man, the politics become secondary if not insignificant.

Latrell Sprewell and his handlers did not expect the audience to forget that he choked his former coach P. J. Carlissimo, and they would never deny Sprewell's identity as a black man with an attitude. But the measure of how much has changed since Ali invented the insurrectionist black man as media icon in the 1960s is that today, as long as he's a winner, Sprewell can believably identify himself with all that's quintessentially American at the millennium and sell product. And he can do it while he is still in his athletic prime and while his most racially threatening actions are still fresh in the public mind. Try to imagine Muhammad Ali doing a sneaker commercial with a theme identifying his persona with the epitome of American values a year after refusing induction into the army in 1964!

The propensity to separate the black performer from his politics (if one can consider Sprewellian antipathy to authority an authentic reflection of black political consciousness) is now deeply ingrained in mainstream popular culture. The basis for the change may well be the verdicts of political history. Vietnam has been recorded as a major American mistake, and those who resisted it on moral grounds, like Ali, are respected if not venerated. Martin Luther King Jr. was so right, he's now a national holiday. Rodney King's beating returned an indictment in the court of mainstream public opinion against the operation of criminal justice against black men—even black men with King's well-known character flaws—that still stands. But it is the translation of these sociopolitical verdicts, through multibillion-dollar marketing efforts, into transracial popular culture that has prepared the mainstream to embrace pop culture figures for whom they may be above and beyond the color of their skin. The lessons of political history, by contrast, seem to be forgotten as soon as they are taught. Think about it: The major use that Americans of all colors will make of the next King holiday will be to go shopping together, quite possibly for sneakers endorsed by Latrell Sprewell. Only in America!

Nonwhite icons do not cross *out* of their race or ethnicity; they cross *into* recognition as singular individuals. It's a recognition that whites of achievement or notoriety take for granted, but it's an elusive and precious prize for nonwhites, especially when, as in Ali's case, it is pursued only on the achiever's own terms. But mixed-race achievers like Jeter and Woods have a unique power to skip the psychological hurdle of crossover altogether. In the transracial marketplace, they can enter the public eye as individuals of African descent without needing the often-insulting fig leaf of crossover in the first place. Their insistence on recognition as individuals from jump street, and the willingness of the public to grant it, tap a mother lode of American identity that, I believe, runs deeper than political race. The individual, argue sociologist John A. Hall and anthropologist Charles Lindholm, is the fundamental unit of American society, not the race or ethnic group. Individualism, in the form of "individual responsibility, personal honor and principled resistance to immoral authority," is a deeper creed than ethnic nationalism, racial chauvinism, and even racism itself.[24] And while Americans do not openly recognize such core values as individualism summing to a common, unifying culture across racial lines, it nevertheless still does.

> One of our students once remarked proudly, "We Americans do not have a culture; we are all different," blithely unaware of the fact that no statement could be more American. [His] blindness derives from assumptions that all persons are equally distinctive, unique and endowed with freedom to pursue their individual quests for happiness and redemption.[25]

As the authors point out, the tragedy of America, and the only exception to their argument that American social cohesion at the dawn of the twenty-first century is stronger than ever, is the historic exemption of African-Americans from the assumptions of inherent individual distinctiveness and endowment. Until recently American identity has presumed that Caucasian people of every ethnicity—including Hispanics to a significant extent—can be seen as "just people" if they present themselves as such, while blacks, in a line of custom and law that runs straight through slavery and the one-drop rule, must always be black people. But as I've said, the alchemy of crossover in the browning of mainstream pop culture has been turning black athletes, performers, and politicians into individuals in the public eye on a daily basis for the last twenty years.

❐   ❐   ❐

Commenting on mainstream style in 1994, *New York Times* columnist Molly O'Neill said that in the 1960s and 1970s she could count on a trip to the mall in middle-American Columbus, Ohio, to make her feel culturally smug and superior to the "whitebread crossroads of the staus quo," where the arc of American cultural diversity was neatly bracketed by "the fashionable Lazarus department store at one end . . . to the sensible Sears, Roebuck at the other.

> So imagine my discomfort seeing a young woman with a blond head full of dreadlocks selling cosmetics at a mall in Columbus recently. Today you don't know where you stand. Hip-hop has unbalanced the cultural compass. When white girls wear dread-locks and black girls go blond, another distinction is being teased apart, hair by hair.

O'Neill went on to call this fashion transracialism a pose, a fad that while temporary and superficial was not "hopeless," since it was "weaving together formerly polarized segments of society." But as the story of Revlon, Cover Girl, and L'Oréal's moves toward institutionalizing a cross-racial approach to beauty products shows, transracial style has proven to be more than a passing fancy to the industry. O'Neill only skimmed the truth in crediting hip-hop with weaving the races together. Hip-hop and the larger trends in American popular culture today do not actually weave black, white, Hispanic, Asian, and other adherents together as it works. Rather, the success of the transracial marketing style reveals the cultural stitching across race and ethnic lines that already existed. The slave/colored/Negro/black servant/blues shouter/rock-and-roll singer/Rastafarian princess has always lurked inside the stereotyped Ohio blond girl of O'Neill's imagination, whether she knew it or not, and Miss Anne's sense of blond femininity-as-privilege has always been part of the American black girl. In transracial marketing America, the distinctions between so-called races are not just being teased; they're being humiliated by history. As Michael Lind declared in *The Next American Nation*:

> We Americans . . . are defined by a common language and culture; and as long as these unite us, we will constitute an ethnocultural nation, no matter what the composition of our gene pool, no matter

what the political entity in which our people reside, or what its ultimate borders might be. There was an American cultural nation on the Atlantic seaboard before there was a republic called the United States; and, we may hope, there will be a flourishing American cultural nation in its North American homeland when the U.S. Constitution has long been scrapped or amended beyond recognition.[26]

Black blonds and white dreadlocks. All-American mulattoes. Black Cinderella and her white sisters. Dr. Dolittle in an Afro. White men who can jump, and hump Latinas, too. The part-Asian Superman and the little white girl channeling Aretha Franklin. Bill Cosby as Father Knows Best. Transracial drag queens riding into a sleepy middle-American town like the Earp brothers and cleaning up its contradictions. A syndicated television judiciary where white petitioners volunteer to let black judges rule. All these things, and permutations to come that we can't even imagine, sell, and each dollar of profit accrues to the proof of Lind's theory of American identity and prediction of a transracial American ethnicity freeing itself from the shackles of centuries-old political constructions of race. As he put it:

[T]he overwhelming majority of Americans—whatever their arbitrarily defined "race"—already belong, not just to a single citizenry, but to a single people, a single cultural nation, defined by common language, folkways, memories, and mores. Centuries of white supremacy have not prevented the formulation of a transracial American culture blending elements of the cultures of many European, African, American Indian, Latin American and Asian peoples with innovations unique to North America. Nor were white supremacist laws against miscegenation able to prevent a substantial degree of racial amalgamation, paralleling the fusion of cultures.[27]

The manifestation of Transracial American identity in the marketplace is perhaps the most unheralded consequence of the triumph of free-market capitalist democracy at the dawn of the twenty-first century. If Lind is right, as I believe he is, then the basis for the transracial commercial mainstream has always been in place, but its emergence was something less than inevitable. It still required a critical mass of competition for the imagination of consumers, a competition too brisk to be fettered by the past. No one will ever be able to mark the exact point on the time line where Transracial America became an absolute commercial reality, says Katz of BBDO. It's more like a successive revelation of a truth that, with each application in the marketplace, becomes a self-fullfilling prophecy. Katz describes a simple, powerful circular logic connecting the transracial imperative at work in advertising and the reality of who Americans are and how we live:

> It wouldn't be done if it weren't true. And if it weren't true, it wouldn't work. And if it didn't work, it wouldn't be done.

6

Youth Culture Leads the Way: Hey Kids Rule!

It's all about the "real."

In the fall of 1999, the Chicago ad firm DDB Worldwide was in the studio ready to roll film on a new commercial for Budweiser. America's biggest beer brand was almost three years into a campaign featuring a craven, egomaniacal lizard and his laid-back partner, but the new campaign coming off the drawing board would be a major departure from the cute, animated reptiles and amphibians that had dominated the brand's image in commercials in the late 1990s. With the client looking on, DDB Worldwide was about to shoot the first of what would be several commercials starring four young black men whose shared vocabulary seemed to begin and end with the slurred phrase "Whassup?!" "Whassup?!" was a common urban colloquial greeting used by males and females of a certain lifestyle persuasion. That is to say, "Whassup?!" began among black hipsters, quickly spread to bilingual Hispanics, and was then making its way toward the white mainstream via white hip-hoppers as well as other whites "urban" enough to be conversant with the black street idiom. But DDB Worldwide, as hip-hoppers would say, was fixing to blow up "Whassup?!" into a signifier for universal male bonding over beer and ball.

Even in 1999, casting a general-market commercial with nothing but noncelebrity nonwhites was almost unheard of. Beer brewers in particular had rarely been known to depict minorities as primary users of their products, except in ethnic-targeted ads confined to minority-oriented media and programming. The typical beer ad was set in a semiprivate, under-thirty social scene—a house party, a favorite bar, a special date, or a family celebration— that was traditionally viewed as too intimate to be credibly portrayed as racially mixed. The beer commercial genre's particular fondness for sun 'n' surf backdrops, heavy on skimpy bikinis and sexy horseplay, generally ruled out any significant representation of nonwhites when the target was a white-majority audience. To be sure, more and more beer brands were quietly integrating their spots in the last half of the decade. Most notable was the fictitious baseball park conjured for the Coors Light brand, in which the protagonist "beer men" as well as the crowd appeared to be a lot more racially mixed than most of Colorado, where Coors is based. Nonwhites were even the principal characters in a few of the most effective spots. But an all-black cast carrying an entire general-market television campaign for a major beer brand was unheard of.

As the biggest advertiser in beer, Anheuser-Busch's marketing had been traditionally conservative, driven from the top down by senior executives who relied on extensive testing, almost frame by frame, for making creative decisions. "It was paralysis by analysis," said Bob Lachky, Anheuser-Busch vice president for brand management. "Breakthrough ideas were hard to come by; you had too many eyes on the process." But the top-down style began to change in 1991 when, at age twenty-seven, August Busch IV took charge of the heart of the family business: the Budweiser brand. The DDB Worldwide spot that Lachky was overseeing that day was conceived and approved in less than two months, without going much higher than his marketing department, said Lachky, and without the input of big shots twice removed by class and age from the target: the barely legal younger beer drinker.

"You can't be running storyboards up to a guy who's gonna be at the country club all weekend," said Lachky, who is white but apparently fluent in Ebonics. He was speaking freely some ten months after the shoot, not long before the campaign won the Grand Clio award for the best commercials of 2000. But that first day on the set, Lachky recalls, he looked over the latest script and saw some revisions that almost gave him a heart attack. The ad's tag line, the word "True" on a simple black background below the red-and-white Budweiser logo and above the Budweiser web address, had been changed—to "Right on," the 1970s mantra of black affirmation. The same substitution had also been made in the few snippets of dialogue that weren't the totemic "Whassup?!"

"True" was so baggy-jeans-and-dance-hall reggae. "Right on" was very bell bottoms and Earth, Wind and Fire. If he hadn't acted, Lachky recalled, his beer commercial would have come out sounding like a new *Shaft* movie thirty years after the original but almost a year before the Sam Jackson remake. Lachky ordered the original wording restored faster than Isaac Hayes's backup singers could coo "shut yo' mouth." Later, he told me, he thanked God for his instinct and the guts to follow it.

> My first thought was "What white guy changed this to 'Right on'?
> This isn't the *Mod Squad*, guys; give us some credit." It cracked me
> up. We'd already bought the "True." But what if we hadn't been
> smart enough to know . . . if we had put "Right on" in it, it would
> have killed it. It would have been a disaster. I mean if ["Right on"]
> isn't on a Curtis Mayfield track, I don't want to hear it in my
> commercial.

The bottom line: Lachky knew it wasn't real and didn't have to think twice about saying so. His decisiveness floored thirty-four-year-old film-maker Charles Stone III, who produced and directed the original short film featuring himself and three other African-American friends on which the wildly popular "True" commercials were, as it would turn out, faithfully based. In fact, it was Stone himself, not some "white guy," who had changed the script, fearing at the last minute that "True" might be too New York regional, too much of the streets of Harlem or Fort Greene, Brooklyn, where he lives, to work in the American beer-drinking heartland. Stone says he second-guessed himself because he underestimated just how thoroughly Lachky and Anheuser-Busch "got it."

> I was impressed. That instance, as well as others that followed,
> showed it was all about following in the integrity of the spot. They

wanted this spot to be all that it could be in replicating the original film. Budweiser felt that if we were going to do this, we should really do it.

Much earlier in the planning, DDB tried to make "True" with a multiracial cast, in an attempt to "diversify" Stone's original vision. But Lachky and DDB quickly saw that that wasn't real, either. "Certainly [the production] got 'true-er' as it went along," said Marty Kohr, the DDB executive managing the Budweiser account. "We went trying to do a more multiracial cast at first. We don't know if it just smacked of an advertiser trying to fill out the population quota, but it just wasn't true."

The "real" in all its aspects—the honest, the authentic, the sincere, the actual, the true, the natural, the faithful, the accurate—is the paramount aesthetic binding the next great American generation. Some researchers and marketers have labeled them Generation Y or Echo Boomers. Others, like Pepsi, have tried to christen them Generation Next. But to themselves the consumers born between 1976 and 1997 are simply the Americans of the twenty-first century, the central artery of the new mainstream. Unlike the late unlamented Generation X (the children of the 1966-to-1975 baby bust), under-twenty-five America is the first group massive enough to displace the baby boomers from the driver's seat of popular culture, according to Bill Katz of BBDO New York.

"Baby boomers are no longer the epicenter," said Katz. "Echo Boomers will be 72 or 73 million, baby boomers are about 69 to 70 million. We [baby boomers] ain't ruling no more. It's gradual, and it's projected out. But it doesn't matter: Baby boomers are not driving the culture anymore. Echo Boomers are driving this culture."

In truth, the next generation hates being labeled with a passion, especially by baby boomers. Such categorization is just another stinging reminder of baby boomers' self-centered, self-referential hegemony. Nevertheless, on the theory of "in for a penny, in for a pound," within the confines of this chapter I'm adopting the conceit of sticking yet another, temporary label on these four-to-twentysomething-year-olds. I call them Hey Kids, after the 1979 Coke commercial of the same name that starred "Mean Joe" Greene. Hey Kids was conceived in the spirit of the little blond boy called "the Kid," who was introduced to the world looking up in wide-eyed awe of the burly black athlete, before one of the largest television audiences in history, during Super Bowl XIII.

Hey Kids are the first American generation certified as ready for non-white role models by corporate mass media.

So what's real, relative to race, ethnicity, and identity, for the Hey Kids now sitting firmly behind the wheel of commercial popular culture?

- The deep sense that *American* is not a synonym for *white*.
- A cultural mainstream that is fundamentally and unalterably racially and ethnically heterogeneous.
- A world is more than the United States, Canada, and Europe; it's the whole world, and Americans of all colors are obliged to find a place in it, not the other way around.
- The expectation of reaching middle age in an America without a clear white majority.
- The sense that identity is rooted in cultures that can be freely traded in the marketplace, not imposed by race or ethnicity at birth.

Consider the next generation's historical and demographic context:

They have never known an America in which popular culture, especially sports, music, movies, television, and the cult of celebrity didn't dominate the imagination of society and set the parameters of aspiration for the American dream. At the same time, they've never known an America in which non-whites didn't occupy a disproportionately large space in that popular culture. They never knew an NBA that wasn't overwhelmingly black, or an NFL that wasn't majority black, or major league baseball that wasn't heavily black and Hispanic. They grew up listening to more R&B and hip-hop, taken together, than rock. They were raised coming home after school to Oprah on television, with Bill Cosby selling them Jell-O during the commercial breaks.

"Oprah is the icon of the hand that rocks the cradle across America," said Belma Johnson, a former producer for the competing talk show hosted by Roseanne Barr. "We're really going to see the effect of this in the next generation, a whole generation of kids who grew up watching their mothers idolize a black woman."

Those are the Hey Kids, perhaps the first generation that can truly be defined by the television they watched. In that sense, they could also be called Cosby Kids, because *The Cosby Show*, not *Seinfeld*, was the dominant sitcom of their childhood. And when the news came on, the first war they remember was sold to them by Colin Powell. America, for all they know, is that old black man who sings the hell out of that gospel song on NBC, the one about God "crowning the good with brotherhood from sea to shining sea," every four years when it's time to feel good about ourselves for the Olympics. And since the terrorist attacks of September 11, 2001, the new generation almost expects to see Powell coordinating the messy details of global war-making diplomacy, and Ray Charles singing that song, again, at the seventh-inning stretch during the World Series. Sure, they have read in history books that Charles couldn't even register in most hotels in Las Vegas until he was nearly middle-aged, much less play them. But they can no better imagine that reality of their grandparents' generation than teenage baby boomers could imagine the absence of electricity that shaped *their* grandparents' world.

White Hey Kids, said Gary Koepke, a principal with the youth-oriented Modernista ad agency in Boston, are seemingly indifferent to race, at least as we have known it.

> I think one of the big things that has changed is that white teens don't see race as much as they used to, if at all. That adds a lot to the realness for this generation. I just think those boundaries are broken It's truly getting integrated. A lot of teenagers in the know just don't see race anymore. People accept good for being good now—you don't have to be white to be good.

It seems to defy credulity, given the boomers' sense of a perpetual struggle for civil rights and against racism. But as BBDO's Katz said, it's not about boomers anymore. Hey Kids do know there's racism out there, but they haven't a clue as to what it's all about, because the text of institutional segregation and the scripts for white racial identity that segregation required were shredded before they were born. We forget that the very concept of a "color line" never really made it out of the 1950s except in parts of the South, and it was legally if not emotionally dead after the passage of the 1964 and 1965 civil rights acts. Without the concept of a color line, Hey Kids have been dis-inherited in the context of American race that their elders took for granted for most of the last century. This fact of Hey Kids identity cuts both ways, as I'll discuss later.

They've never know an economy that wasn't dependent on truly global trade for growth—especially trade with Mexico, which has never been out of the news for the generation that began paying attention in the 1990s. They have never known a world in which Japan didn't have the second-largest economy or in which the prospect of China's economic output surpassing even the mighty U.S. economy as the world's largest wasn't inevitable. They've come of age with the largest boom in immigration in U.S. history and the only one dominated by Asians and Hispanics. They've come of age at the time when France's best-known figure skater is of African descent, England's most famous writer is an Indian, and a Miss Italy was ethnically Latin American. So much for the conceptual integrity of "European" in European-American identity.

The nonwhite-majority American future predicted for 2050 is already much closer to reality for people under twenty-five; they're already only two-thirds white. Almost a third of teens report that "a lot" of the friends they regularly spend time with are of another race or ethnic group.[1] Some 73 percent say interracial dating is "no big deal," with 17 percent, 33 percent, and 15 percent of whites reporting dating experience with blacks, Hispanics, and Asians, respectively.[2] Nine out of ten kids under age twelve say they have friends of different races, and four in ten expect to marry someone of a different race.[3]

None of this means that the social politics of race, and the related political economics of wealth and class divisions, will be disappearing overnight. The same polling that found that interracial dating was no big thing also found only that 24 percent of teens thought dating across racial and ethnic lines made America a better place. Some 65 percent of respondents felt that increased interracial dating made no difference at all. In fact, a 1997 poll found a surprising 68 percent of Americans aged fifteen to twenty-four felt that racial separation was okay in America as long as opportunities were somehow the same for all.[4] That result was up from 41 percent in 1991. It seems inconsistent, but it's not surprising. After all, this group has no memory of the one-hundred-year run of the "separate but equal" doctrine, much less an appreciation of why its utter repudiation in law was central to the modern civil rights movement. In some ways, members of Generation Y are not necessarily any more socially or politically liberal than their baby-boomer parents, and in one important sense they may be less so, according to generational historians Neil Howe and William Strauss. They argue that the next generation doesn't really much buy into the group-rights model for resolving the problem of racial inequality: They are leery of orthodox multiculturalism and frequently oppose affirmative action in practice if not in theory.

But at the same time, Howe and Strauss point out, Hey Kids don't define race and culture in the same black and white terms—literal and figurative—that confined the thinking of previous generations. The authors call today's teenage cohort Millennials, taken from the title of their latest book, *Millennials Rising*:

> The racial issues for Millennials are all mixed up. They're not black and white and they don't like seeing it in black and white. They kind of want to get past [racial] bean counting . . . [but] they're prepared to date, marry, and work for people of different races more than any other generation. The moral high ground is different; charges of racism can fly from anywhere. When you talk about African-Americans, for example, what are you really talking about? For a Millennial they might be Somalian, Haitian, or Jamaican . . . they might be professionals of some kind. And the idea that being one quarter black makes you black is ridiculous to them.[5]

The next American generation may not lead the electorate to vote for a new racial world order at the ballot box anytime soon. And they may or may not vote with their feet to live in racially diverse neighborhoods or otherwise break longstanding patterns that tend to socially isolate one group from another. But more than any previous generation, they have been reared to vote with their wallets big time, and their notion of consumer sovereignty especially disrespects racial boundaries. As consumers, they've internalized and consolidated their boomer parents' hard-won right to "do your own thing," and they've taken individualism a step further into mixing and matching multiple overlapping identities across racial and ethnic lines.

White youth have never known a time when the latest hip-hop or rap wasn't positioned right next to the newest rock, R&B, or country music in the record store, so they feel free to come home with all styles of music. This holds true even for youth that MTV research chief Todd Cunningham calls "extremists," the ones research shows to be devoted to genres like heavy-metal rock or gangsta rap that aren't easily dissolved into mainstream pop.

> The interesting thing we find is, all the people who like the extreme kinds of music—whether it be extreme rap, extreme rock, extreme country—all those people have much more in common than we might have all thought in the past. . . . There has been so much divisiveness in the media about people who like rap versus rock, and [we assumed] that at the extremities of that preference, [con-flict] would be more noticeable. But it's not the case—in fact, they like each other's kind of music. They enjoy communicating the same way, mostly because of the passion that's behind each of the genres. The blurring of lines is everywhere, whether it's Shaquille O'Neal doing a movie and being a basketball star and hawking products everywhere . . . to Will Smith doing similar things.

In other words, Cunningham concluded, young fans of either hard rock or hard rap are not blinded by race to the common pain, frustration, and rage about things adults just don't understand that drives each other's music. This tendency, much more pronounced among white, Latino, and Asian youth and less so among blacks, parallels a tendency among Hey Kids to interpret the world around them in terms of class more than race. This ten-dency, the unintended realization of the generations-old dream of the Amer-ican left, may have revolutionary implications when Hey Kids come into full political power, according to Strauss. Once again it's about the "real." As any die-hard leftist will tell you, what's real is workers versus bosses, not black versus white. Strauss told me he thinks the next generation is programmed, in part by by their consumption, to be the first American cohort to embrace this truth and the class consciousness it implies.

> We [baby boomers] grew up with this black-white dichotomy in the shadow of the postwar black migration north. The gaps in

income [between whites] were much narrower. The only dichotomy the Millennials know is the spread between rich and poor. The leading color issue for Millennials is green. I guarantee you that college campuses are going to be come cauldrons of class conflicts. They'll be reinventing what we used to call the Old Left.

Hey Kids' musical tastes inform their fashion and style preferences much more than music did in generations past. They've never known a time of songs without accompanying videos; music for them is as much seen as it is heard. So as with music, perhaps *because* of the music, the racial origin of a particular style of clothing and dress is no impediment to acceptance and often is a boost to its cachet in the marketplace. Once a fashion is on display in the stores, that racial identification becomes almost transparent to teens and young adults, even when the blackness of, say, a pair of extrabaggy jeans on a bare washboard-stomached black man sporting a do rag is quite opaque to the older customers and other adults who control merchandising decisions.

In the fall of 1998, the first year his FUBU line of "urban" sportswear was featured in the back-to-school showcase windows at Macy's flagship store in the heart of New York's garment district, CEO Damon John reflected on the resistance from middle-aged white men FUBU had met on the way up to competing head to head with brands like Calvin Klein and The Gap. In the traditional assumption of whiteness as universality, baby-boomer marketing managers never perceived these labels as racial, but FUBU, which after all did initially stand for "For Us By Us," was pigeonholed as "urban" because its creator and its initial market were black. John grew up on the same black middle-class streets of Hollis, Queens, New York, that produced rapper LL Cool J. He started the business, whose 1999 volume was reportedly $350 million, in 1992 as a teenager selling homemade baseball caps on street corners. Now his office in the Empire State Building overlooks Macy's and the rest of the garment district, just a few blocks west.

One store said to take our hang tags [with the black faces of the four FUBU partners] off the clothes, because "we want to sell to forty-year-old white people, and they won't buy it if they see those guys on there." We've had people say, "We don't have *those* kind of people in our store." They were like—there's gonna be a shootout in their stores. And I'm taking about major department stores. Now they're some of our biggest customers. Maybe the buyer wouldn't agree to it at first, but the president said, "Try it." He said it because a lot of these department stores saw that the specialty stores, who were carrying what they called underground or urban lines, were beating them to the cash register. The department stores . . . felt that blacks didn't buy from their stores and white kids wouldn't dare wear it. But after it started passing the register, they realized that the bottom line is the bottom line.

But while fifty- and sixty-something adults try to second-guess them, the youth themselves barely recognize the translation of socially constructed racial categories into fashion marketing niche labels. Since the late 1990s, a representative slice of young America has been "feeling" the "urban" FUBU brand, from the small-town white heartland communities served by The Buckle (a specialty store chain based in Carney, Nebraska) to major "inner city" sportswear stores like New York's legendary Dr. Jay's, whose flagship location is also just down the street from Macy's. But in the beginning, Damon John told me, even he assumed his customer base was limited to people like himself.

That was my first problem. When we thought our customer was just all black guys—out of our ignorance—we didn't realize that there were kids growing up in Des Moines with the same social problems we have here in Hollis, Queens. So they can relate to the music, and with the music the fashion is so closely related. As long as they feel the product is authentic, coming from other urban guys who understand them, our customer, whether white, black, or Chinese, isn't offended by this whole urban thing—they understand what it is. When that white suburban kid buys it, he's the same kid that watches MTV or BET [Black Entertainment Television]. This kid, believe it or not, may have grown up with Wu-Tang Clan and Puff Daddy, and he sees those artists wearing these clothes. These are the artists he emulates. We had a couple of kids e-mail us saying, "Hey, I'm a white kid. If I buy FUBU, am I a wannabe?" We answer, "What is the purpose of your buying? If you're buying to be associated with other people, you're wrong. But if you're buying because you like it, understand it, feel it, you're right."

Like his core customers, John dismissed the validity of race-freighted labels like *urban,* because they exist only to provide a comfortable frame of reference for less enlightened retailers and marketing executives. *Urban* has little to do with what's real for the new youth generation because it's a category imposed from above, almost by default, based on race. Hey Kids make their own categories from below, based on their own sense of identification with particular youth cultures. To paraphrase an old-school rap song, it's not where you're from when you wear the clothes that matters, it's "where you're at" in your sensibility. John continued:

> What I always say to people about "urban" is that before we were out, urban lines to us, the young American hip-hop or inner city crowd, were Abercrombie and Fitch, Levi's, Adidas, et cetera. I personally used to wear a lot of Oshkosh and Lees. Now [older] America's perception of urban is a young kid with pants hanging off their ass. But look closely: some of those pants are Calvin Klein. When a white kid dresses the same as a black kid, he becomes a skate customer—not an urban customer. When an Asian kid dresses like that, he's a retro customer. And when a black kid dresses like a black kid, he's urban, or a crook, or a thug—something in that area. Hispanics get thrown into the same thing.

Once again it's all about the authentic, the "real." From the moment commercial hip-hop culture rose above the radar as force to be reckoned with, skeptics insisted it was no more than a passing fad that wouldn't stick—that is, it was not "real." Much like jazz culture in the 1920s, rock and roll in the 1950s, and hippie culture in the 1960s, hip-hop was dismissed as merely the latest vehicle to express a generation's moment of rebellion against its parents for rebellion's sake. But going on twenty years later, hip-hop is still consolidating its hold while evolving within the mainstream. The reason, argues marketing and demography writer Mark Spiegler, is because the roots of hip-hop's cultural output are fundamentally different from those of a James Dean film in the 1950s or even a Beatles album in the 1960s. For all that they captured and inspired in their time, Dean's *Rebel Without a Cause* and the Beatles' *Rubber Soul* came down from studios. Hip-hop comes up from the streets for distribution by studios, and even then the culture is relentlessly self-aware, always checking itself against its own reality.

"Hip-hop springs from the experiences of young blacks living in cities," Spiegler wrote in 1996.[6] "It's based on a real culture, giving it more permanence than earlier teen trends. People who want a part of hip-hop culture always have something new to latch on to, because the culture is always evolving." And as it evolves, the more Darwinian savvy marketers have learned to adapt in order to cash in.

Coca-Cola has enjoyed phenomenal youth market success in advertising its Sprite brand by using young black athletes like Kobe Bryant and Grant Hill and by infusing the campaign with an antiestablishment tone that reeks of black rap music. Yet Sprite is in no danger of being seen as the "black" brand in the marketplace. Sprite is the brand for cool individuals who think for themselves enough to know that brand "image is nothing," to reprise its late 1990s slogan, and "thirst is everything."

"You have to realize that for these kids, individualism isn't a vector. It's a baseline," demographer Strauss told me. "They don't know anything else but market-oriented individualism."

Strauss's "market-oriented individualism" is another way of describing the triumph of the new commercial mainstream, in all its multihued glory, over political, intellectual, or socially ordered identity movements. Today's young people don't follow politicians, as the Nixon or Kennedy youth did before them. And they take few cues from activists or ideologues from any part of the spectrum, from Ralph Nader green to Pat Buchanan red white and blue.[7] Nothing like the nonmarket-based hippie movement of the 1960s is driving youth culture today. Instead, the single biggest force in youth culture—hip-hop—is the most commercialized, inherently entrepreneurial youth culture ever. The youth marketplace is cleared, in the economic sense, by a new set of values that for the most part flow up from the generation itself, not down from the moral, intellectual, economic, or political authority of earlier generations. Chief among these values is relevance to Hey Kids' special reality. Hey Kids, marketers say, recognize that traditional, socially constructed race has very real consequences for individuals in society but that the construct itself isn't real, and therefore marketers shouldn't respect it when addressing them in advertising. Hey Kids have no equity in perpetuating the status quo of whiteness as norm and nonwhiteness as "other," and they aspire, with mixed success, to break with that paradigm entirely.

To compete with Sprite for Hey Kids' lemon-lime soda affections, Pepsi's Mountain Dew didn't affect a hip-hop pose, but it did tap the group's sense of multiracial reality, said BBDO's Katz, whose firm created the "Do the Dew" television campaign for the brand in 1999. In a signature commercial that had its debut during the 2000 Super Bowl, a cheetah races across an African plain leaving a trail of smoke. A wide shot shows another smoke trail coming from behind and gaining on the cheetah; its a "dude" on a mountain bike. He overtakes the cheetah, tackles it, reaches into its mouth, and pulls out a Mountain Dew can that, from the teeth marks, appears to have been already drained. "Bad cheetah," scolds the dude, who is white. Then the camera pans to a precipice where the dude's partners, one black and two white, are looking on. "See, that's why I'm not a cat person," the black one says. Katz told me:

> Extreme sports. Mountain Dew—a hillbilly image. Who gives the punch line? An African-American is the dude who gives the punch line. Why? Not because Mountain Dew and BBDO made a conscious effort to patronize African-Amercans. Not because lobbying groups lobbied both companies to include African-American talent. Not because of any other politically correct agenda. Because that's what's going on! That is what that crowd looks like when you go down there and you see them. That is how diversity has naturally, not unnaturally, pervaded Echo Boomers' societal makeup. It's real; if you didn't do it, it would be unbelievable. It is natural; it is a reflection of reality. You ask, how does it affect marketing and advertising? One way it affects it is, it has to be real.

Experts say Hey Kids are most distinguished from previous generations by an optimism born of a sense of their own specialness. They see themselves as chosen. They're the generation that will harvest the social, scientific, and economic revolutions of the last quarter of the twentieth century, while shedding the excess baggage of greed, hedonism, and hypocrisy, especially in the media marketplace. Their love affair with the "real" is grounded in a feeling of invincibility and empowerment. They feel absolutely entitled to be who they are and not what baby boomers were or what boomers think they should be, said MTV's Cunningham. Hey Kids' relentless self-acceptance creates a high value for tolerance of racial and ethnic diversity. The events precipitating the current war on terrorism may have shaken some of that certainty, but the result may be that a determination to advance change in the world order galvanizes a generation. Marketers suspect that Hey Kids already find the reigning conceptions of American racial categories irrelevant to the emerging global youth culture. And they, the marketers, are already playing heavily to that sense of generational exception. So a 2000 television campaign pitching a juice drink product to teens features a United Nations of American adolescents enjoying a montage of healthy outdoor-lifestyle activities, with much interracial touching and palling around. A young teenage voice-over seems to speak directly to boomers on the adolescents' behalf. It repeatedly asks, almost chants, "Are you ready for us?"[8] The voice-over message is remarkably political for an orange drink. Closely paraphrased, it says: *The headlines today are all about you boomers, but we Hey Kids are coming on strong. We may not have control of any institutions yet, but we've got Sunny Delight in our veins, and that's more than enough. And by the way, we're all different colors together, and we don't give a damn. We're evolved beyond all that.*

Just where did Hey Kids come by their evolutionary values? Their revolutionary boomer parents! While the boomers in their youth took to the streets and set out to torch the cultural and political conventions of their World War II–era parents' generation, Hey Kids, with some very important qualifications, fundamentally embrace their parents' postdisco sensibilities. That is to say, Hey Kids identify with the norms that were in place after the boomers sowed their wild oats. Research, MTV's Cunningham told me, actually reveals a kind of partnership between Hey Kids and their parents that's unique among generations.

> This generation . . . really, really connects with their parents in a big way. They respect their parents and even talk of them as role

models. A lot of that is because their parents grew up in a modernist society, with modern marketing, modern ways of thinking, modern ways of communicating. They respect their kids, they watch the same shows, wear the same clothes, and listen to a lot of the same music: there's not as much of a generation gap.

At the same time, Hey Kids are very much disposed to take their parents, and boomer culture in general, at its word about tolerance, the dignity of the individual, and the whole Martin Luther King dream vision of America. They take these principles, however unproven, as their basic social inheritance. White suburban teenagers have come to openly embrace rap and hip-hop culture in large part because their parents didn't dare prohibit them from consuming a product so self-consciously black and urban in its content and imagery. Hey Kids' love of rap and hip-hop, said Cunningham, may in fact be the logical outcome of parenting that glorified the value of all things true, natural, and authentic while inculcating a healthy disrespect for authority and artifice. Their parents' organic vegetables, acoustic blues, and natural fibers were the perfect pre-sell for the homespun, urban grassroots brand image of rap and hip-hop. According to Cunningham:

> A lot of the reason for [Hey Kids' embrace of rap] is that it represents realness to them. And actually that quality was passed on to them from their parents. Their parents grew up in a world of "Don't talk about sex, don't talk about race, don't talk about the things that you like." Their parents were the ones who were dropping acid, burning their bras, protesting the war, smoking pot, whatever, to express themselves publicly. So [in Hey Kids] you're just witnessing the generational evolution of that movement.

Indeed, by now the statistics showing that white suburban youth consume the largest share of rap/hip-hop music are old news. But the question of why or what it really means is rarely pressed. According to rap-music-mogul-turned-urban/youth-marketing-entrepreneur Russell Simmons, "The real core hip-hop community shares the same core values; the kids in Beverly Hills identify with and understand the struggle of kids in Compton." Few marketers are as qualified as Simmons to compare the youth vibrations in gangsta rap to those in L.A.'s legendary platinum ghetto, but I'm skeptical about the depth of the commonality. Many young people, of all races, say they don't really pay close attention to the content of the lyrics in rap music, and when they do, it seems to me, they are quite capable of distinguishing their individual circumstances from the obligatory scenarios of deprivation, oppression, and social isolation that animate rap. More important, Hey Kids are well aware that by the time it reaches them, whatever was real about urban (or black) poverty and pathos has already been commercialized several times over. I think the values Simmons sees uniting inner city and outer suburb are really *commercial* in nature, not social (which is not to say that commercial values have no social dimensions).

In an age dominated by media and information consumption, commercial values increasingly inform if not control our perspectives on social reality and relationships between people. While hearing the latest rap phenom rhyme about survival and triumph over the ghetto or serve notice on white middle-class adult society for its wicked ways, the white middle-class teen listener is also well aware that the rapper may be declaiming from the safe vantage of being a millionaire, replete with bodyguards—and real estate in places like Beverly Hills. Indeed, boasts about "livin' and lovin' large," all tricked out with furs, diamonds, and other totems of conspicuous consumption, are the most ubiquitous clichés of the genre.

This fundamental contradiction in rap/hip-hop would seem the height of hypocrisy and an affront to Hey Kids' iconic sense of the real and the true. But the fact is that they are, as they say, very cool with it. Because the rap blaring from their speakers confirms not only that the conditions of the inner city are real but that they've inspired a creative cultural response that results in a product everyone wants to buy. Success itself is a shared commercial value that cuts across racial lines, *especially because it cuts across class lines.* Remember, while the average white youth may have more money than the average black or Hispanic youth, the majority of white Hey Kids are not upper-middle-class affluent; they dream about "gettin' paid" like anybody else. For those who are more affluent or who possess a social awareness of their own white privilege, their membership in the hip-hop nation as consumers affirms a sense of participating on a leveled cultural playing field that is very important to their identity. The real transracial message of hip-hop's often rank commercialism, stripped to its core, says: *We may be coming to the game from different places, bringing different things to the table, and facing different obstacles. But we want the same things, especially the same brands, for the same reasons; they're cool and powerful. And we are almost cocky about our ability to get them.*

One of many things boomer analysts don't get about hip-hop is how it's quite detachable from what political liberals recognize as social consciousness. The easy cleavage between medium and message explains the most incongruous segment of the hip-hop nation, the white youth known as "wiggers." The term, coined by William "Upski" Wimsatt, a white Chicago writer on hip-hop culture, refers to whites of generally working-class, racially isolated provenance who hold reactionary views about the social complaints of nonwhites yet tend to make the same fashion statements as the rappers on MTV, whom they idolize. Wiggers "are pure consumers—they're really into rap, but don't know much, so they're easily manipulated," Wimsatt said in a 1996 magazine article.[9]

Pioneers of commercial hip-hop culture like Simmons didn't set out to fuse the identities of black/brown inner-city and white suburban youth, but their genius was to recognize the transracial nature of the demand for their products in the youth market. Something was going on out there in real space that was bridging the gaps between adolescents of different races in the post–civil rights 1980s. With all the focus on the near collapse of inner cities in the 1970s and 1980s, the suburbanization of black and Hispanic middle- and lower-middle-class families has been a much-overlooked catalyst for change. A decade ago the 1990 census found that nearly one-third of African-Americans were living in suburbs, yet we still persist in equating "suburb" with "lily white." The fact is that Hey Kids have grown up with suburbs that have been integrating since the 1980s and in many cases developing within the suburban enclaves pockets of concentrated black and Hispanic populations that echo the flavor of the inner city.

Hip-hop pioneer Bill Stephney grew up in suburban Nassau County, on Long Island. It's no coincidence, he said, that most important commercializers of rap/hip-hop in the 1990s—including Sean "Puffy" Combs, M. C. Heavy D, Russell Simmons, his younger brother Joseph Simmons of Run DMC fame, Queen Latifah, Lauryn Hill, and many more—grew up or went to high school in the suburbs in the 1980s. Stephney, whose current business is producing sound-track albums for films, including the 2000 remake of *Shaft*, has been one of hip-hop's most thoughtful seers ever since he helped found Def Jam Records with Simmons in the early 1980s. He likes to tell the story of how, when he was in junior high school, black male fashion peer pressure dictated wearing imported knit sweaters and shoes with inch-thick off-white "marshmallow" soles and expensive natural fiber pants, especially silk and wool blends. "But then," Stephney says, "there was this handful of black kids in lumberjack shirts, work boots, and oversize jeans and overalls. And we would call them 'whiteboys.' That was 1975."

Where did these black "whiteboys" get this renegade style? From their white classmates and neighbors, who themselves borrowed their Carhartt hooded sweatshirts, overalls, and other rugged gear from their construction-worker fathers, uncles, and big brothers. One of hip-hop's most enduring basic fashion statements thus comes from mostly white-ethnic construction workers, whose unions, ironically, are still notorious for excluding blacks. Another irony is that, as Stephney said, "fifteen years later, if a white kid puts on the same outfit, he might be accused of being a black wannabe; it's all so crazy fluid!" His point is that today's hip-hop youth culture flows through multiple pipelines that link the urban and the suburban, the white and the nonwhite, the affluent and the poor in a way that is much more organic than the rock culture of the 1950s and 1960s that linked baby boomers.

The parents of white boomers, looking to put as much distance between their children and the browning inner cities as they could, fled in large numbers to what were truly all-white suburbs during the 1960s. While boomer teens still rebelled, they did so mostly in the privacy of their own rooms and in their own all-white schools. They were armed during their formative years with only the music and the pop culture that were marketed to them by a handful of mainstream AM radio and television networks. They lived mostly out of range of low-powered black radio; even FM rock radio didn't come on strong until the late 1960s. There was, to be sure, the slow but accelerating browning of top-forty radio, led by the Motown sound and other rhythm-and-blues acts as the 1960s became the 1970s. But boomers' access to non-white cultural output was limited to the narrow range of music that World War II–generation business executives deemed acceptable for crossover.

Programming decisions were driven mainly by financial considerations, but relatively little muscle pushed the wider range of black or Latin music into the mainstream, since segregated white boomer teens did little to demand it. Many boomers picked up wider exposure in college and the in the military; the gospel of James Brown became a frequent late addition to their rebellious canon. But their identities were still rooted in the experience of the music they brought to college as freshmen: the Beatles, the Beach Boys, and the Rolling Stones. Later, as they came of age, pop culture was defined by boomer artists producing not-so-revolutionary music for other boomers (think the Eagles, David Bowie, Cher), but the fundamental division of preferences along racial lines and the denial of nonwhite cultural roots was still in place.

By the time the boomers started having children in great numbers, rock's potency as the music of generational revolution was pretty much spent, and what was left of it had been heavily colonized by black pop acts like Michael Jackson, Stevie Wonder, Lionel Ritchie, and Earth, Wind and Fire, or by neoblack dance-oriented youth music of the late disco era. Unlike their boomer parents, then, Hey Kids had much more to choose from, with their parents' blessings, when rap and hip-hop first caught fire from the still-warm ashes of funky disco like "Good Times" by Chic, the song that powered the first rap megahit, "Rapper's Delight." And Hey Kids had powerful FM black music stations, often owned by large publicly traded corporate chains, whose signals were inescapable in every major market. And when cable television brought them MTV and BET by the mid-1980s, even the white innovators were typified by Gen-Xers like Madonna, whose sound was produced by black boomers like Nile Rodgers and Bernard Edwards of the aforementioned Chic. In all media the major marketers were ready to put sponsorship muscle a-plenty behind anything that young people showed any interest in buying.

So much for the supply side. As for demand, a significant number of white Hey Kids came up sharing hallways at school with black and Hispanic kids. When they got their first jobs in the 1990s, they worked side by side at McDonald's and Burger King. Wherever they went, they were exposed to the sights and sounds of hip-hop culture, in the flesh as well as the media. It's as if the cultural river that was economically dammed up at the top of the AM dial in the 1960s burst with full force by the early 1990s. Hey Kids grew up swimming in it. Hip-hop is not like their father's James Brown collection on the side. It's the medium in which they've been cultured.

Unlike what remains of "pure" white rock—that which is completely devoid of urban influence in its sound and presentation—hip-hop is preternaturally commercial. Rock trends like grunge have come and gone without leaving a mark on fashion or style merchandising, much less general-market advertising: There are no "grunge brands" to speak of. But new hip-hop-modified goods and service brands (like hip-hop movies, hip-hop sportswear, hip-hop romance novels, and hip-hop dating services) that sell themselves as such come into being every day. Hip-hop lends itself well to almost any commercial concept because no marketing plan that turns a buck is too broad to fit under its tent. Despite its black face, hip-hop expands as necessary to accommodate an entire generation, not just one race. It is the ultimate in what advertisers call "aspirational" branding mediums, Simmons told me, because hip-hoppers aspire to imprint their lifestyle on every kind of consumption imaginable. He was talking about dRush Communications, the urban/youth-oriented advertising agency he started in 1999 in partnership with Deutsch, then the nation's largest independent ad firm. Coca-Cola was dRush's first big client.

> When we say aspirational, we mean, you could aspire to be raggedy and cool and rich at the same time. Hip-hop aspires to a lot of the glamour of American life. Yet hip-hop is really about everything on television. It's so brand conscious and brand aspirational. (Hip-hoppers) like Coca-Cola—not the Un-Cola. The jokes about Brand X have always been in the black community. They don't want Brand X because they already feel like Brand X. And they've sold that attitude to the world.

❐   ❐   ❐

Not only does recorded hip-hop and rap music outsell rock, but hip-hop sensibility is the hands-down winner in selling goods to the Hey Kids generation. "One thing hip-hop doesn't have is the notion of selling out," said Lance Jensen, thirty-six, cofounder of Modernista, the Boston ad agency whose clients include MTV. "There's nothing to sell out to. Hip-hop is a commercial venture up front. There's no embarrassment there about getting rich."

Before starting Modernista in February 2000, Jensen made a name for him-self as the creative force behind Arnold Communications' award-winning "Drivers Wanted" Volkswagen campaign of 1999. The campaign is widely credited with making Volkswagen the most top-of-mind car brand among teen-to-young-adult Americans. Overall VW sales went from 50,000 a year before the campaign to 70,000 per month in early 2000. The success of Jensen's work underlines Simmons's assertion that hip-hop's place in the worldview of the next generation is much deeper than the hot musical style of the moment. One of the more memorable commercials shows a young white couple cruising down a street in New Orleans' French Quarter on a rainy day, while an omnipotent beat synchronizes everything from the windshield wipers to some delivery men unloading a truck. But none of Jensen's ads has a rapper or a deejay or any overt marker of rap/hip-hop musical culture in sight. What they do have, admiring advertising experts agree, is an uncanny way of channeling—you guessed it—what's "real" for under-thirty people.

People of color figure prominently in Jensen's commercials, but not for their political, social, or niche-marketing value. They're there because, in Jensen's creative opinion, they evoke some truth that the client wants to pro-ject about the brand, a truth that wouldn't be revealed with an all-white cast. In one spot a black senior (but not *too* senior) is seen coolly slipping out of his nursing home. Nattily attired, he is met by a twentysomething black man in a Volkswagen, perhaps a grandson or young nephew, and they're off on a road trip to Las Vegas. It was "a simple story about a grandson picking up his grandfather and hanging out," said Jensen. "Black, white, that's not the point. It's a human story. The purpose was to show that VW is always focused on people and the freedom it can bring."

But it was decided to cast the commercial with black characters from the start, Jensen told me, "because we were trying to develop a character for the grandfather—like someone who might have been a musician, maybe a jazz or blues man, who despite his age hasn't given up on his lust for life." As it turned out, the actor playing the older man, "has this incredible gravitas; the guy just kind of oozes history." What makes the commercial hip-hop, or at least consistent with the Hey Kids worldview, is the very weight of the older man's presence, the thing Jensen aptly understood as "gravitas." He cast the commercial with the same eye for cultural authenticity as his target audience.

Without really thinking about it, without intending to make a statement for the audience to interpret, Jensen picked up on a truth about American identity that resonates for Hey Kids as well as their parents. In the commercial the World War II–generation black bluesman is now revealed for the archetype of American culture that he is and has always been. The archetype-icon makes its way into mass market advertising today, thirty years after blues-based rock and roll first took over pop culture, because Hey Kids have no memory (and little effective knowledge) of the racial baggage that the general market was still carrying around in 1965. They have precious little appreciation and no feeling for the fear, loathing, bitterness, and rage associated with the social upheaval that ultimately allowed that blues man to end up comfortably installed in that hypothetical, predominantly white nursing home somewhere in the Southwest, of all places. Perhaps for that reason, they have little disbelief to suspend about the fact that he is there at all. They have no uncomfortable emotional investment, one way or another, in the very sight of this black man to get in the way of the product-identification message. Instead the culture, the real transracial American culture, comes through to make a German car come off as American as the 1999 version of apple pie (which itself, of course, was a German import anyway).

The commercial makes no political point, said Jensen, and none is taken, at least not by viewers under thirty-five. Nevertheless, Jensen feels that the browning effect of youth culture on general-market advertising and other forms of mass media foreshadows an impact on society far beyond the bump in sales for a growing range of products. In the world of choice that the Hey Kids have inherited, consumers choose the commercials they'll watch, largely on the basis of whether the ads are bringing them something that is true and valuable to who they are or want to become, without regard to race or ethnicity. Accordingly, creators of commercial culture are free, if not compelled, to remove their parents' and grandparents' blinders and reinterpret the world for Hey Kids and for everyone else who consumes and wants to feel young. Inevitably, Jensen told me, society will come to see itself the way young people want to see themselves. He feels it's a very heady, exciting time to be making advertising.

> There's no doubt that the hip-hop culture and aesthetic is the most vibrant thing going on now—especially for younger people.

Everything is sort of being remixed into this new aesthetic, even the technology that allows you to do it. I think it bodes well for the future of this country. Whether advertising is getting it from the culture or leading it, imagery is very powerful. Positive imagery can have a powerful effect. I think you're remiss as an advertiser if you aren't aware of the powerful effect you can have.

Gary Koepke, Jensen's partner at Modernista, put it in more personal terms. He's the father of two teenagers,

and they're both white. My son and daughter would be insulted to think of race as an issue, and it's not from anything I've taught them. Images have a lot to do with that. [The images of transracial youth culture] may not be literally and figuratively true, but perception is the first step toward that reality. Images are leading that charge. And you can't underestimate the impact of the Internet in this. Where you live in the meat world doesn't necessarily dictate where your head is at on race. I think it's less about being white and more about being American.

7

Majority Minority:
The Short Life and Death of the
Great Racial Oxymoron

In August 1996, while still in the throes of preliminary research and delib-eration to validate the premise for this book, I attended the annual con-vention of the National Association of Black Journalists, which was held that year in Nashville. Since its founding in 1975, the NABJ convention has grown into, depending on your point of view:

1. A large, prosperous association of more than two thousand mostly suc-cessful black professionals who, with little to do but network, drink, hobnob, and tell stories for a week, would be almost indistinguishable from a similar group of white journalists on parade, except, of course, for the color of their skin.

2. A self-satisfied collection of African-American journalists and commu-nications and marketing professionals who are more smugly devoted to maintaining the not-inconsiderable patronage of the corporate media elite that foot the multimillion-dollar bill for the convention than they are to the NABJ's founding mission: telling the stories of black communities that white journalists are ostensibly disinclined or merely unable to tell from a "black perspective."

In either case or both, I have been a proud member of the NABJ for twenty years and the convention has always been an annual source of inspiration for my work. But that year it wasn't doing much to boost confidence in my still-evolving vision for *American Skin*. My view, lubricated by too many shots of Jack Daniel's, that the next big thing in the assault on racism should be a focus on the illegitimacy of the concept of race itself, had been met with polite indifference that bordered on hostility from some acquaintances who were marketing professionals. They especially didn't like a race-bending ani-mated Levi's jeans commercial running at the time that featured the rapping of dance-hall reggae star Shaggy narrating the exploits of a hypermacho clay-mation hero rescuing a screaming blond from a burning building. The hero, Clayman, is white, sort of, with dark hair that's done up to look part greaser and part dreadlock, and decidedly thick lips to go with a strong-jawed Elvis sneer. At the climax of this thirty-second mini-movie, I loved it, especially after, when he grabs the damsel from the roof and uses the jeans to slide down a telephone wire to the next building, causing two chickens perched on the wire in his path to instantly evacuate themselves in shock, before being fried by the friction as our hero blazes by. If crack came in a testosterone flavor, this spot was like taking a hit, at least to me. The marketing professionals thought it hypocritical for a self-consciously antiracist marketer like Levi Strauss to exploit the supermasculine black male stereotype—even if it was being projected onto a nonblack character. Of course, my fellow convention-ers were in the business of marketing to the African-American consumer seg-ment; they get paid to convince large corporations that they can increase their sales to African-Americans by understanding and exploiting inherent cultural differences between blacks and whites. The idea that blackness and whiteness could be merged in this way, thus becoming much less difficult to differentiate, much less exploit, was just not consistent with their business plans.

That night I got one of my first chances to chat at length about the book with one of my editors from the *Wall Street Journal*. He was one of hundreds of whites who parachute into the weeklong convention every year for a day or two and experience what I'm told is a uniquely disturbing disorientation at suddenly being a racial minority in a professional environment and thus being rendered socially invisible. At the NABJ convention, only the most arrogant, powerful, or genuinely "comfortable around blacks" whites do much speaking unless they are first spoken to—except, of course, when talking to other whites. Perhaps because of this racially jarring context, the editor seemed very receptive to my theories of an emergent transracial American identity. He was particularly excited about the racial transformation involved in the repositioning and branding of a nearly all-black National Basketball Association in the 1980s. But as the conversation wore on, I again felt the vague sensation of polite resistance that I had sensed from my black marketing friends. He really only *got* the part of the story that used professional basketball as an example, and that was because he was a fan. My arguments about the moral and cultural illegitimacy of white identity, like my discussion of the race-bending impact of hip-hop on American commercial popular culture, had fallen on nearly deaf ears.

Nevertheless, I pressed on into the night, drinking too much, eating too little, and talking myself into doubt. I woke up the next morning famished, with a cotton mouth, a leaden head, and spirits to match. I dragged myself to one of the lobby restaurants and sat down feeling near dead and demoralized. But an hour or so later I left my table with my faith in the dream of a new American identity beyond whiteness renewed. My revival had begun when I noticed that my order was being taken by an attractive thirtysomething Asian woman. Her English suggested she was a recent immigrant, perhaps from Vietnam or Cambodia, but just barely. As she spoke, her accent rounded out so fast, taking on the familiar cadences of the not-so-deep New South, that she seemed to be assimilating before my eyes. She started me off with a bolstering bowl of chicken soup, then recommended a delicately spiced spring roll stuffed with smoked shrimp, with a succulent barbecue sauce on the side. I don't recall the entree, but I've never forgotten the tableau. In the next America that is now, there's every reason why a new Asian-American might be serving an African-American journalist spring rolls in barbecue sauce at a black convention in a first-class hotel restaurant in the home of country music and big hair. But what really got me was how grits 'n' gravy "y'all come back now, ya heauh" southern gracious she was, and how natural and comforting it felt to me as a New Yorker of Jamaican descent who never met a southerner, except in movies or on television, until he reached college. I've since learned much more about the economic and demographic trends that conspired to bring us together that morning. Even then I knew I wasn't in the real Dixie heartland but somewhere that more

closely resembled a scene in a movie directed by James L. Brooks or maybe
Spike Lee. It's a movie set in America-the-imagined, that place of wonder
that revels in the harmony of its contradictions. My new American-Asian
waitress didn't change the reality that either my white editor or my black
colleagues took home from Nashville. If she served them, they probably
barely noticed her. But that doesn't make her any less real a character, maybe
better than real, playing a vital role in today's real American dream.

❐   ❐   ❐

I've discussed at length the historical roots of America's miscegenated cultural identity. Its foundation is made from an unstable, uneven, and unequal
alloy of black and white. Its chemistry was radically altered by the influx of
vast numbers of new immigrant converts to whiteness from southern and
eastern Europe in the early twentieth century. Still, the bipolar geometry of
black and white in American identity remained essentially intact; "white,"
however revised, was still the norm, and black, steadfastly determined by the
one-drop rule, was the "other." Now, since the early 1980s, comes the impact
of a new high tide of immigration—this time from Latin America, Asia, and
Africa—that has barely begun what is projected to be a very slow ebb. By
1970s-America definitions, these newcomers are supposed to be more categorically, irredeemably nonwhite than any Jewish peasant or Italian laborer
fleeing Europe a hundred years earlier. But just as no one in Washington
anticipated that the Immigration Reform Act of 1965 would open the door to
a late-century flood of nonwhite immigrants, today's powers that be, and all
the academic, social, and political pundits that speak for them, haven't got a
clue about where the newest Americans are going in what Colin Powell, the
first black (by way of Jamaican immigrant parents) secretary of state, called
his "American Journey." And none of them knows where these newcomers
will take the meaning of American identity in the process.

I'm not entirely sure where it's going myself, but I have faith in a general
theory, and that faith is grounded in my belief in the price-, value-, and
perception-setting power of the markets. But first we come to terms. Words,
as usual in discussions of American race and ethnicity, fail to capture the
shifting, indeterminate nature of new American identity. The term *minority*
in particular has been chewed to a pulp in the maw of mainstream media,
politicians, and other interested hacks. *Minority,* the concept, has also been
savaged by demographic facts on the ground. We still talk about blacks, His-

panics, and Asians as "minorities" in cities like New York, Atlanta, Houston, and Chicago, where they are actually in the numerical majority. Most glaringly, we still consider them "minorities" in California, even as headlines declare that, by the numbers, they are not. Clearly, the meanings of *minority* and *majority* are no longer related to simple math.

The closest the major media can come to explaining the implications of the 2000 census results in California is to declare the oxymoronic advent of the minority majority state, now that Hispanic, Asian, African, and Native Americans collectively outnumber whites. Like a white editor at a black journalists' convention, mainstream media and the chattering classes cling tenaciously to the notion that whites must always be seen as the general majority—the norm—even when they are, in a particular situation, the minority. This desperate delusion holds true even when the particular situation is as vast as the state of California. A goal of this book is to discredit and dispel such delusions, so for the purposes of this chapter, I'll use the term *new majority* to refer to native black, Hispanic, Asian, and Native Americans and immigrants from everywhere that's not Europe. *New majority* is a woefully PC and, in truth, reactionary coinage, but it does serve to shift the paradigm, if only a little bit, especially as I'd like to use it here. Because for me and for this discussion, the new majority is dominated by its fastest-growing components: post–World War II Hispanic and Asian immigrants and their children. It's the margins of growth that get the most attention from the markets, as economically rational individuals and firms make business decisions. If you're a home builder, you put your next dollar of investment where the number of new families is growing fastest, not where the largest number of families already live. Focusing our definition of *new majority* on the segments with the hottest marginal growth is also consistent my view that, PC notwithstanding, the "new majority effect" is really about the rapid penetration of Hispanic, Asian, and other non-European immigrant stocks into the mainstream, not about native American blacks. After all, there is nothing dramatically new about the presence or proportion of black Americans in the United States per se. True, the black population is growing faster than the non-Hispanic white population, and black incomes (and related indexes like home ownership) have closed a great deal of the gap with those of Anglo-whites in the last twenty years. Nevertheless, African-Americans, as things stand today, are increasingly only honorary members of the so-called new majority coalition because, as the rest of the new majority hurtles toward its merger with the old majority, many things are being changed, but the construction of African-Americans as "wholly other" in American identity seems to remain intact. In other words, I think *new majority* should be taken more literally than the mostly black sponsors of the term ever intended or imagined. The new majority is not about "people of color" numerically displacing non-Hispanic whites. It's about Hispanic- and Asian-Americans redefining whiteness as they enter its normative grace. I'll have more to say about this ironic contradiction later.

❑   ❑   ❑

The most striking manifestation of the new majority effect at work is in the creation of certain markets for goods and services. Among my favorites is the takeover of the American motel industry not just by Asian Indians but by a single subcaste of Asian Indians in which the surname Patel predominates. Somewhere in the 1990s industry data first revealed that just over half the motels in America are owned by people of Indian origin. According to a *New York Times* feature story, "about 70% of all Indian motel owners—or a third of all motel owners in America—are called Patel." Hence the not-so-facetious headline, "A Patel Motel Cartel."[1] The Indian dominance in motels represents what the author, Tunku Varadarajan, calls an example of a "nonlinear ethnic niche," in which a particular ethnic group "becomes entrenched in a clearly identifiable economic sector . . . for which it has no evident cultural, geographical or even racial affinity." Other examples include the Korean presence in the deli/convenience store/fruit and vegetable store businesses in New York and Los Angeles and the Pakistani dominance in New York's newsstand business. New York's porn-video stores, Varadarajan points out, happen to be run mostly by Sri Lankans. The particulars of how these seemingly incongruous ethnic niches came about are as varied as the ethnic groups and the economics of the different industries. But one significant common feature is a kind of pioneer dynamic. Once a handful of, say, Korean immigrants begin running fruit and vegetable stands in a big city, their success provides a template for subsequent Korean immigrant entrepreneurs. The other important commonality in these ethnic takeovers is the opening of a market opportunity in a particular industry that both attracts and enhances the odds of success for the earliest immigrant pioneers.

In the case of the Indian motel owners, the opportunity came in the 1970s, when the founding generation of the postwar motel industry were nearing retirement age, and when oil shocks were casting a big shadow on a business heavily dependent on consumers taking automobile vacations. More important for this discussion, the children of these mostly WASP motel owners weren't very interested in taking over the family business. The owners had almost no one to turn to but the light-brown aliens with vaguely British-sounding accents. Thus the Indians had the good fortune to buy in at the bottom of the market. At first the industry treated them coldly, which forced them to start the Asian American Hotel Owners Association (AAHOA), a trade group, to protect their interests. The *Times* feature story details the Indian group's triumph through the eyes of Mit Amin, a prosperous owner of a bed-and-breakfast in a fashionable section of Atlanta.

> Today, the A.A.H.O.A. has 5,000 names on its rolls—and an annual budget of $4.5 million. The market value of properties owned by association members is $38 billion. They pay $725 million a year in property taxes and employ 800,000 people. "The hotel establishment once didn't want to know about us," chortles Amin. "But now we *are* the establishment."[2]

Indeed, the American Hotel and Motel Association, the primary lodging-industry trade group, elected its first Indian chairman in 1998.

In assessing the meaning of this and other "nonlinear" ethnic takeovers, it's important to consider what they do not mean. The motel business has not "changed" as neighborhoods are said to "change" when whites flee or are otherwise displaced by nonwhites. The consumers of motel services are still predominantly white. There is nothing particularly "Indian" about your average Patel-owned and -operated Best Western motel; its culture is as American kitsch as ever. The Indians have not had to defend their industry from a perception that motels have somehow "gone down," as, say, the National Basketball Association has had to do since the league became so clearly dominated by black players in the 1980s. Motels have not become an "Asian" business sector, like Chinese restaurants. Yet the Indians running the motels have not exactly become "white," either.

What has happened is that Indian-owned and -operated motels have become American, and Americans have become people who stay with Patels while on their way to the Grand Canyon on a family vacation or when they get lucky on prom night in North Carolina. In less than a generation's time, Indian-operated motels have become a national American norm. Moreover, the number of regional norms—like Mexican-American construction firms in the Southwest, Caribbean nurses on the East Coast, and Filipino nurses and doctors on the West Coast—is growing as well. They are norms in the same way that American motels, construction firms, and nurses have always been "normal": the race of the people providing the services is almost as incidental as it was when they were most often white. In other words, brown (but not necessarily black) is as normal as white in more and more of the arenas that constitute the American way of life. One major proof of that normality, the *New York Times* writer discovered, is the extent to which the pre-existing white establishment ceases to question the hegemony of the new majority in an area where the norm was once white.

> Eventually, the mere perception of dominance becomes self-fulfilling. A number of moteliers to whom I spoke said that white American hotel brokers would often sound out Indians first if they have a property up for sale. David Mumford, who has been in the brokerage business for twenty-one years, said that this was "*completely natural*, given the track record of Asian Indians." His company has a database of more than 7,000 "buyer-seller" prospects"—about 1 in 4 of whom have Patel as their surname.[3]

The reality of this "norming" validates the slow but steady stream of creative decisions made by advertisers and producers of movies and television to depict nonwhites as ordinary stakeholders in the American good life that I've discussed in earlier chapters. And the reality of trends like the Indian motel takeover, a truth still stranger than everyday popular fiction, gives Hollywood that much more confidence in pursuing its transracial vision in new productions. The Indian motel manager (or Nigerian taxi driver, or Korean manicurist) who's really just like you, or is on the way to being just like you, only with darker skin and a hybrid accent, is fast becoming a stock figure in popular culture. More nuanced portrayals show the new American (or newly discovered American) as having a mixture of religious and social-cultural attributes that are sources of internal contradiction and conflict. And just as in the immigrant identity movies and plays of the 1930s and 1940s, the conflict is usually resolved against conformity with the expectations of the immigrant community or old-country culture in question and in favor of individual choice. And the ultimate result of that individual choice, more often than not in this quintessentially American genre, is a "mixed" marriage. Thus, at the end of Mira Nair's 1992 film *Mississippi Masala,* the conflicted young Indian immigrant heroine Mina flees the small southern town where her family owns a motel (of course!) to marry a hardworking black carpet cleaner played by Denzel Washington. This well-reviewed and moderately successful film brought the reality of the Indian-American hotel business into our consciousness several years before journalism caught up to the story; once again technology, globalization, and Hollywood's thirst for new stories quickly came together with the aspirations of a new majority, here represented by Nair, to stake a place in the American whole. It took several decades before the turn-of-the-century European immigrants felt both free and empowered to tell their own stories on their own terms, but Nair was able to to bring her movie to the market just sixteen years after she emigrated from a small town in India to study at Harvard. Such is the momentum of transracial change in the global economy of commercial pop culture.

Back in reality, the *Times* story ends with an image of Mit Amin savoring his collection of Mercedes, BMW, and Rolls-Royce luxury cars, well aware that such conspicuous consumption was not the way of the founding generation of motel Patels, like his father who staked him in the business with a gift of $50,000 in 1990.

> "An old-fashioned Patel would say, Why so many cars? But I'm just enjoying my achievements, right? It's a generation thing," he says. "My dad never went out to dinner, never indulged himself. He saved every penny. That's how he had $50,000 to give me."[4]

To be sure, the same norming privileges afforded to Amin and other new majority success stories are not being extended to Mexican migrant laborers in Florida or to Vietnamese slaughterhouse workers in Iowa, at least not yet. But this may have more to do with society's blind spots about class than about race. Pop culture tends to reflect the larger reluctance in society to identify with the working poor. Even when they are imagined to be mostly white, like, say, "redneck" laborers in some southern town, they are almost never depicted as being "just like us." In fact, they rarely get close-ups at all. But close up or not, those blue-collar Asians and Hispanics are rapidly becoming part of the heartland, too.

❐   ❐   ❐

The headline in the *New York Times* Sunday Styles section read, "For Women Great and Small, Briefs Can't Get Much Briefer."[5] Below, an apparently white, well-dressed woman is seen stretching a lacy pair of thong panties in an upscale Macy's department store. She regards the trendy lingerie with a mixture of fear and fascination on her face and in short order, the article suggests, resignation, as she will likely take it to the cash register and then home. Thongs accounted for 40 percent of the underpants sold by the Victoria's Secret chain in 2000, which sold some 20 million of the stringy things in 1999. "Even at Macy's, where the average shopper is older—in her 30's and 40's—thongs make up 20 percent of the total sales for women's underpants. . . . That is a 100-percent rise in a year," said the *Times* article. But a photo of mannequins from the Macy's underwear boutique is worth more than a thousand words of explanation of the plight of this shopper and all the old majority white women she may represent. Two "flesh"-colored (i.e., medium-pink Caucasian flesh) female dummies, nude but for bra and panties, are seen from behind. The one on the left wears traditional black panties that fully cover a backside that, while not stereotypically flat, has no particular camber to it. The panties hang about even with hips that only barely flare from the typical narrow mannequin waist. But the one on the right was custom made to display a tan thong that reveals two near perfectly shaped hemispheres of an ample yet taut behind, sculpted enough to let the center flap of cloth nestle between the cheeks. The right dummy's behind is not quite "high" enough, as in an old African-American descriptive, to set a cup of coffee on, but it's high enough that the top of the thong's waistband is naturally hung across the small of the back. The left dummy's waistband would barely top the crack in her behind (if she had one). This "Jennifer

Lopez-ization" of fashion and style is in some ways the ultimate victory in the decades-old war against a modern female-body standard of beauty that excluded not only Afro-Latino women from consideration as ideal but a majority of women of European and Mediterranean ancestry with hips or behinds substantially larger than the prepubescent fantasies of Calvin Klein and his ilk. The change is not a triumph of political will on the part of African-American or feminist activists. (The latter probably feel more outraged than affirmed by the thong thing.) It's the triumph of a marketplace reaction to the direct and indirect influence of shifting demographics on fashion and fashion retailing.

Hip-hop popular culture has been moving the focus of young male attention southward from breasts (the stereotypical white male obsession) to the places between the knees and the waist (the stereotypical black male obsession) for almost twenty years. As hip-hop both melds with and supersedes rock as the dominant fashion leitmotif, behinds are more out front, so to speak, than at any time since the "bustle" fashion of the late nineteenth and early twentieth centuries. The *Times* reporter supplied some recent pop history context for the thong:

> Another factor is increasing Latin American and African-American influences on fashion and beauty that emphasize the posterior. Whereas low-slung bikini briefs came into fashion during an era obsessed with the Beach Boys and the slim figures of young white California girls, the thong rose during the rap era, in the early 1990s, when Luther Campbell and his 2 Live Crew first filled videos with thong-clad women shaking it up at the beach. Now, Foxy Brown celebrates her own buttocks in a recent remix of Sisqo's "Thong Song."[6]

But unlike the turn of the twentieth century, when the aesthetic of ample curves was personified by the full-figured, very WASP actress Lillian Russell, retailers today are responding to something more than the manipulated fashion fantasies of a limited class of white women. Today's retailers are actively accounting for the integral physical as well as the cultural presence of new majority women in their marketplace, moving the dials on what constitutes "mainstream" fashion shapes, cuts, and colors in the process. What goes for fashion-forward Victoria's Secret, a mainstream specialty chain dressed in libertine's clothing, also goes for JC Penney, at the geographical and emotional center of American fashion identity. Since the 1980s, Penney's fashion merchandisers have come to understand that regional and local cultural influences, national pop cultural trends, and demographics interact in ways that are sometimes unpredictable and that vary greatly by market, but the result is almost always same: the color of the new majority is rubbing off on the old.

In the late 1990s, for example, Penney featured the Sandra Salcedo line of clothing geared toward Mexican-American women. It is cut for smaller but not necessarily child-size figures and is often trimmed with lace or beadwork reminiscent of some traditional Mexican clothing styles. But the line was also "career oriented," for women working in traditional American office environments. The Mexican-American woman, who represents the core Penney shopper in southwestern markets, was "attracted because of the sizing and the decoration; she is happy she doesn't have to hem everything she buys," said Beverly Anderson, Penney's manager of women's fashion apparel segment marketing in a 1997 interview. At the same time, the Salcedo line, which was found on the same racks as the rest of Penney's women's clothing, was a hit with non-Mexican-American women, too. Anderson said that after generations of denial, southwestern fashion markets have finally accepted a kind of Mexican-American cultural identity that's independent of ethnicity. "If you live in the Southwest and you see the Salcedo collection," Anderson said, "even if you're not Mexican-American, you will probably be attracted to it because you have been in the culture for so long."

For similar reasons of historical cultural affinity and demographics, the Salcedo line also did well in northern California. But in sprawling Los Angeles, with its nearly 50 percent Hispanic population that's predominantly Mexican-American, the Salcedo line didn't do nearly as well and was carried in few of Penney's southern California stores. Why? Because cosmopolitan Los Angeles is far more influenced by "urban" popular culture, said Manuel Fernandez, Penney's manager of sports and fashion segment marketing at the time. Despite the fact that Los Angeles is only about 12 percent black, its fashion culture is closer to that of demographically blacker eastern metropolitan areas like New York, Washington D.C., and Atlanta than to that of Texas. As Fernandez explained to me:

> You can't just ask about ethnicity, you also have to ask where they live—because they will be largely influenced by their environment. What we're finding, when we really get down to it, was that there are a lot more regional differences than ethnic differences, *but the regional differences are created by the diversity*. As a mass merchandiser, it's our responsibility to figure out what all these nuances are. It's evolving, but at our company we get a lot of input from our stores out in the field. (emphasis added)

Penney's Beverly Anderson credited the influence of new majority women in the marketplace with making brown a year-round mainstream-fashion hue. "Brown was traditionally a fall color only," she said. "But women of color were wearing it all the time for years, because it looks good on them. Suddenly while sitting in one of our marketing meetings, we looked around and realized that it's become a mainstream fashion color. Everybody wears brown now."

Most of the lessons Penney has applied in its ongoing melding of the new and old majorities were learned from its early-1990s experiments with stand-alone fashion boutiques stocked with clothing lines specifically targeted at African-Americans and/or Hispanics. By 1997 Penney all but abandoned such ethnic-segmented marketing. In effect, it made a business decision both to follow and to lead the new majority into the mainstream, rather than to try to attract them and then herd them into separate areas of the store. I'll discuss at length this pattern of moving from indifference to ethnic targeting and then to mainstreaming in the next chapter, but it's important to note here that Penney eventually repositioned its explicitly African-American-oriented boutiques, making them less ethnically specific while still featuring the wider variety of colors, patterns, and cuts that new majority women—and the women they influence—favor. The boutiques, and a related catalog, are now called Fashion Influences.

"What has happened with Influences is, it has become very high fashion," said Anderson. "The reason for its success is that it built a customer base, and a large part of that base is not necessarily African-American but is very fashion-forward. These women wait for the catalog." Anderson noted that a great number of reorder calls for the Influences catalog come from stores in decidedly nonblack markets. "When customers look at an African-American model," she said, "I don't think they necessarily think that it's an African-American-specific fashion anymore, because we're now so used to seeing diversity in everything." For example, Ashro, a line targeted to African-American women and found only in the Influences boutiques, has been "tremendously successful" because its vaguely "Afrocentric" motifs are increasingly seen more as "art to wear" than as statements of ethnic affinity or pride.

This might help explain the nonblack women who are sometimes prominently seen wearing Egyptian-flavored prints at the supermarket while shopping for tortillas, Chinese oyster sauce, Jamaican beef patties, and that new all-American staple, salsa. By now most observers should have "digested" the pop "true fact" that Americans today eat more salsa than ketchup. That factoid was reported in the early 1990s as business pages began reporting the mad dash by major food conglomerates to enter "ethnic" food markets. Actually, in 1993 Americans consumed almost three times as much ketchup, by volume, as salsa. But in dollar volume, sales for the category known as "Mexican sauces," including taco, picante, and enchilada sauces as well as salsa, rocketed past ketchup somewhere in 1992 and haven't looked back. And, new economy or old, it's the volume of dollars that counts. The combination of high retail markup prices for Mexican and other new majority cuisines and their fast growth at the supermarket has quietly reordered business and marketing plans throughout the food industry. In 1993 no less a white-bread food maker than venerable Campbell Soup paid $1.115 billion to buy Pace Foods of San Antonio, the world's largest Mexican sauce maker at the time.

The great Mexican food rush is another example of the new majority impact on "mainstream" markets. The first step is the recognition of large numbers of new majority customers showing up at stores in neighborhoods or even whole regions where they were once were absent or were little recognized as consumers. In this "plantain effect," the spread of new majority households into new neighborhoods and new regions, especially in the suburbs, in the 1990s led to a widening range of produce and packaged goods on supermarket shelves far beyond the barrios and other immigrant ghettos.

The photo accompanying a 1994 Associated Press wire story about the sudden rapid growth of "ethnic minorities" and their discovery by supermarket chains and other retailers says it all. A white store clerk at a Winn-Dixie in north-central Florida is seen piling dozens of plantains high on a produce display, handling the green to yellow-brown fruit as gingerly as if they'd been imported from Mars. The caption takes pains to note that plantains are "a fruit used in many Caribbean recipes." New majority households tend to be larger and younger and as a result are greater consumers of food than old majority households.[7] As their numbers have grown exponentially in the suburbs, in some cases accounting for the entire population growth during the 1990s, local supermarkets are motivated to accommodate their unique tastes. At the same time, the stores, often with the aid of national manufacturers, are scrambling to figure out how make traditional "nonethnic" fare more accessible, if not attractive, to the newcomers.

One strategy for "mainstreaming" new majority shoppers at the retail level is to integrate ethnically identified items like, say, Goya brand legumes and related sauces and seasonings, with the similar but nonethnically identified inventory. Strategy Research, a Miami market research firm that has specialized in Hispanic and other minority marketing data, calls this integration of product lines "intermerchandising." According to Strategy Research vice president Dave Thomas, early 1990s research showed that while grouping Mexican-American-favored products in one tight area made them easier for Hispanic shoppers to find, especially the newest immigrants, Latinos really wanted to see Hispanic cuisines and brands stocked in their natural, nonethnic-specific categories. Thomas explained to me:

> Scanners are helping focus real scrutiny on this. Some southern California stores are pioneers; they have lot of data about how movement is a function of shelf placement. We gave [a cross section of shoppers] hundreds of goods and asked them what they'd like to find next to each other. Many Hispanics expressed a preference to find their ethnic foods next to their general-market counterparts.

Thomas's client, an unnamed southern California food chain, decided to try stocking some of its Hispanic-Mexican fare into "nonethnic" aisles, "and lo and behold they found an 8 to 10 percent sales increase across the board." That was in 1993, and while the ultimate equilibrium of intermerchandising is still complicated by the shifting mix of attitudes and levels of acculturation among new majority members, the trend remains clear. Not only do new majority immigrants and their children like to do their shopping in a mainstream that reflects their tastes, but old majority shoppers perceive easy access to new and different if not exotic varieties of foodstuffs as a marked *enhancement* of the quality of their consumer life. In this context, I might add, the term *old majority* refers not exclusively to whites, but to all fully acculturated native-born consumers, including blacks. African-Americans may not immediately welcome the sight of a great many new Mexican immigrants at their favorite supermarket, but they sure do appreciate those little dark green Haas avocados that have become almost as ubiquitous on the East Coast as they have been in California for decades. Traditional supermarketers have little to lose and much to gain from following their natural economic instincts (and from ignoring more xenophobic or racist instincts) and steadily changing the mix to accommodate the fastest-growing part of the market. The "ethnic" food aisle will by no means disappear in the near future, but experts say the evolution is going on at a fairly rapid clip. The "foreign food" (to use a term no right-thinking supermarket manager would even think of putting on a sign anymore) lane has become much less foreign to the average consumer in recent years, especially as some of its staples steadily migrate into other aisles where the new majority is happy to see them and the old majority is more likely to give them a try. As Thomas put it:

> There are people who will never look in the Chinese aisle but will try the Chinese mustard if it's in the condiment aisle. Tortillas are huge now; they're almost not Hispanic-oriented products anymore. They're outselling bread in some stores, and not necessarily because of the Hispanic patronage dynamic at work.

If the evolution of Mexican food, or rather the Anglo-Mexican store-bought cuisine that we call Mexican, is any guide, tastes inspired by emerging Hispanic, Caribbean, and Asian America will have a bigger impact on the mainstream than ethnic Jewish, Italian, or other turn-of-the-twentieth-century immigrant groups did, and in a much shorter period of time. The reason, again, is the overriding economic imperative of big business to profit by efficiently exploiting America's most unique and still dynamic resource: its racial and ethnic diversity. The research, development, and marketing behemoth that is today's multinational food business simply didn't exist in the 1910s and 1920s. The Mexican-American supermarket food category, with U.S. sales of $1.6 billion in 1996, began with mid-1980s "southwestern chic" fad and ended in an answered food industry prayer. The core sauces have sharp, distinctive tastes that are low in calories and fats—and more important are low in ingredient costs, creating high profit margins. The profit to the manufacturer on a typical jar of salsa, for example, is estimated to be over 30 percent, higher than soda, coffee, and even some brands of cigarettes.[8] Perceived as healthier and certainly more interesting than ketchup, salsa first moved out of the ethnic or "Spanish" aisle to be with its sugar-laden relative in the late 1980s. Then American-style tortilla chips, born in the salty snack aisle and pumped up with high-tech pressurized bags, began to muscle in on the venerable potato chip. As it did, it forced grocers to make room for salsa on the snack aisle shelves, too. By the late 1990s a narrow ethnic specialty supplied by a handful of regional food firms had become a full-blown American food category dominated by multinational firms like Pillsbury, now a unit of General Mills. These firms quickly raised their sights above and beyond the fast-growing Hispanic consumer base, applying technology and marketing creativity not only to blanket the United States but to develop a world market—including Latin America—for a product that would be almost unrecognizable in Mexico. It's not surprising: in Pillsbury's case, the entire operation is directed from its headquarters in that bastion of southwestern culture, Minneapolis. As the *New York Times* noted in 1997:

> About the only thing missing from the boom is Mexicans, who have less and less to do with defining this country's—and now the world's—taste for their native food. There are no Mexicans on Pillsbury's 20-member Old El Paso [brand] development team; its leader was born in India.[9]

Of course, Mexican-Americans with intact cultural memories of the real thing wouldn't be caught dead giving Taco Bell burrito kits (from Philip Morris's Kraft Foods unit) any respect, though they still might pick some up for dinner in a pinch. But it doesn't matter. Multinational marketers are not only effectively marketing to the expanding population of assimilated Hispanics who, according to the *Times* article, "see the products as mainstream American food," they're marketing that image in Latin America, building awareness for the category at the very source of Hispanic immigration.

As big business hijacks Mexican cuisine for its own purposes, it's effectively transforming part of Mexican-American or Hispanic identity, but not in the old melting pot model. I've discussed assimilation of new immigrant groups and the reverse-acculturation effect their presence continues to have on the larger native-born society. But we need a new word for the post-reverse-acculturation response by big marketers like Pillsbury and its effect on new majority identity formation. Let's call it *acculturated secondary assimilation*. It explains the preference that Asian-Americans have for Japanese- and Korean-made automobiles, models that mostly aren't even sold in their countries of origin and that are marketed here in the most all-American fashion, with no reference to their Asian provenance. In this instance Asian multinational car makers, working with American multinational ad agencies, have expanded the definition and the image of the American good life in a way that fits the product and have simultaneously widened the American identity space in the direction of so-called Asian-Americans. In other words, "Asian" cars and "Mexican" food are both really recent commercial culture icons cooked up by multinational manufacturers and marketers in response not to any Chinese, Japanese, Korean, or Mexican reality but to a perceived opportunity in a competitive business environment. It's much like the U.S. government's creation of "Asian" and "Hispanic" as official categories for Chinese, Japanese, Guatemalan, Argentine, and so on, people in the 1970s. The federal government created new official "brands" of American identity to turn the post–civil rights era social crisis into an opportunity to expand its political franchise in a way that was managable and acceptable to the old majority. What's fascinating is how these parallel artificial worlds of commercial and social identity almost immediately began an interaction that continues to this day. One significant and often overlooked link is government-mandated affirmative action, which has placed varying degrees of obligation on manufacturers and marketers of all kinds to do business with firms based on the official minority status of their ownership. But I think the dynamic has long since taken on a commercial culture life of its own. We—the Census Bureau and Madison Avenue—really think we can convince a second-generation Columbian-American that he's "Hispanic" and that "Mexican" supermarket food out there will confer upon him a lifestyle that's completely and authentically American!

Of course, the people who make the stuff, as quoted in the *Times* article, know better and, in any case, have much wider ambitions for their creations:

> Pillsbury executives have no illusions about the authenticity of their cuisine. "We're interested in mainstream America," said Christopher Policinski, a vice president of Old El Paso. "Internally . . . we always put the word 'Mexican' in quotes." Indeed, Pillsbury sees Mexican food as "a hybrid phenomenon," Mr. Policinski said, "where Mexican components are being integrated into fusion cooking." How integrated? "On the West Coast," he said, "people are using tortillas as a new kind of white bread. They're putting peanut butter and jelly on them."[10]

He was referring, of course, to a West Coast in which Hispanics already hold a demographic plurality and are heading for the majority. No wonder another food executive predicted that in twenty years we won't even recognize what they'll be calling Mexican food. In fact, as *The Wall Street Journal* reported, a new category of so-called fusion foods, like Southwestern Lasagna, "a gooey blend of ricotta cheese or vegetables and salsa sandwiched between tortillas," and Thai Jungle Salsa, "a chunky mix of soy sauce, grilled onions, and Thai peppers," are moving out of the high-end restaurant and specialty-store niche and into the supermarkets.[11] That spring roll stuffed with smoked shrimp and barbecue sauce that raised my spirits back in Nashville may soon be coming to a frozen food aisle near you. In a happy non-coincidence, the commercial fusion foods are being developed by the kind of small food business players, many of them Hispanic- or Asian-owned, whom multinationals once squeezed out of the now-mainstream market for "ethnic" foods. This kind of competitive response, gambling on products developed with the ethnic blender turned up a notch, could only happen in America.

❐   ❐   ❐

One of my favorite barometers of new majority cultural pressure is the headline count in various *New York Times* sections devoted to art and entertainment.

Periodically, and with seemingly increasing frequency, I turn up an issue like that of August 14, 2000, a Monday Arts section in which every story but one was about nonwhite artists or performers, or non-Western culture in the mainstream marketplace.[12] Usually these stories reflect yet another example of new majority cultural crossover that's becoming so common as to be unremarkable in and of itself. It's no longer news that, say, Indian music or black comedians or Latin American films are being taken seriously by critics at important cultural outlets like the *New York Times* and by the predominantly (though by no means exclusively) white and affluent audiences they serve. It's just color penetrating the mainstream market. But beneath the headlines, in some areas of high and low culture, there is still new news; in some key mainstream cultural niches, the new majority has *become* the market. As recently as the 1960s, for example, the hobby of car customization, an esoteric but vital branch of American automobile culture, was the nearly exclusive province of young white men, especially on the West Coast, where it was known as "hot-rodding." But since the 1980s it has been taken over by the Chicano-Latino culture known as "low riding," whose signature aesthetic involves rigging a car's suspension so that the body appears to glide an inch or less above the surface of the road. The *Times* article, under the headline "Victory to the Low and Slow," details the "mainstream" acceptance of the style born in the southern California barrios. The author points out that the readership of *Lowrider* magazine, the bible of the movement, is only 58 percent Latino today, while "fully 25 percent" are white.[13] But the point and the news, for me, was that Latinos rule a segment of American culture that is otherwise defined as "mainstream."

The article went on to mention that when the Petersen Automotive Museum in Los Angeles put on a low rider exhibit in spring 2000, museum attendance doubled. The Petersen's experience reflects a larger impact that the new majority is having on high culture institutions that were historically the least responsive to recognizing blacks, Hispanics, or Asians as important, much less primary constituencies. But high culture institutions in more and more American cities have been coming to just such a recognition of the new majority markets that often quite literally surround them. The underlying trend is (unlike most others in this book) driven as much by politics as by market economics. Simply put, it's been nearly impossible for symphony halls and opera houses built in central cities before the era of white flight to pick up and follow their old exclusive patrons to the suburbs. Those that have survived the perigee of urban decay in the 1970s and early 1980s find themselves much more dependent on subsidies from local governments that are heavily influenced or dominated by some combination of African-, Asian-, or Hispanic-American taxpayers. The plight of institutions like the Detroit Symphony, the Houston Grand Opera, and the Washington (D.C.) Opera exposes the description of these major American cities as "majority minority cities" for the oxymoronic fraud that it is. The managers of these institutions have learned that they can't afford to buy into that lie. Instead, they recognize that the future of old majority high culture rests with the sufferance of new majority political clout, if not their outright embrace as consumers. As a result, the face of traditional high culture is increasingly multiracial. Think about it: Has anyone mounted a production of *Aïda* since 1990 that didn't cast Aïda as a black woman? The canon is not only being reinterpreted and recast in color, it's steadily being amended as cultural traditions rooted in new majority communities are hastily added to it.

The Detroit Symphony was shamed into recognition of new majority reality in 1989, when it still counted just one black member out of a hundred or so in its ranks. While it was traveling on its first European tour in some time, a black state senator back home in the 70 percent black city decided to get the debt-plagued orchestra's attention by holding up its subsidy check, according to a *New York Times* account.

> In Madrid, the musicians met with Deborah Borda, who was then executive director. She spelled out the options. "It was either set aside the audition process and hire a black musician on the spot or buy your own plane ticket back to the U.S.," she said. . . . Shocked by the rebuke from its own city . . . and roundly criticized by the American orchestra community for allowing itself to be hijacked as an instrument for social change, the Detroit Symphony went home to ask how it might increase diversity without sabotaging its own artistic mission. Staffing and board membership and guest artist rosters were overhauled to accept more blacks.[14]

The St. Louis Symphony got its wake-up call in 1991, when the 47 percent black city rejected its bid for increased public funding, in effect preferring some museums and the famous zoo over the orchestra. That same year the president of the Monsanto Fund, a key private sector supporter, tied its next support check to efforts to bring the orchestra closer to the city's people. It's no coincidence that the Monsanto Fund's president at the time, John L. Mason, was black. In 1993 the orchestra published a remarkably frank five-year plan for improved relations with St. Louis's black community. The plan was to "turn active dislike into mere disinterest, benign neglect into modest participation, and mild interest into active association."[15] The Houston Grand Opera, for its part, committed itself to representing the new majority in 1993, when it mounted an experimental opera called *Frida* based on the life and work of Mexican painter and Southwest cultural icon Frida Kahlo. The production, incorporating traditional and reimagined Mexican folk music, puppetry, and a mariachi band, may have severely taxed the imagination and skill set of the Houston Grand Opera staff, but its top management saw it as a risk that it had to take. The wager, according to a *New York Times* account, paid off:

> Hearty crowds with heavy Hispanic contingents appeared, a relief to David Gockley, the general director of the Grand Opera. Mr. Gockley thinks his organization has little time to secure its position with the burgeoning minorities. His plan is to make the case for opera to nontraditional audiences *by redefining opera itself.*[16]

In 2000 MTV raised the profile of what might become the first successful new majority classical form when it broadcast a "hip-hopera," based on Bizet's *Carmen*, called *Mob Story*. Starring Destiny's Child pop star Beyoncé Knowles (currently the celebrity model for L'Oréal's Feria blond hair coloring) and young black heartthrob actor Mekhi Phifer, the success of the commercial-free broadcast suggests that the new form may survive to share space with stricter interpretations of Bizet's classic opera at a major big-city high culture venue near you. When it does, you can be certain that the productions will be targeted not to the "minority market" but to the "emerging market," a new catchphrase that signifies the same truth as "new majority," without threatening the old majority's sense of social security or hegemony.[17] The critical, nonrhetorical distinction between "emerging markets" and "minority markets" is the fact and recognition that as new majority markets "emerge," they overshadow and ultimately subsume the old majority's once-singular importance to those who provide goods, services, and capital to the market.

Take the residential mortgage market, for example. The housing boom of the 1990s was largely fueled by new majority members, especially recent immigrants, coming into ownership for the first time. Blacks and Hispanics alone accounted for 42 percent of home ownership growth between 1994 and 1997, according to a study by Harvard's Joint Center for Housing Studies, even though they make up just 24 percent of all U.S. households. The numbers partially reflect pent-up demand that began to be released by a series of high-profile state and federal government moves against housing and lending discrimination. But they also reflect a major market-moving decision by the Federal National Mortgage Association, known as Fannie Mae, to redefine the profile of the typical American homeowner to comport with the reality of the new majority. Fannie Mae, the nation's primary purchaser of residential mortgages in the secondary market, is the five-hundred-pound gorilla in American home finance because its underwriting criteria essentially define the secondary market for American home loans. In 1994 Fannie Mae began funding a $1 *trillion* (that's a 1 with fifteen zeroes behind it) commitment to help 10 million "underserved" families buy their first homes by the end of 2000. Fannie's initiative, backed by a long-running, extensive media campaign that disproportionately depicts nonwhites as the typical first-time home buyers, fairly rewrote the business plans of national mortgage lenders like GMAC Mortgage, the home lending unit of General Motors. Fannie Mae inspired GMAC to take a marginal "community lending" program aimed at minorities, quickly rename it the Emerging Markets Initiative, and make it the foundation of an effort to break into the ranks of the top-five mortgage lenders in the United States.

Sitting around a conference room table at their Horsham, PA, headquarters, GMAC Mortgage president Mike O'Brien and the managers of the initiative recalled how the Fannie Mae commitment triggered a process of rethinking the very nature of their business. Before, they had viewed their customer as a middle- to upper-income suburbanite, a white baby boomer who had landed his first mortgage before the Carter administration. Of course, by the 1990s, "when you compete in that suburban arena for the 'hot prospects' . . . there's a hundred competitors trying to slay each other to get at that customer," O'Brien told me.

Then came the epiphany:

> The single biggest *ahh-ha* for me came while reading about the housing cycle in the 1990s. All the experts said we were heading for a decline after boomers passed through. The *ahh-ha* was Fannie making this $1 trillion commitment—a tremendous, audacious statement, really a lightning rod. I mean, how do you line up this big goal with a cycle that says the market is getting softer? That's when I started to become much more aware of the buying power that's outside of historical measures.

Put another way, that's when O'Brien realized that the geographic and racial center of his market had moved sharply toward urban and some suburban areas characterized by browning new majorities. It was, for O'Brien, like a chance to go back to the markets of the 1950s and 1960s that built the postwar mortgage industry. Only now the market's most prominent members were blacks, Hispanics, and Asians, consumers who were long considered "suspects" instead of "prospects" in the conventional industry wisdom, just by virtue of skin color. Now O'Brien fairly rhapsodized about how the "passion" of new immigrants and upwardly mobile African-Americans for home buying was so much greater than that of their traditional customers, who had long taken home ownership as a right and thus for granted. That passion "means they're going to accumulate the necessary savings and prioritize," said O'Brien. "It may be the first time in their whole family history that anyone has owned their home. These are the customers I want to find and work with."

To be sure, Fannie Mae chairman Franklin Raines, who is black, has an underlying goal of closing the gap in the rate of home ownership between minorities and non-Hispanic whites. But his approach had much more far-reaching consequences than a typical affirmative action or entitlement program. As the head of a private, Big Board–traded corporation—the largest of that kind headed by a black man—Raines had to validate his initiative on relatively pure market-economic grounds. Fannie Mae in the 1990s constantly experimented in developing and then supporting new loan products designed to meet the needs of the new majority home buyer. As it turned out, while the "underserved" homeowner market was (and is) disproportionately black, Hispanic, and Asian, its majority was (and still is) non-Hispanic white. But these were not George W. Bush's father's non-Hispanic whites. For one thing, Raines's systematic market research determined, they were heavily into professional basketball, not baseball. Thus Fannie Mae became a major sponsor of televised NBA games, spending $30 million in advertising in 1998. Think about it: The average member of the new majority housing market is an urban renter. Whether they're half-generation new immigrants from Taiwan, third-generation black Harlemites, or residents of a "white ethnic" enclave in New York, their common denominator is an urban culture that's exemplified by the NBA. Interestingly, the NBA in the 1990s and college basketball both rated high with nonurban working-class aspiring homeowners who are white, too. The images in the Fannie Mae ads cut across all races, genders, and ages, "yet if you ask people 'who's in them,' they say 'people like me,'" Raines told me in an interview. The new products pioneered by Fannie Mae and adopted by firms like GMAC Mortgage, like the very popular 3 percent down Fannie Mae Flexible 97 mortgage, have turned out to be "absolutely applicable" to the overall mortgage market, according to Leon Wilson, who was then GMAC Mortgage senior vice president for emerging markets. "As we become better at understanding our customers' needs," Wilson told me, "we develop a culture that is more accepting of differences beyond race."

Insofar as it was "accepting of differences beyond race," Wilson seemed assured that GMAC Mortgage had already committed itself to looking past the racial differences between the old and the new majority and was moving toward seeing their other sociofinancial attributes—credit profiles, bill-paying habits, savings patterns—as part of the new "norm" in its marketplace. His assumption is telling because just a few years earlier Wilson, who is black, was breaking new ground—and making his bones in the industry—with pioneering community-lending programs in Boston. There his primary objective was to mitigate long-standing patterns of discrimination against African-Americans. Race, as opposed to barriers of culture or even economics, has always been the fundamental obstacle to recognizing African-Americans as members of any majority—old, new, borrowed, or blue. But for one new majority member group, perhaps the most important part of the emerging majority, the very idea of racial difference from whiteness itself is being dissolved.

◻   ◻   ◻

Though their intellectual and political leaders tend to deny it, the people we now call Hispanics are well on their way to being the next "white ethnic" group in America. They are the first such group not to hail directly from Europe, and for that very reason they hold the seeds for the eventual destruction of whiteness as we've known it for more than two hundred years. Hispanics may be the bridge over which all non-European Americans—including Americans of predominantly African descent—may one day walk into an Americanness that has little or no remaining basis in Anglo whiteness. Hispanics could well be the way the new majority becomes simply the majority. It's not going to be simple, and the dynamics of the process are still so unstable as to leave the outcome uncertain. But one thing that is certain: Hispanics and other non-European immigrant groups have not come to the United States to be part of an amorphous racial minority coalition called "people of color." They bring nothing from the cultures of their homelands to support such an identity. And while the experiences of American racism and the left-leaning intellectual cant disbursed in higher education may cause them to see some value in such a coalition, the benefits of merging with the emerging Transracial American mainstream, however uncertain, will likely far exceed the current value found in identifying with multicultural minority status. Think about it: Why would upwardly mobile (and no matter how low they start, most immigrants can credibly see themselves as upwardly mobile) Hispanic- or Asian-Americans want to aim for the ground-floor status that African-Americans are still struggling to reach as a group, when they can see a way to the very top floor via individual staircases that are mostly of their own making? And even if they do get a helping hand from affirmative action here or there along the way, no one is going to require, as a consequence, that they support any particular agenda based on racial minority identity. For this reason, as I've said earlier, African-Americans are coming to the sobering conclusion that their membership in the new majority—a concept, ironically, pioneered by black activist thinkers—is becoming more and more honorary than substantive, because the Euro-Indian-Asian-blooded members have far greater social mobility.

The mainstream of black thought and sentiment still constructs itself as "wholly other" from a monolithic American whiteness. How accurately this construction reflects reality, especially the "white monolith" part, is perhaps the most critical question that I will consider in Chapter 9. The mainstream of the so-called Hispanic lifestyle—the Hispanic-American dream, if you will—may construct itself with a Latin flavor that's fluent in both English and Spanish. But while Hispanics value a sense of being distinct and apart from "Angloness," not unlike the Québecois in Canada but with far less fervor and no subnational ambition, they do not see themselves as wholly other from a "white monolith." To the contrary, the fine print under all the charts and figures in newspaper and magazine articles digesting the 2000 census data remind us that Hispanics "can be of any race." It's true, but only under the assumptions Congress and the Census Bureau chose to make when they created the "Hispanic" category out of the thin and racially polarized air of the early 1970s. While the 2000 census offered Americans an unprecedented fifteen races to choose from, including "other," and all possible combinations thereof, 94 percent of the people who said they were "Hispanic" also said they consider themselves to be just one of two races. About 49 percent said they were members of some "other" race. Some 51 percent said they were white.

So though their leaders are reluctant to address the fact, Hispanics are an increasingly important part of the "white monolith." Among the more interesting aspects of the melding of the new majority and the old is the way Anglo-white America is also coming to grips with the fact and the nature of Hispanic whiteness.

Earlier in this chapter, I mentioned the oxymoronic splendor of the "majority minority" state. Today California is even more literally the "Golden State," as so-called non-Hispanic whites dip below 50 percent of the population, and the same is happening in cities like New York City and San Antonio and Houston. The 2000 census confirms that the old (read: Anglo-white) majority is being eclipsed in some of the biggest states and most major metropolitan areas. Once large numbers of blacks moved north after World War II and then pushed into previously segregated urban areas in the 1960s, whites who had remained in the cities after their relatives left in the first great wave of suburbanization quickly followed those relatives into "naturally" segregated suburbs. In recent years periodic waves of white immigration from California to much whiter mountain west states like Utah, Nevada, and Idaho have been heavily reported. But the latest census makes clear, at least to me if not to the vast majority of journalists causing forests to be felled for this subject, that if the old majority is running from the combined presence of blacks, Asians, Hispanics, and others, it really has no place to go, except perhaps to a shrinking number of countries in Europe. Wherever a large economic infrastructure is in place (as in New York, Chicago, Los Angeles, Houston, Dallas, and Miami), the new majority is already there in force. If they run to some fast-growing smaller town, they'll generally find that the new majority—*primarily* in the form of recent immigrants and long-time Hispanics—is crossing those borders with them, if they aren't there to greet them. After all, "magnet for immigrants" is almost the definition of *boomtown* today and is likely to remain so.

Whiteness would seem to be cornered between the proverbial rock and hard place. But history teaches the careful observer never to underestimate the flexibility and resourcefulness of American whiteness. It abhors the loss of majority status as nature abhors a vacuum. And like nature, I believe, whiteness has already begun to fill that void with something, or someone, to equalize the pressure: Hispanics, the pseudo-race and ersatz nationality that never was, the quasi-ethnic group that will soon be at the center of the new American average.

Hispanics are already ground zero for the life-or-death political struggle to control California, Texas, and Florida, three of the four most populous states in the country. The political demography news stories are all about the vanishing non-Hispanic white as a proportion of more and more political jurisdictions, especially districts that were recently overwhelmingly Anglo-white and Republican. If the media trend continues, they'll have to name a new news beat: political ecology. But before they do, I think, the system will adjust by incorporating what has been apparent to Republican strategists for quite some time. Running out of non-Hispanic whites? Replace them with Hispanics, half of whom count themselves as white and the other half as "whites-in-waiting." Republicans have credible hopes of gaining more and more Hispanic support by appealing to their often-reported conservative social values. Democrats are learning that, unlike the African-American vote, they cannot take Hispanic loyalty for granted. But pragmatic political conventional wisdoms aside, Republicans have a shot at gains and Democrats run a risk of real slippage with Hispanics because of one and the same fact of American racial history: Hispanics are not a race, and their vote, to the extent it can be characterized, is not racial but ethnic.

Moreover, and most important, the already-weak bonds of this quasi-ethnic group are quickly dissolved in the new majority stew. Amid the glut of predictable 2000 census news analysis, Harvard sociologist Orlando Patterson made the profound—and profoundly politically incorrect—point that the rumors of the white majority's death in America are greatly exaggerated, because Hispanics are already poised to effectively maintain the white demographic majority for many decades to come.

> Even with the most liberal of assumptions, there is no possibility that whites will become a minority in this nation in this century. The most recent census projections indicate that whites will consitute 74.8% of the total population in 2050, and that non-Hispanic whites will still be 52.8% of the total. And when we make certain realistic sociological assumptions about which groups the future progeny of Hispanic whites, mixed couples and descendants of people now acknowledging two or more races are likely to identify with, there is every reason to believe that the non-Hispanic white population will remain a substantial majority—*and possibly grow as a portion of the population.*[18]

Patterson ties a nice sociological bow around facts on the ground that thinking observers of American race (and especially African-American observers) recognized decades ago. Not only are the majority of Hispanics effectively white, but as they choose to marry so-called Anglo-whites (or for that matter other "white" Hispanics), their children are even whiter. Patterson notes that recent studies indicate that second-generation Hispanic whites "are intermarrying and assimilating mainstream language and cultural patterns at a faster rate than second generation European immigrants of the late 19th and early 20th century."[19] The same studies find similar patterns holding for Asian-Americans: about one-third marry non-Asians, mostly non-Hispanic whites. Again, as with Hispanics and unlike blacks, the one-drop rule does not apply. The child with one Asian and one white parent can always be at least half white, could never be accepted as properly, purely Chinese, Japanese, and so on, in the land of his Asian parent or grandparents' birth, and might actually have a hard time confining themselves to such an identity here.

In real life a union between even an olive-skinned Hispanic and a pale Anglo-white is less and less considered to be "interracial," much like a marriage between a Jew and a WASP along about 1963. Post-1980s popular culture has long since gone reality one better: In movies and even on TV, a relationship is recognized as a interracial only if one partner is black. Thus one unacknowledged aspect to the "breakthrough" film career of Jennifer Lopez and those of a growing host of Latina "it girls" like Cameron Diaz, Salma Hayek, Jessica Alba, and even the undisguisable Rosie Perez is that they can bed white guys or otherwise (except Rosie) just plain *be* white (i.e., apparently Caucasian with nothing to suggest they are ethnically or culturally different from all the non-Hispanic whites around them) in movies. The pop culture market apparently thinks nothing more of it than if their last names were Ciccone or Kinski. Asian men can still rightly complain that they never come close to getting the white girl on screen (though, ironically, a great many of them do in real life), but so-called Hispanic men enjoy the same white privilege as the new crop of Latina divas—that is, when they get to be on screen at all.

As the most numerous and genetically Caucasian constituency in the putative "people of color" coalition, Hispanics have had the most important role to play in legitimizing the new majority's ascendance. But I predict Hispanics will also be the group most responsible for smothering nascent "minority majority" political states in their infancies. Think about it: In metro Miami, where Hispanics outnumber Anglo-whites as well as Afro-Caribbean blacks, only the blacks see themselves, and are also seen, as a minority group. As the minority majority fails to materialize, so also goes the possibility of tenure for a truly new majority. *When it's all been said and done, America won't be coming into a new majority so much as a renewed majority.* The only question is exactly what part, if any, whiteness will play in a majority that fully includes most of the genetic heritages of the Far and Middle East, the Asian Pacific, and Native and Latin America. The Hispanic undertow in the renewed majority tide is broad and at the same time so subtle that, I think, most Americans will barely notice the water that's already in up to our collective shins. Indeed, the fact that even politicians have already caught the wave it means that the forces melding old and new majorities in commercial pop culture must perforce be so far gone as to be irreversible.

My revelation about the shift in the center of gravity toward Hispanics came at the movies on the opening weekend of the 2001 release *Spy Kids*. The matinee at a multiplex in a semiurban part of otherwise suburban West-chester County was brimming with kids and parents. While waiting in an interminably long popcorn line, I noticed that the crowd seemed to fairly reflect the southern Westchester mix of one-third black, one-third white and one-third "other," and that the largest chunk of the latter appeared to be His-panic. Closer inspection revealed that a lot of the apparent plain old majority whites were Hispanic, too, like the brown-haired guy who chatted me up on the lousy concession service in an accent more redolent of an Italian-American enclave in the Bronx than of Puerto Rican East Harlem. When I finally got my popcorn, I thought nothing of it and rushed back to the seats where my three-year-old daughter, my neighbor, and her two children were already past the opening credits. In a setup that could pass for Disney circa 1972, we learn that Daddy (played by Antonio Banderas) and Mommy (Carla Gugino), are former secret agents who retired to be normal middle-class (meaning upper-middle-class) parents to their kids, a girl of about thir-teen and a boy of about ten. The family name is Cortez, and Banderas has a fairly thick yet nonspecific Spanish accent, but these details are barely noticed at first. My mind only registered "white family." After all, Banderas, married in real life to Melanie Griffith, is from Spain and is technically not "Hispanic" as far as the government is concerned.

Only when the plot of this modest budget kiddie-Bond flick was well into its second act did the new majority revelation hit home. Seeking refuge from pursuing bad guys at the door of a computer-controlled safe house, the girl, Carmen (Alexa Vega), is asked to identify herself. When she says, "Carmen Cortez," the computer responds with an error message and insists on her "real name." After a brief show of protest, Carmen, who to this point seemed the quintessence of the Gen-Y "Valley Girl," hauls out one of those heavy-duty eightfold Latina names that begins with Carmen and ends with Cortez, followed by her mother's maiden name, in a light but clearly fluent Spanish accent. In my own head, and faintly with my own ears, I heard someone saying, "Whoa! She's a Latina!" Later in the chase, before the ultimate showdown in the bad guy's fortress, the action moves to the downtown area of a city that's almost surreal in its nonspecific Hispanic-Americanness. All the kids in the playground are speaking Spanish, though our heroes aren't, and all the signs are in Spanish. But there is no way to know if it is a city in San Diego County, California, or somewhere in middle-class Latin America proper.

In the end, apart from one passing reference by Banderas to Latinos being very emotional about family, nothing about the film made it "Hispanic" in the way that's consistent with the image of a "minority group." Interestingly, Banderas's reference comes as he embraces a long-lost brother whose brown skin, accent, and demeanor comport with the more familiar stereotype of a working-class Chicano male. Only when the closing credits rolled did I realize *Spy Kids* was written and directed by Mexican-American filmmaker Robert Rodriguez (*El Mariachi, From Dusk till Dawn*) and that the actors playing the "spy kids" (who, of course, rescue their parents) had Spanish surnames, too. The not-so-atypical suburban audience behind me, heavily laced with Hispanics who are also white, was ecstatic with their applause. Most of the critics, I later learned (virtually none of them Hispanic), also raved about *Spy Kids*, with little or no mention of its vaguely Latino identity. It went on to gross over $100 million in its first run, leading the box office for its first two weekends running. But long before I saw the numbers, I remember telling everyone who'd listen that I'd just seen the future. It's white, sort of—with a Spanish accent and Latino-American family values.

Spy Kids *didn't have one black face on screen long enough to remember if it had even appeared.*

◻   ◻   ◻

In the long term, I like to think that the black absence from such a sociocul-turally defining moment as the success of *Spy Kids* will be seen as an over-sight. But in the short run it reflects the distinct possibility that the ultimate merger of all Americans into one ethnicity will be a two-step process, the first of which does not include traditional black Americans. In a 1998 essay titled "The Brown and the Beige," Michael Lind argued persuasively that while high rates of intermarriage between Anglo-whites and Hispanic-, Asian-, and Native-Americans will effectively merge these groups in our lifetime, Americans who make the conscious choice to identify themselves as indivisibly black, or are otherwise compelled to accept such identification, will remain apart from the majority that I've termed "renewed" and that Lind calls "beige":

> In the 21st century, then, the U.S. population is not likely to be crisply divided among whites, blacks, Hispanics, Asians and American Indians. Nor is it likely to be split two ways, between whites and nonwhites. Rather, we are most likely to see something more complicated: a white-Asian-Hispanic melting-pot majority—a hard-to-differentiate group of beige Americans—offset by a minority of blacks who have been left out of the melting pot once again.[20]

My analysis of trends in commercial popular culture suggests that marketers have already incorporated the emergence of a renewed beige-American majority. At the same time, however, American mass commercial culture continues a two-hundred-year-old dependence on African-America for its distinctive vitality. While *Spy Kids* blazed a trail for beigeness in the spring of 2001, the individual talents of a bevy of black comedians, including Eddie Murphy, Martin Lawrence, Chris Tucker, and others were being loaded into big movie guns aimed at another big summer-movie box-office season. These movies were not being targeted to any particular racial or ethnic group, any more than a Pampers commercial featuring a Latina-looking mom or the second (2001) season of the Budweiser "Whassup?!" commericals were. They merely reflect what the renewing majority of the market wants to see, in a context they can accept. A version of *Spy Kids* that was identical except for the lead characters being black would have been accepted, too, I think, but the characters would have been seen as black, not as beige. And the filmmaker, if he too was black, would probably have insisted upon having them seen that way.

The African-American's place in what Lind calls "Transracial America,"[21] which we both want to see coming, remains, ironically, uncertain, given the considerable cultural and political leadership that blacks have contributed and will continue to contribute to bringing it to fruition. To be sure, there is a certain chicken-and-egg quality to explaining the contradiction. The thing that separates black Americans from all so-called immigrants of color, and the thing that dooms the "people of color" coalition to a historical footnote, is not the African-American experience of slavery. It's the subsequent formation of an identity rooted in a sense of racial minority status that's unique in the world. This identity flows directly from the legal, social, and political shackles that have historically all but precluded the possibility of tossing the one drop rule into the fire and jumping into the American melting pot with abandon. We black Americans are culturally and emotionally unprepared to fully imagine ourselves as part of any majority, even when it's just us. In black-run cities like Atlanta and Detroit, black identity centers on an ineffable but indelible sence of minority status that is almost alien to Cuban-American Miami or Mexican-American San Antonio. How can African-Americans, as a group, ever see themselves as part of a majority that includes whites, Hispanic, or otherwise? Only by being willing to elevate individual identity a little bit higher than group identity, as every other group in the United States slowly but surely does. It's been nearly fifty years since *Brown v. Board of Education* and thirty-six years since the passage of the Voting Rights Act. A full generation of black Americans has seen barriers to individual cultural freedom only go down rather than up in their lifetimes. The defining question about blacks in twenty-first-century America is no longer the one that W.E.B. DuBois posed "what America will do about the color line." The question is who will continue to hold that line tightly stretched across black America's throat and why. The marketplace of commercial culture, I believe, is already mostly letting it go—with some important exceptions—and as it does, American norms, political and otherwise, will follow suit.

There's no question that black America has been held captive by the one-drop rule. The question is whether, after all these years, the captive and the captor have changed places. In the next chapter, I'll discuss the promulgation of an unmeltable black identity in the marketplace and the infrastructure that is now struggling in vain to maintain it.

8

The Rise and Fall of Ethnic Marketing: What Race Had to Do with It

Before sorting the facts and the fictions of ethnic marketing's long slow rise through the 1970s, its sharp mid-1980s upward spurt, and its sharper early-1990s decline, it's important to remember that minority marketing has meant many different things to its key constituencies: minority-owned media and marketing firms and their political/civil rights allies; government overseers of affirmative action policies; corporate marketing, community relations, and other executives; mainstream media and marketing firms; and finally minority consumers themselves. Over time their goals and expectations have both coincided and clashed, as differing agendas crossed paths with the profound demographic, political, technological, and cultural shifts of the last two decades of the twentieth century. Still, when future histories take the measure of the ethnic-marketing era, they will agree on one thing: It jumped off when marketers started to recognize the power of black consumer markets and respect its advocates, and it faded when the same marketers became more thoroughly convinced of the power of nonwhite cultures themselves, especially black culture, over all American consumers.

Somewhere in the middle, ethnic marketing got an important second wind from the sharp growth in Hispanic and Asian immigrants. Today, as African-American ethnic marketing heads for a long slow sunset, targeting

specific minorities with sizable investments in advertising and special promotions in ethnic media is more and more about reaching Hispanic- and
Asian-Americans in Spanish and in Chinese and other Asian languages. This
chapter is therefore almost entirely devoted to African-American target marketing because, while Hispanic and Asian targeting owes its ongoing vitality,
and viability as a business, to language barriers associated with specific ethnicities, black target marketing is about race and the politics of race in business as well as in culture. I will, however, return to the distinctions between
race targeting and language targeting near the end of the chapter.

Modern ethnic marketing—variously called target or multicultural marketing—has its roots in the ambitions of the black men who sought to pick
up the pieces of the civil rights struggle after the deaths of Malcolm X, the
Kennedys, and Martin Luther King. Surveying the post–King assassination
riot-torn landscape of black America and accepting the reality of Republican
president Richard Nixon and the Silent Majority backlash, these men publicly and loudly concluded that the only place to lead the black community
now was to the bank. They also concluded, in the privacy of their own
circles, that they would be first in line to cash the checks; that's what American capitalism was all about. The point cannot be overstressed: Black ethnic
target marketing was always a subset of a larger agenda of black wealth creation. The goal was never to maximize the welfare of the black consumer, as
measured by satisfaction with the goods and services available to this economically emergent class. The goal was to maximize the community's
wealth, starting with those entrepreneurs who were most capable of harvest-
ing the accumulated political gains of the civil rights struggle. What grew
into ethnic target marketing has always been a means to the same end and is
rooted in a political demand for economic empowerment. It is no coincidence that when *Black Enterprise* magazine founder Earl Graves made one of
his first successful advertising sales calls on a *Fortune* 500 corporation, he took
with him, not marketing or sales professionals, but civil rights activists
turned politicians:

> In the summer of 1971, the vice president of marketing for Hertz-
> Rent-a-Car Company received an odd request for a meeting with
> three black men, two of whom were legislators from Georgia. . . .
> One was State Representative Julian Bond, who had been a found-

ing member of the Student Nonviolent Coordinating Committee (SNCC). . . . Another was John Lewis, who had been the leader of SNCC and was also antiwar and civil rights activist. Julian led off our presentation. He spoke briefly on why he felt it was vital that corporations such as Hertz be responsive to the minority market. John Lewis followed with his own version of the same theme.

Then my door-busters got out of the way so I could get down to business. I reeled off statistics about the nation's emerging black middle class. . . . Meanwhile, Julian and John sat quietly . . . as I hit the Hertz man with figures on the number of Hertz cars rented each year by minorities—statistics he had never heard before. Finally, I went for the gold. Looking the marketing boss in the eye, I demanded that he show his appreciation and awareness of his loyal African American customers by purchasing full page color ads in several issues of *Black Enterprise* during the next several months. He didn't know what hit him. He said yes, and Julian, John and I got out of there before he could change his mind.[1]

Hertz, Graves noted, was still advertising in *Black Enterprise* in 1997, when his semiautobiographical black business advice book was published. The political part of Graves's original pitch, though frayed at the edges and faded like an old photograph, still has traction. Being seen as supporting the black community by supporting Graves's magazine is worth the price, even at the premium cost per thousand readers that the smallest (370,000 guaranteed circulation in 2000) of the big-four black-owned magazines offers advertisers. In fairness, Graves, and all the founding fathers of the magazines positioning themselves as the gateways to the loyal attention of black consumers, were fighting a nearly straight-uphill battle against a fundamental indifference to their arguments whose racial basis was sometimes not even thinly veiled. The dramatic results of the 1980 and 1990 censuses and any number of research studies in between, coupled with new and newly accessible technologies for exploiting such data, would later give black-owned media much more powerful tools with which to press their pure business case. Aggregate black income was rising faster than the national average in the 1980s, and it could more easily be proven in quantitative terms that black people buy almost everything white people do and in some key product areas disproportionately

more. It could also be argued, though with much less analytical rigor, that
while black consumers are well and easily reached by mainstream television,
newspapers, and magazines, a message delivered in *Black Enterprise, Essence,*
or *Ebony* is much more effective, despite a lower frequency of delivery,
because they are the chosen, trusted guardians of the black community's
welfare.

But Graves, a tough talking ex-Marine, had to build his business on what
was readily available to black entrepreneurs at the time: white guilt and
government-mandated affirmative action. Disgruntled former *Black Enterprise* staffers, and they are legion, say Earl Graves Ltd. never did bother to
learn and adopt standard industry best practices for selling a magazine to
advertisers, because Graves, perhaps concluding early on that the written
rules would never be fairly applied to his business, had already perfected the
strategy of aligning support for *Black Enterprise* with support for the black
community and the tactic of promoting his business as one of the community's few legitimate primary conduits for communicating that support. The
other two dominant black magazine publishers have been more subtle and
less overtly political in advocating their own cause, but they are no less committed to the notion that their publications offer a significant, however intangible, additional value to advertisers because their black-owned books
were perceived as the community's own, and black folks are strongly motivated to believe, trust, and support their own. Even as late as 1999, long after
it became apparent that black women rely on a host of woman-oriented
information sources with little or no racial identity value attached, at least
inside the covers, *Essence* cofounder Ed Lewis defended the integrity of
the core argument he and the others used to justify their their books to corporate advertisers. In an interview for one of my "Business & Race"
columns, Lewis said:

> We've often said that black women read these [*Cosmopolitan, Vogue,
> Mademoiselle,* etc.] magazines. But if you want to effectively reach
> them, you should be in the magazine they see themselves in consis-
> tently, month in and month out. I believe the argument [that an ad
> in *Essence* means more to the black reader than an ad in *Cosmopoli-
> tan*] is more convincing than ever. Certainly our ad pages have

grown—as the industry has. I want to believe they're not [buying ads] out of social reasons.

At the same time, about six months before Lewis and cofounder Clarence Smith sold 49 percent of *Essence* Communications to Time-Warner, effectively becoming a unit of the world's largest mainstream (read: white) communications firm, Lewis complained that selling advertising remained unreasonably difficult, as whole categories of products still refused to come into the book. But according to Clarence Smith, in a separate interview with me, *Essence* was commanding a premium price for its ad pages and carrying more than a thousand of them per year.

What gives? How can ad pages be flourishing while whole categories— notably banking and financial services, import luxury cars, travel, consumer electronics, and major fashion names like Levi's—remain immune to the central logic of black-owned media's sovereignty over black consumers? In general, beyond the particular situation facing black-owned media, why has rising recognition of disproportionate black buying power and rapid spending growth in products like luxury cars and financial and travel services not translated itself directly into growth in business for advertising and marketing firms specializing in black consumers?

The answer is that the advertisers, with the advice and counsel of their general-market large advertising agencies, never much bought black-owned media's affinity marketing argument. I was told this by Byron Lewis, founder and CEO of UniWorld Group in New York. UniWorld has been one of the largest, oldest, and best-known black-owned ad agencies since the modern era of black media/marketing began in the early 1970s. It is also one of only four black ad agencies of any size left standing in 2001, and then, like the other three, only by dint of significant equity investment, if not constructive control, by large white general-market firms. UniWorld is 49 percent owned by WPP Group. Not withstanding Ed Lewis's desire to believe otherwise, UniWorld's Byron Lewis insists that the primary motivation for most of the advertisers buying space through his agency has in fact been "social," a response to perceived political pressure to keep faith with the black community by aggrandizing its entrepreneurial representatives. Research, of course, has also helped persuade more and more firms, in certain competitive mass-market categories, of the black consumer's importance to their bottom line. But even the beer, soft drink, and fast-food companies, long the backbone of any black- and later Hispanic-owned or -oriented media business's revenue stream, never spent product-advertising dollars with minority media on a pro rata basis (i.e., if blacks drink 20 percent of the product, then 20 percent of the total ad budget would be spent with black-owned media and/or created by black ad firms). Most corporate marketers, as the 1980s began, were just responding to subtle and not-so-subtle political pressure, periodically laid on by Jesse Jackson or the NAACP, with a suitably political response: community-relations programs. Corporations learned to give up corporate image advertising dollars rather than the far more numerous, bottom-line, brand-advertising dollars. The message in these ads targeting blacks and, to a lesser extent, Hispanics in English was "I acknowledge your importance, and I salute you and what your leaders tell me I should salute." Lewis told me that at a certain level the black media and marketing communication venture was never a business-based enterprise. Instead, he said, it was "a conscience-based business."

> The general agencies didn't even come into that; there wasn't enough money in it. You work the black papers—you do *Ebony, Jet, Black Enterprise*—yes, you could do black-owned radio—and the word was *black-owned*. That was the key thing. Because [slapping the table for emphasis] that's how they kept their licenses, and good standing for government contracts. They were able to say, "We advertise on black-owned stations, we hire black contractors." They were quotas—I really don't want you to be misled on this point. That was the primary thrust, with some exceptions, of how [minority-targeted] advertising got started, how black media got business, and how black agencies functioned.

The fact that corporate America never broadly bought the argument for marketing to blacks in a "black way," that is, in self-consciously black-owned media using creative calculated to be "culturally relevant" to African-American consumers, doesn't mean that that argument was invalid on its face. From the beginning certain categories and firms—Anheuser-Busch in beer, Philip Morris in cigarettes, Coke in soft drinks, Smirnoff in spirits, and McDonald's in fast food—recognized the crucial share points and fractions of share points against cutthroat competition that could be gained by target marketing—or lost by letting a competitor beat them to it. What those firms had in common, said Lewis, was a distribution structure that closely tracked the movement of unit volumes from the grassroots, on a store-by-store, neighborhood-by-neighborhood basis. "Wherever the clients knew, from their retail involvement, that the black customer had a critical business value," said Lewis, "they became the first mass marketers to be in black media on a consistent basis."

Other factors also propelled the spread of target marketing against the inertia of indifference or the outright rejection of mainstream marketers. UniWorld got its first break into making lucrative television commercials targeted to the blacks and Hispanics for Avon in 1976, primarily because the cosmetics firm's huge direct marketing force included a disproportionate number of black and Hispanic women. Even when they failed to commit their main marketing budgets to minority markets, in the affirmative-action-friendly Nixon-Ford years more and more firms saw the value of establishing good minority community-relations programs. Community-relations programs necessitated increased hiring and promotion of minority executives into visible positions to represent the company to minority communities. It's an almost funny joke now about all the vice presidents of something with "community" in the title from the 1970s and early 1980s whose primary function was to smile for the cameras while handing out checks to the NAACP or the United Negro College Fund. They were, as Doug Alligood of BBDO New York used to joke, "vice presidents of being vice president."

They were, at first, almost exclusively black, because blacks were by far the largest recognized minority group (Hispanics still being somewhat unrecognized at the time) and, more important, because the political clout in favor of affirmative action was exclusively wielded by black politicians and activists. To this day no Hispanic or Asian leader comes close to striking the kind of fear in the corporate heart that Al Sharpton and Jesse Jackson do—or used to. Nonblack minorities, especially Hispanics, grumbled, took notes, accepted the leavings, and bided their time as the African-American agenda dominated the nascent ethnic-marketing industry. The high point was best symbolized by the aggravated state of commercialization of Black History Month in the late 1980s. By 1992 the late, legendary black advertising pioneer Caroline Jones was moved to complain about how every corporation in America was calling her to do something for February—then seemed to forget her number for the next eleven months. That year, when every other campaign seemed to star the then recently retired Supreme Court justice Thurgood Marshall, I quoted Byron Lewis in my *Wall Street Journal* column calling Black History Month "recession proof" and "part of their annual planning" for companies in the market "for the long haul."

Looking at it from a more recent vantage point, one that even he couldn't fully see coming in 1992, Lewis is a lot more candid and just a little bitter about the truth of the matter.

> It was "If we're gonna show our appreciation to black consumers and be visible to black consumers, why don't we take advantage of Black History Month?" So the majority of token efforts went into the merchandising of Black History Month. In January–February everybody got a little something, but it wasn't really advertising to reach the market from a business perspective. It was "We care." It was the ancillary budgets, with some exceptions. None of it was because they thought it was necessary. None of it because they thought they had to do something special. They were forced to.

To be sure, Lewis's business had grown from nothing to a multimillion-dollar enterprise by 1992 and like most of the fairly closed circle of black media/marketing magnates, he was fairly wealthy and, perhaps more important, extremely influential as a black community communication gatekeeper. Together with the activist leadership that helped them get off the ground, the black media/marketing leadership came close to controlling the cultural, political, and social agenda of black America. They were, and continue to be, showered with all manner of awards and accolades from a host of black institutions and causes that they favor, and by the white mainstream corporate sponsors that ultimately pay all the bills. After so many years at the head of the table they constructed, perhaps they could be forgiven for becoming almost reflexive in identifying and actually equating their own economic success with that of the black "community" as a whole. But not quite.

The example that sticks out the most in my mind is a Christmas 1995 "Letter from the Publisher" by *Black Enterprise*'s Earl Graves that basically enjoined readers to be sure to spend their holiday dollars in ways that built the black community. How were they to know with whom to spend such community-building dollars? Well, the front-of-the-book piece with Graves's picture told them, the first place they should look was to the companies that advertised in *Black Enterprise*. After all, the piece suggested, these firms support *Black Enterprise*, and *Black Enterprise* supports black America.

Graves, of course, was never called on the logic of identifying his own magazine business—one of just three private black firms that still control the lion's share of all advertising dollars flowing to black-targeted magazines—with the good of the black public. Like the publishers of *Essence* and the venerable mothership of all black publications, *Ebony*, *Black Enterprise* has thrived on representing the obligation that white corporate America has (or at least says it has) to support black America. Robert Johnson's Black Entertainment Television has held a similar position in black-targeted television all by himself. To an extent, these firms have always passed on some of that support, in charitable contributions, business opportunities, and a certain kind of public advocacy and leadership for causes like ending apartheid in South Africa. But for all their good works and better intentions and for all the self-serving awards, they cannot escape the judgment that while they lay some justifiable claim to *represent* the black community as a market, they are not *accountable* to it. They are not even accountable to the public debt or equity markets, in which African-Americans also participate, for how they manage their businesses or disclose business information.

Interestingly, in the many interviews I've done with the big-three publishers and BET's Robert Johnson (whose holdings have also included print vehicles), they have never acknowledged a contradiction in stewardship without accountability beyond the judgment of subscriptions, newsstand sales, and ratings. In an unforgettable 1998 interview, *Ebony* founder John H. Johnson addressed the subject with astonishing candor. But before we hear him, it's important to first understand who John H. Johnson is.

He started *Ebony* (then titled *Negro Digest*) on a shoestring in 1949 (he launched its remarkably durable sister publication, *Jet*, in 1951) and built an empire almost entirely below the white institutional radar. *Ebony* is still the number-one monthly black magazine, with a circulation of about 1.7 million, and Johnson Publishing has a perennial lock on one of the top three or four spots on the annual *Black Enterprise* list of the largest black businesses. To say that he is revered by the boys' club of black media and marketing entrepreneurs, many of whom got their start directly or indirectly because of Johnson, is a severe understatement. He is worshiped, even by the most jealous of the children born of his entrepreneurial spirit. Grown men who decades earlier cut their teeth with Johnson, then went on to success in their own right, still refer to him as "Mr. Johnson" even when he's not in the room. He rarely gives interviews, to black or white media; he's never seen a great need for exposure in anybody's pages but his own.

For twenty years, until *Essence* and *Black Enterprise* came along, Johnson had the black magazine business entirely to himself. And for twenty years, he makes a point of noting whenever I've heard him speak, he never got so much as a bank loan, much less equity capital, from white institutions. I asked Johnson to comment on a controversy surrounding the fast-rising tide of "white" capital trying to flow toward media businesses targeting black consumers. Johnson said it was a free country and that up-and-comers with hot ideas were free to get backing from wherever they could. He gave faint praise to the apparently successful *Vibe* magazine, then three years old, only lightly damning its nonblack ownership, because *Vibe* was making it without directly competing with him or the other major black-owned titles.

In truth, his own efforts, and those of BET's Robert Johnson, to score with magazines aimed at the younger and male black readers that have flocked to *Vibe* had already failed miserably. Nevertheless, he made it clear that if he had a viable product serving that black segment, he would take great offense at someone like, say, Time-Warner, a major investor in *Vibe* at the time, helping a young black entrepreneur to compete against him. "I don't think a black person ought to be part of any white-media-bankrolled competition against other black media," Johnson told me, seeming to take pains to direct his fire at the would-be upstart black publisher, not the white capital. He went on to say that the very fact of black ownership was as essential to the value of a publication like *Ebony* as the content.

> I think that, innately, a great many black people distrust the white majority—and they believe what we say. Because they don't think we have any other motive; my success is their success.

At that point I had to ask Johnson about what seemed to be a legion of young black entrepreneurs who had come to him over the years, like Dorothys to the Great and Powerful Oz, seeking backing for new, presumably noncompeting magazine start-ups, only to come away empty-handed. In ten years covering the business and race beat, if I had a dime for every black entrepreneur who had a tale of woe and disillusion after finally gaining an audience with John Johnson, or any of the big-four black media magnates, I could retire—or start my own magazine! Johnson's flat response was that none of the ideas brought to him were ever good enough. "I'm not gonna invest in something I don't believe in," he told me. I followed up by asking why, after nearly a hundred years of publishing experience between them, the big-three publishers had produced only four successful titles to serve a black population of over 35 million that, many argue, still has a considerable unmet demand for more and better black magazines. He responded by suggesting that the four titles, while not competing with one another, were doing a superior job competing against everyone else—including white media.

"After all this time, why is there only one *Wall Street Journal*?" Johnson asked in the interview for my *Wall Street Journal* column. "I think it's because you do a better job, and I think [there are only four major black magazines] . . . because we do a better job. Chew that and swallow it."

"But," I persisted, "if the established black publishers have the stewardship and special loyalty of the black consumer market, and if they expect to be protected from competition funded by white capital, don't they have a parallel obligation to innovate, to do among themselves what more open competition would otherwise force, for the good of the black consumers?" In the early 1990s, for example, the original publisher of *Heart & Soul*, a now modestly successful health-and-fitness book aimed at black women, was forced to seek backing from the white-owned Rodale Press after he failed to reach an agreement with any one of the major black publishers. Why, I asked Johnson, wasn't he the one to help launch something like *Heart & Soul*?

> A good answer is, we didn't want to start one. I once rejected the idea of starting a black *Playboy*. It might have made money, but I didn't want to do it. *The race can't tell me what magazines to start. It can only tell me what people do or do not want when I start it. Why do we black publishers have to start everything?* (emphasis added)

His last question was emphatically rhetorical. And though I could have challenged it by the facts of his earlier statements, I chose not to; his question really did answer for itself, and it told me something I will never forget. Indeed, the black "race" does not tell Johnson or any black media entrepreneur what to do, any more than the white "race" tells the publishers of *Time* or *Vanity Fair* what it wants in a magazine; that's what market forces are for. But as long as anyone remembers, certainly for all of John Johnson's lifetime, the market had always failed the black consumer. Mainstream white media and marketing capital had mostly ignored the black market, leaving the field potentially wide open for an entrepreneur like Johnson if he could do it entirely on his own. Later, as Byron Lewis said, affirmative action and the post–civil rights political climate provided the foundation on which the post-1960s black media firms could be built. But affirmative action is not the market; it's a political response, not a market response. The failure of affirmative action, in this context, is its assumption that the market, for ownership as well as consumers, is naturally segregated based on skin color and that its needs can be effectively met by accommodating the demands of its unelected leaders. Affirmative action saw no need to examine Johnson's assumption that, as far as the black community was concerned, "my success is their success."

Much as affirmative action in the societal sphere displaced and then almost silenced the much more challenging ideal of genuine racial integration as a goal, affirmative action in support of black-targeted marketing spared mainstream white media and marketers the challenge of really integrating everything—from the workforce in big advertising agencies and corporate marketing departments, to the look and feel of television commercials, to the roles available to people of color on stage and screen—everything!

White America, corporate and otherwise, was clearly and solely to blame for over seventy years of market failure before the brief heyday of affirmative-action-driven target marketing from the late 1970s to the late 1980s. But black media and marketing entrepreneurs must take a share of the blame for what the market has failed to deliver since then. However noble their assumptions when they began, as their wealth and ambitions for the flow of marketing dollars against their target increased, so did their vested interest in controlling that flow, by keeping white corporate capital out, to keep themselves running the game. At the same time, they never—with the partial exception of BET's Bob Johnson—thought it necessary to run their firms in such a way as to tap significant white capital, public or private, to widen the range and raise the quality of their products. Black consumers might have grumbled, but in the face of continuing indifference from the mainstream of media and marketing and the sense of political abandonment that set in with the Reagan years, the producers of black media were still seen as a bulwark of black pride. And they knew it.

They could have invested in new magazines or "superstar" black talent (in the days when they could have done so at a relative bargain price) or in emerging technologies (when they were still cheap, too). They could have made it their business to pay whatever it took to hire the well-educated talent that started coming out of top schools by the late 1970s in a steady flow. If they were sure they didn't want Wall Street, and that the feeling was mutual, they could have figured out how to consolidate to create firms of scale that could make it to a new level without reliance on the public equity markets. The could have moved aggressively in the 1980s to capture the genuine diversity of black aspiration and the real experience of a burgeoning black middle class that was moving beyond the sense of limitation and isolation that dominated its thinking just a decade earlier. They could have innovated to catch those new black dollars as soon as they were earned.

But they did not—or perhaps in fairness, they *could not*—escape the limitations of their race-based business model once it was in full operation. Instead, the powers of black-owned and -targeted media and marketing put most of their energies into maintaining and expanding their share of the affirmative action quota being dispensed from above, and they put the remainder of their clout into expanding the entire affirmative action pie through politics. Instead of focusing on satisfying black consumer demands, they focused on conditioning the demands of black cultural politics (well within their capabilities, since they controlled media credibility in that area) and then satisfying those demands. Instead of owning the black market itself, they aimed for what Byron Lewis called "ownership of the black psyche," and for a time, it seemed, they had it.

There's an infamous story in black media and marketing circles about a remark made by a hapless Revlon executive in the early 1980s to the effect that, if it wanted to, Revlon could knock out all the leading black-owned hair-care-product manufacturers with a flex of its marketing muscle and vast capital resources. It is somewhat ironic, given Revlon's recent financial woes, but it was deadly true back then. However prescient, it was also stunningly impolitic, and it provided the shot in the arm that gave the black-owned hair firms, which had a little more than half the market at the time, their last-lease extension on life as they had known it.

Before going on, I must point out that the unique demand for black hair products created the only sizable black-owned manufacturing industry in American history, with an informal but vital relationship with the new black media firms of the 1970s that almost approached vertical integration. Mostly based in Chicago, like *Ebony,* the black hair care firms were the charter advertisers in *Essence* and *Black Enterprise* when they began. Johnson Products (no relation to Johnson Publishing, which also confused matters with its own small hair and larger cosmetics line) will always be better remembered in the black market as the founding sponsor of *Soul Train* than for being the first publicly traded black-owned firm. Black hair firms provided the only revenue stream available to black media firms that was not driven by any affirmative action mandate, and as such they reflected the very height of pride in black accomplishment to date.

So the barons of black hair, including Soft Sheen, Johnson Products, and Proline of Dallas, used the misguided alleged Revlon comment as a spur to rally black opinion to the cause of supporting black-owned firms. It worked, but only for a hot minute. Despite only lukewarm editorial support from the major black media it had nurtured just a decade years earlier, the black hair industry bought some time to hang on to the exploding profits from the infamous Jheri Curl. The "curl" was by far the most successful product developed in the late 1970s that offered the politically incorrect benefit of removing most of the natural kink from black hair. And for the first time, black men were major consumers of the product, potentially doubling the size of the market not only for the straighteners but for the highly profitable maintenance products that the processed hair required. But even as they were winning that battle to innovate and market, the black firms were about to become the first major casualties in the larger war that has since devastated the very concept of black target marketing and even black-owned business itself.

The curl first took off after an exceptionally glossy *Ebony* cover with the Jackson Five sporting the 'do, a few years before Michael took over the world as a solo act. But right there in Chicago, under the nose of Soft Sheen, the dominant Jheri Curl maker, and *Ebony*, another brother named Michael was starting to make a name for himself as a media and marketing icon. Everyone knows what "His Airness" did for the processed hair look. And that, of course, was the least of his impact on mainstream marketing culture and the larger revolution Michael Jordan both inspired and personally represented. While the black-hair-care barons were so worried about the threat of white capital from firms like Revlon, Michael Jordan slam-dunked the foundations of their industry. Actually he did it with an assist from black filmmaker/comedians like Spike Lee, Eddie Murphy, and Keenen Ivory Wayans, who savaged the icky-sticky curl unmercifully in their breakthrough work. Almost overnight, by sometime in 1986, no self-respecting, upwardly mobile black man would be caught dead with a Jheri Curl. The overall market for black-hair-care products, which had experienced record growth in the beginning of the 1980s, took a nose-dive. When it recovered, not only were longtime white-owned brands of traditional, pre-curl products, like Alberto-Culver's TCB and Carson Products' Dark & Lovely stronger than ever, but new white-owned brands, most notably African Pride (yes, African Pride), had capitalized on the boom in braided hair styles and were dominant players in that niche. The old black hair business was also wounded by the rise of a broad selection of "ready to wear" hair products like hair weaves and extensions, whose distribution was dominated by Asian immigrants. By 1999 almost all the biggest names in black-owned hair care found themselves with no better options than to be acquired by large multinational corporations, including Soft Sheen, Johnson Products, and Proline.

The Jordan effect on the industry was inadvertent and was certainly unmotivated by any prospect of financial gain. And of course the trends that swept up the black-owned hair business were much bigger, with much deeper economic roots, than Jordan's fashion leadership at the time. But it's still no coincidence that Jordan, Lee, Murphy, and Wayans were in the first wave of a sea change in the relationship between African-Americans and mainstream commercial culture. And it's no accident that the black-hair-care business was first to succumb to the trend that has since confined what remains of the black-owned media and marketing industry to a diminishing role as niche players in what was supposed to be their own market. The black hair firms, as it happened, were especially dependent on the pre-Jordan, pre-transracial commercial culture status quo for their existence. To the extent that they used black celebrity talent to promote their product, it had always been "black stars" like singer Anita Baker, whose appeal and marketing potential, despite enormous talent, was largely confined to the black community. Michael Jordan represented the biggest of several black commercial icons whose power was primarily based not in the black market but in the much larger mainstream market. Even a consolidated black hair industry could not have paid Jordan enough money to grow his hair or to limit his potential as a national and multinational marketing icon by endorsing a black niche product. Think about it: In 1980 a great many successful black artists would have been elated for the opportunity to appear on *Soul Train* and grateful for the sponsorship of Johnson Products that made it possible. By 1990 being on *Soul Train* was merely part of a much larger marketing plan that included reaching that *portion* of the black audience that could be snared only by a such a racially targeted vehicle. The standard for success was now making it to MTV.

The opening up of mainstream television and movies to black entertainment talent was paralleled by the opening up of some new corporate ad budgets to buy more pages in the big-four black magazines. On top of the affirmative action motive, which was still in effect, some major mainstream fashion and beauty names—Revlon, Cover Girl, Maybelline, and later Tommy Hilfiger come to mind—found value in extending their branding messages to African-Americans in targeted vehicles. More than any increase in sales, these marketers wanted to buy mind share with the emerging arbiters of what was cool, especially younger African-Americans. They were willing to pay top dollar, and the black publishers were more than willing to sell them space. *Essence* even relaxed an informal rule against using white models in ads. The resultant run-up in ad rates worked a hardship on the undercapitalized black hair firms, which were already reeling from the Jheri Curl bust.

Mind you, black hair products are still a very viable, profitable business that must of necessity be targeted to African-Americans. But as the worm turned, the black-owned industry was no longer a cause in the black community, no longer the only billboard you might see in the ghetto for something that wasn't tobacco or alcohol. Hair care was just another product—except that now it had to compete with Nike for that billboard space, and with Revlon for that precious (because it's still the only black women's book with national reach) double-truck ad space in the front of *Essence*. For reasons that were obvious, the black media and marketing magnates didn't bang the drum that loudly on behalf of their black hair brethren as they tried to fight back with a succession of "buy black" campaigns, which failed. But what was not obvious to the black media barons at the time was that competition from the suddenly browning commercial mainstream was steadily undermining their position, too.

The story of the rise and fall Black Expo USA almost perfectly captures the shearing effect that the forces of transracial commerce had on the old order of black marketing. Billed as "The Biggest Economic Event in the History of Black America," Black Expo USA began in 1988 by promising a wide range of small black-owned and, more important, black-minded businesses access to tens of thousands of black consumers over the course of a long weekend. The consumers, drawn by ads promising top-name entertainment and celebrities, fairly filled major convention centers in sixteen cities in 1992 at the height of Black Expo's success, with more than 400,000 paid admissions. While there were already a number of other local black expos, some many decades old, Black Expo USA founder Jerry Roebuck, a former concert promoter, aggressively built it into a national force with brazen salesmanship and a keen understanding of what drove the Black Expo business: saturation coverage from black radio. By this time the dominant station with the African-American market in most cities was black in every detail, except that it was owned by a white radio chain. Most such stations were more than willing to heavily promote Black Expo in return for the perception of being strong supporters of the community and of the values of black entrepreneurship that Black Expo espoused. They also got a few ad dollars, but that was almost beside the point. Black Expo was good content. Many stations did whole shows live from Black Expo, drawing ever-bigger crowds as the event progressed.

By the mid-1990s, while still positioning the event as bringing black merchants together with black consumers so as to keep the flow of dollars "in the family," the real money was in the larger and larger corporate sponsorship deals Roebuck was able to swing with brands like Coke, Pepsi, and Chrysler. When Black Expo suddenly folded in 1997, in a wave of unpaid bills and bitter accusations all around, insiders reported that a great many of the thousands of small entrepreneurs who had paid between $300 and $800 for a booth over the years had come away feeling they'd been ripped off, because, in the end, they were just one of a host of little guys selling the same T-shirts, books, or artwork on the basis of black affinity, heritage, and culture, while competing for attention with well-funded corporate entertainment or other special events that dominated the floor space. It's now clear that Black Expo USA was doomed to be another victim of the browning of mainstream commercial culture. At a time when you could see more and more of any black talent you wanted on a dozen different television stations and movie screens, who needed to go back to a crowded convention center for the second year? And when black consumers in every major metropolitan area with a decent-size black population and especially in the browning middle-class suburbs of Atlanta, New York, Washington, Chicago, Dallas, and Detroit found more and more malls catering to their needs, the only value in patronizing Black Expo's small black vendors was sociopolitical.

But Black Expo USA's end really began after a 1994 run-in with parts of the black community in Atlanta. In 1993 Atlanta's V-103FM, the black music station then owned by the Summit Broadcasting chain that had been Roebuck's Black Expo partner there, made a deal with Atlanta's Coalition of 100 Black Women to do a woman-and-family-oriented expo called For Sister's Only. The event was similar to Black Expo but with a greater focus on women-and-family-friendly issues like breast cancer screenings and nutrition. The coalition, a chapter of a national nonprofit black civic group, also received a $50,000 donation from V-103 to do more good works. It was more money than the group normally received at one time from any source—and was definitely $50,000 more than Jerry Roebuck had ever given it. The second For Sisters Only was deliberately set for the fall of 1994 so as not to compete with Black Expo, which was to be held in the spring. But Roebuck went ballistic. He accused the station of stealing his idea and of perpetrating a fraud by suggesting it was doing something for Atlanta's black community. He took to any media that would hear him but especially to black media to inveigh against

the facade of For Sisters Only being for the betterment and advancement of black women. It is not. We are misled into believing we're helping our community—that it's a black-run thing. Black Expo as a business is about strengthening our community, helping our businesses survive and get exposure. Now its message and mission may be diluted by a white company whose only interest is to make money.

When it was pointed out to him that he too was in business to make money and that, as a New Yorker, he wasn't really part of the Atlanta community, his answer was "I consider all of African-America, and Africa and the Caribbean too, as my community." Roebuck, I think, sincerely believed that the white-owned radio station had no right whatsoever to compete with a black entrepreneur in marketing to the black community, echoing the sentiments that John H. Johnson expressed to me a few years later. Privately, Roebuck also castigated the leadership of the Coalition of 100 Black Women for selling him out to a white-owned firm. Publicly he threatened to sue Summit Broadcasting (an empty threat on its face) and also campaigned in black media to get support for a big protest at the event itself. His early saber-rattling was enough to convince Summit not to go ahead with plans for a For Sisters Only expo in New York, where its black station, Kiss-FM, was in the process of FCC review of a pending sale to Emmis Broadcasting. At Roebuck's urging, the regional office of Jesse Jackson's Rainbow/PUSH Coalition picketed the September 1994 For Sisters Only expo in Atlanta—a spectacle that, I think, was the high point of folly and hypocrisy among the owner/leaders of the nominally allied black ethnic-marketing businesses.

"We even had Al Sharpton getting out of a white limousine, saying the coalition had prostituted itself," recalled Bunny Jackson Ransom, an Atlanta public relations entrepreneur when I interviewed her in 1997, at the time of Black Expo USA's ultimate demise. Ransom, former wife of former Atlanta mayor Maynard Jackson, was president of the Coalition of 100 Black Women during the 1994 dispute. "There were several complications inherent to the traveling Black Expo that we tried to explain to him [Roebuck] at the time he attacked us," said Ransom. "We were trying to make money for a cause, not for a profit. We were the cause!"

Ironically, Ransom noted, For Sisters Only had its biggest success the year it was picketed; it went slowly downhill every year thereafter. Back in 1994 she had tried to explain to Roebuck that in a remarkably short space of time, perhaps less than ten years, the expectations of the Atlanta black market had shifted in ways that played to the strength of mainstream marketers and mainstream media, and that the radio station had responded. In 1994 it was clear, at least to Ransom, that the market didn't need a black entrepreneur in between white capital, represented by the radio station, and its community event. Yes, it's true that Roebuck showed the radio station the value of promoting such events and how it could be done. But after that the radio station knew his role was expendable, and so did the community, as represented by the Coalition. By 1997 it was clear that the consumers' concern was with the product—the value they got for their admission dollar—and not for the politics of who owned it.

And in 2001 a check of the V-103 website showed that For Sisters Only was still going, with major corporate sponsors including KFC, Sprint, Ford (Lincoln), and Kroger. It billed itself as a "celebration of the power of Atlanta's African-American consumers" and their $18.8 billion buying power. The site promotes the opportunity for expo visitors to purchase "high quality goods." While there is a limit on the size of the firms that can rent space—at $895 to $1,000 a pop—the site makes no reference to black entrepreneurship and contains no nationalist cant about collective community economics; in fact, small vendors of any race are welcome to participate. The Coalition of 100 Black Women, if it's still involved, is not mentioned.

Jerry Roebuck may have been exceptionally brash and impious, compared with the older and better-established black media and marketing entrepreneurs and related public relations and consulting firms. But the lesson from his comeuppance is the same as that of the black-hair-care barons. In less than a generation since Martin Luther King was killed, the black consumer has come to assign little or no intrinsic value to race pride of ownership, or to cultural political correctness, in making consumption decisions or pledging brand allegiance. It's not that these things don't matter to black consumers— they do, but only at the margins, when all other things of monetary value are equal. And of course they are rarely equal, because this is capitalist America. To use Byron Lewis's terms, the black consumers psyche can only be rented with dollars directed toward the production of the goods, services, and brand images that African-Americans want to buy, regardless of who directs them and the political correctness of the product. The massive consumption of a great deal of hip-hop culture, with race images and messages that make NAACP types faint, is a screaming case in point.

Black-oriented—but not necessarily black-owned—media and black-targeted events and promotions will always play a role in delivering brand messages to the black market, but they will never play the primary role, and they may yet become even more marginal.

Why? Because the triumph of African-Americans in commercial popular culture has defeated the black-owned media and marketing industry's goal of gaining hegemony over the black marketplace. Increasingly, in fact, the future of targeting the African-American consumer is now in the hands of a new generation of minority marketing professionals at mainstream corporate marketers and, to a lesser extent, mainstream ad agencies, who are more like creative technocrats than entrepreneurs. Doug Alligood, senior vice president for special markets at BBDO, New York, told me that the key difference between the old entrepreneurs and the new professionals is in their attitude.

> The older mind-set was "The black community belongs to us; anyone else is an interloper." Today [the new black marketing professionals] have come to realize that the black community doesn't belong to *anybody*. The black community will go where it gets satisfaction; it is up for grabs.

At first the discovery of the crossover value of blacks in pop culture seemed like a boon, Byron Lewis recalled, because one of the first places it was recognized was in black radio ads like the kind he was creating for Burger King in the mid-1980s. As the hip-hop-formatted black radio stations (increasingly owned by large white chains) were gaining nonblack youth audiences, so were the black-targeted commercials. When marketers saw these commercials move the needle with white suburban youth, he told me, they took a new look at UniWorld's product.

> At that point they said, "Let UniWorld and black agencies do this music, because they can do it, and there are still the affirmative action mandates. Let that be their role." That didn't mean general-market firms couldn't do it, but they were kind of held off for a while.

Similar opportunities were opening in television. Chicago's Burrell Advertising, which has always seesawed with UniWorld for the title of largest black ad firm, made great breakthroughs with black-targeted ads for McDonald's that consistently tested well with young whites. These black crossover commercials were perfect for big parts of the new Fox and later WB and UPN network schedules, with their heavy youth and minority audiences. They also found increasing use on a wider range of programming that was reaching large numbers of some combination of younger and minority audiences. If they were not a national buy, the commercials often made their way into the mix in major urban markets like New York, Los Angeles, and Chicago on everything from professional sports to *Seinfeld*. The clients did increasingly insist that the work of the minority firms be closely consistent with the campaign images and tag lines in the general-market campaigns. But otherwise a window of opportunity opened for the black ad firms to compete with the big white firms using the newly discovered cachet of the culture they knew best. For Lewis and UniWorld, the window was open widest in 1993, when Burger King, in the midst of a management shakeup and between ad firms, invited UniWorld to bid for its entire interim general-market campaign, and UniWorld won it. "So from October 1993 through August 1994, we produced the national creative campaign for all markets for Burger King," said Lewis. "It was very, very flattering."

But even at that moment of triumph, Lewis saw the handwriting on the wall. Mainstream ad agency competitors' minds and checkbooks were now eager and open to take advantage of the trend and to sharpen their positions on the cutting edge. While Burrell Advertising made crossover-type commercials for Coke's Sprite brand using relatively hard-core hip-hop icons like rapper KRS 1, Coke's general-market agency had NBA star Grant Hill endorsing the product in its commercials and establishing the wildly successful "Obey Your Thirst" campaign message. The clients, said Lewis, never changed their view that the black firms' primary expertise was reaching the black market via black media. Meanwhile, their general-market agencies proved that they could use the flavor and sometimes even the substance of black culture in general media to sell not only to the majority but to blacks as well. And the general-market agencies were already positioned to extend their new creative expertise to a host of product categories that black agencies never got to touch, like financial services, prescription drugs, consumer electronics, and high-tech corporate image ads. No black agency had a shot at making those award-winning-cool Volkswagen ads that featured black characters or funky beats. It's not that they were excluded from the business, but that almost overnight African-American stars and black culture were far too big a commercial force to be controlled by black agencies, which were still relatively small shops compared with the major international players. They had no monopoly on the ideas, and—in perhaps the most bitter pill for Lewis to swallow—they had no particular lock on the talent itself, which, as in so many professional areas in the post–civil rights era, had many more bidders than back when Lewis and the other black industry leaders got started. The brain drain from the black-owned industry remains severe, he told me, and seems irreversible.

> While we are the dominant influence on those television sets and the dominant influence on the music . . . we don't *own* it, because it has crossed over into the mainstream market and the mainstream media. [General-market] advertising competitors say, "We can do that as well." The mainstream talent is black now, but no black agency that I know of has ever worked on a consistent basis with a major black superstar, because the mainstream money is in the white agencies. The black agencies have no way whatsoever of competing within this tide, because we're small, and because of the money that it takes to pay this talent—we don't have it in our budgets.

So the point is this: To profit from meeting the unmet black demand for attention from mainstream media and marketing, the leaders of the black target marketing industry developed what I'll call "commercial blackness" in the mid-1970s. Commercial blackness was about having a certain look and feel to black magazine editorial copy, black radio deejay chatter, and the ads that supported them both. It was almost entirely dependent on a fairly tight network of politicians, activists, and civil rights organizations to back up demands made by the leading black media entrepreneurs to compel more white corporate capital to enter the market—but only after passing through several pairs of black hands. Of necessity, old school commercial blackness was political—it defined itself by a fairly tight code of cultural and economic nationalist sensibilities and rules. For example, to be an officially black film, as far as the Black Filmmaker Foundation is concerned, two out of three of the film's director, producer, or writer must be black.

At the beginning black identity itself was naturally placed at the center of commercial blackness. After all, in the early 1970s the very term *blackness* was only just entering widespread polite use with a positive connotation. Who better to commercialize it, filling in the details of what was and was not black as they went along, than black media and marketing people? As Lewis recalled to me:

> When black magazines started, they were needed, because nobody was taking about blackness. That's why Earl [Graves] is a genius. Earl created black business, if you want to say it that way.

But the mainstreaming of black icons and black culture has made the old political blackness an endangered species, because to make it in the mainstream, the culture and the icons must be separated from the politics of blackness. In transracial commercial culture, Oprah, Bill Cosby, the brothers in the "Whassup?!" Budweiser commercials, Kobe Bryant, the black comedian in the 7-Up commercials, Samuel Jackson, and all the rest are clearly black in the way they walk, talk, run, and jump and especially in their attitude. They even, implicitly or explicitly, spoof white folks. But by definition, as mainstream stars, very few if any aspects of their appeal can be confined to their own racial group. The old school was about black talent modeling (as in "role modeling") blackness for the benefit of black audiences; the new school is about black talent simply being their black selves for any and everybody who tunes in. Even rappers, whose content is as specific to a certain black community experience as popular culture gets, as Lewis pointed out, don't market themselves according to the rules of the old political blackness. The day I interviewed him, he'd just returned from a much-hyped "summit" of hip-hop movers and shakers on issues of their concern. As usual, discussion centered on the threat of censorship and the general misunderstanding by social critics—especially black social critics—of hip-hop culture. Their indifference to any obligation to use their clout in the service of the black media industry made Lewis just sigh and shake his head.

> Nobody's politically black anymore—only [Reverend Al] Sharpton. Political blackness is old-fashioned. Not only that, it's not commercial. Politically black is old school. I gotta tell you, even the rappers aren't politically black, because they see that their opportunity to be movie stars—to tour the big venues—is with the white audiences. The rappers send almost no money back into the black community. They're beyond what we call the traditional black community—the inner city. Their fundamental culture comes from there, but you will not see a good base between them and black churches, for example.

"When I started this business," Lewis explained, slowly slapping the conference room table for emphasis, "blackness was a political situation. There wouldn't be black agencies if the civil rights agencies and affirmative action didn't create this niche for us. But as we become more successful, the culture is too big for that. They don't need us, truth be told."

He was speaking about black Hollywood, but his feelings clearly extended to all segments of the black talent base. He went on to paint a very dark picture for the few remaining black ad firms. In the previous three years, he said, three out of the four of any size remaining had become units of large multinational agencies. In keeping with the one card they still possessed that could not, for the time being, be trumped, they were all still 51 percent black-owned, allowing them to continue to qualify for credit toward clients' affirmative action goals.

❐   ❐   ❐

When Lewis began, UniWorld also provided help for a number of clients in targeting Hispanics. This policy was entirely in keeping with the idea that blacks and Hispanics have more in common with each other as people of color—especially Caribbean Hispanics—than they do with the white mainstream. While there may be a certain truth to that logic, the fact was that blacks were much better positioned to exploit the affirmative action opportunities becoming available, inasmuch as they had been the most vocal and organized in opening them up in the first place. Time, however, was on the side of the Hispanic ad agencies and the Spanish-language broadcast media. The number of Hispanic ad agencies has grown explosively in the 1990s, as the Spanish broadcasters they support have grown in reach and market power. It has often been reported and re-reported that the dominant Spanish radio or television station in New York, Los Angeles, Dallas, Houston, or Miami regularly weighs in at number one in ratings. Of course, given the fractured nature of major metro broadcast markets, it may take as little as a 5 percent share to be number one in radio, and no more than 15 percent in television. Still, the numbers seem to support the view that the future of minority-targeted media and marketing lies with Latinos—provided those numbers are counted *uno, dos, tres.*

Language, Lewis told me, is the reason there are now more Hispanic ad agencies flourishing in any one major Hispanic market than there are black agencies flourishing nationwide. The Association of Hispanic Advertising Agencies (AHAA), founded in 1996, boasts well over forty member firms. Membership is not constrained by Hispanic ownership status; indeed some of the biggest Hispanic agencies, including Conil (New York) and Bromley Communications (San Antonio), are units of mainstream general-market agencies. Bromley, the largest Hispanic agency, is 49 percent owned by the multinational BCom3 Group but is still 51 percent Hispanic owned—just enough to qualify for set-asides when that matters to them.

When the AHAA was formed, the Hispanic agency heads took pains to differ with Lewis's belief that Spanish—the inescapable fact that a significant portion of the market can be reached only via Spanish-language media—is the primary reason the AHAA agencies flourish. Anyone, including mainstream agencies, can translate words into Spanish, runs the Hispanic agency party line, but it takes deep cultural understanding and sensitivity to effectively translate feelings into Spanish. In some cases no effective translation is possible, and the Hispanic branch of an overall ad campaign must part ways with the mainstream English branch. For example, one Hispanic agency told the California Milk Marketing Association that its now-famous "Got Milk?" campaign and slogan wouldn't fly with Hispanics because the straight Spanish translation suggested a query about whether someone was lactating.

Instead, the slogan, loosely translated into English, became "Have You Given Them Enough Today?" Directed to mothers, it played into images of nurturing and family that are said to be central to the Latino psyche, as well as a bit of maternal guilt. Hector Orsi, president of La Agencia de Orsi in Los Angeles, one of the AHAA's founders, said that despite their perpetual movement toward greater U.S. acculturation, Hispanics will always be different in ways that begin with the language but go much deeper. Mainstream agencies, out of self-interest, tend to doubt his contention, he said, telling their clients to wait for most of the Hispanic marketplace to acculturate to their general-market campaigns. Hispanic agencies, in their view, were good only for people too green and too poor to be reached in English. Orsi told me,

> The attitude that I found generally in the business was that we had a ten-year window of opportunity in which to make out like bandits, after which all Hispanics would be tall, blue-eyed, prosperous, and English speaking. And of course they were wrong. No matter how much English you learn, you don't forget your Spanish, and you don't stop reacting to it. Even when they understand English . . . Spanish is not a language of ignorance—it's a language of choice.

There's something hauntingly reminiscent of the old lions of black media and marketing in the spirit of Orsi's claims, if not their substance. In my interviews with him and with other Hispanic advertising leaders, they firmly (but always politely) insist on defending their claim to cultural hegemony, a thick-walled fortress of identity that they maintain will always surround the Hispanic consumer market. And of course, they are the only true keepers of the keys to the kingdom. But, unlike the black-owned ethnic-market entrepreneurs, the Latinos have language and cultural differences that are distinct enough, at least for a sizable portion of the market, to give them a genuine advantage over purely Anglo-minded general-market competitors. While Hispanic political activists still try to reinvent the black political strategy for dislodging mainstream marketing dollars, the fact is that Hispanic entrepreneurs and professionals, if not the Hispanic community overall, have never really bought into the righteous victim identity that has always powered the black strategy. When it comes to "mao-maoing" Anglo-white America, most

Hispanic business leaders I've interviewed privately conclude, with sheepish regret, that their people are just too polite and say—at least to this black reporter—they wish they had an Al Sharpton. Quite a few others, however, openly disdain affirmative action and any suggestion that their status as minorities should be used as a basis for collective identity and private gain. *Hispanic Business* magazine publishes an annual list of the largest Hispanic-owned firms based on revenue, similar to the one that *Black Enterprise* made into the primary benchmark for black-owned firms. The editor once told me that the biggest problem with *Hispanic Business*'s list is that there's no telling how much of Hispanic entrepreneurship is not represented, because so many firms, if they can be identified as Hispanic at all, don't bother to return requests for information.

Hispanic, as we are slowly, finally, coming to recognize, is not a race. *Hispanic,* I must add at the risk of criticism, is not really a culture, either. *Mexican-American* is a culture. *Puerto Rican* is a culture. *Hispanic* is a term of art promulgated by the federal government to designate people of Latin American (but not Spanish) descent as an official minority group for affirmative action purposes. The only problem, as I've said, is that Hispanic people did not come to the United States to become a minority group à la African-Americans. And despite facing a certain amount of the same racism as blacks, they are not about to accept the historical racial perceptions and prejudices of some whites and white institutions as their reality.

There is a good amount of truth in what Orsi said about the Spanish language. But only time will tell how durable that truth will prove. Indeed, if Orsi, a dapper little man with big brown eyes who vaguely resembles David Hyde Pierce, the actor who plays Niles Crane on *Frasier,* is at all representative, Hispanics haven't become tall, blue-eyed Englishmen in the ten or so years that marketers have been wooing them. But he is prosperous, and he is effectively a white person of Latin American descent. So is every Hispanic media and marketing executive I've ever met. They are privileged success stories, in the classic American bootstrap mold, just like their African-American counterparts. But unlike the Earl Graveses or Robert Johnsons of the world, they legitimately aspire to fully enter the American mainstream in the same way that Italians, Jews, and every other European ethnic group entered it: through whiteness. And they know their market is heading that way, too. The only difference is that they will be more bilingual for much longer and will remain much closer, literally and emotionally, to their ancestral homes. Marketing to them, targeted or not, will evolve in a way that's consistent with these facts.

A June 2000 Associated Press wire feature story led with how Bromley Communications won the general-market account for the San Antonio Symphony's campaign to change its stuffy image. The nut of the story: As Hispanic agencies hone their English-language product aimed at bilingual and English-dominant Latinos, they're getting more opportunities to hit home runs in general-market campaigns. The story quoted the president of the AHAA saying that San Antonio Latinos were so "acculturated" that you had to target them in English as well as Spanish. But of course, even in English, the communication must still be "in culture," said Daisy Esposito-Ulla. Although it is doublespeak on her part, this remark does reflect the larger state of American cultural flux in which Hispanics play a pivotal role. The article cites a Simmons survey indicating that English is the preferred language among San Antonio and San Francisco Hispanics.

> And the cultures of San Antonio, Miami and other markets are so heavily Hispanic that the "culture has intertwined" and ads created with Hispanic market sensibilities can effectively reach other groups, Esposito-Ulla said. That phenomenon has led to a national ad campaign with a bilingual talking Chihuahua as spokesman for Taco Bell and Tex-Mex flavored ads for TacoCabana with actor Cheech Marin switching in and out of English and Spanish with the tag line "Mas food, less dinero."[2]

The ironies here, from the point of view of veteran black marketers, add up to the ninth circle of hell. While Hispanic culture may be lately "intertwining," African-American culture is both bred in the American bone and is more dominant than ever in history. Yet after thirty years in the business, Byron Lewis says it's just a matter of time before big white agencies effectively squeeze him out of the only part of the business he could ever get in. Meanwhile the Associated Press article about Hispanic agency crossover quotes Al Aguilar of the firm Creative Civilization in San Antonio. Aguillar is one of the three founding partners of the agency that preceded Bromley; like Lionel Sosa, he left to start another successful San Antonio ad agency. In the 1980s, Aguilar said, he would have been limited (presumably by racism) to targeting Hispanics in Spanish. Now he saw his firm, and himself, as squarely in the general market.

"We just happen to be Hispanic. It's a bonus," he said.

I doubt we will ever hear that from Earl Graves.

9

American Skin

In the beginning, somewhere in the fall of 1992, I was amazed by signs that, in the commercial popular culture that surrounded me wherever I went, my vision of the American dream seemed to be coming true in my lifetime.

But that's not why I had to write this book. The mission of this book has been sustained in me for nearly a decade because, as excited as I have been about all that has been and continues to be wrought, precious few people I have met or known seem to share my vision. And if they were excited in any way by, say, yet another black or brown face in the media spotlight representing the American everyman or everywoman, they barely let on. Even the supreme and very open exultation among my black friends and colleagues during the first flush of Tiger Woods "Tigermania" in 1997 died down to a very private, personal roar among black folks, like some pleasure reserved for the privacy of one's bedroom. We're still sky high over Tiger when he triumphs, and even though we know he cannot possibly win them all, or even win at the incredible pace he set in 2000 and early 2001, we will tune in to every competition he's in and willingly wager all our pride on his performance. But we talk very little about our investment in Tiger, and much less about a new commonplace thing like, say, a black woman modeling a mink stole in a Macy's ad or Jennifer Lopez hosting *Saturday Night Live*.

I had to write this book because I really believed that the changes, taken together, meant an answer was coming to the question posed in 1994 by the writer Jim Sleeper: "Is there an American identity skin that's thick enough for all of us to live in?"

Everything I thought I saw said the answer was an emphatic yes, though Sleeper, a friend and intellectual fellow traveler, wasn't so sure himself. Nevertheless, I thought and still think that Sleeper's question both updates and retires W.E.B. DuBois's now-classic assertion that the disposition of the color line was the question of the twentieth century. After all, when DuBois made this assertion circa 1903, the year *The Souls of Black Folk* was published, the twentieth century had not yet properly begun in terms of American popular culture. The world's mightiest marketing and communications businesses had not yet been born, and even when he died, just months before Martin Luther King's triumphant 1963 March on Washington, they were only just starting to bring their massive resources to bear on erasing sections of that color line that, as recently as the early 1980s, were still considered all but indelible.

But when I heard black people talking about the significance of all these changes, usually because I forced them to, their average attitude was somewhere between indifferent and dismissive. The same could be said for much of the writing of the black intelligentsia on the subject, except that it ranged from dismissive to downright scornful. Some black culture critics find no difference between the triumph of Chris Tucker at the box office and minstrelsy, albeit updated for a new century. And you don't have to be a published black public intellectual to point out that America's profound faith in Oprah's psychobabble and its fascination with Puffy's—er, P'Diddy's— hip-hop soap opera have not made one whit of difference in the sociopolitical relationships between whites and nonwhites. At least as far as the average black man-on-the-street can see.

White people seem to have seen little more of what I see. In some ways they manifest even greater enthusiasm for the triumphs of Tiger and of Michael Jordan before him. If they're into any kind of black-dominated music—and they all are—they don't have to be prodded very much to tell a black acquaintance (or even a sympathetic black stranger) about their allegiance to their favorite recording artists. But when pressed, they don't see that race has very much to do with any of it. They are, of course, aware of the racial uniqueness and triumph of Tiger and Oprah in the history of sports and entertainment celebrity, respectively. But even that awareness, and their broad but thin satisfaction at being part of the audience for such a change, seems to be quickly fading over time. After this many seasons, in golf and on TV, Tiger and Oprah just happen to be black, as far as they're concerned. Familiarity with the phenomenon of the mainstreaming of color does breed contempt, I think, in a distinct minority of whites, though they would never directly express it to me, a black man. But worse than contempt, familiarity seems to have bred in the majority of whites I've talked to the same range of indifference-to-dismissal that it does in African-Americans.

The dismissal end is the easy part to deal with, because no matter which race or group the dismisser belongs to—black, white, Hispanic, or Asian— he or she comes from the same place, the progressive left. The dismissal begins and ends with the point of view that nothing of political substance is changed by any of this, except perhaps that the culture produced by the most disadvantaged communities of our society is being exploited and expropriated by large corporate (read: white) entities on a massive scale while those communities continue to languish or worse.

But *indifference* to the idea that something significant is taking place, resistance to excitement beyond race pride or endorsement of symbolic social progress, is much harder to digest and requires examining. I see the nature of this resistance as divided between two categories of Americans: those who believe or assume they have white privilege, and those who do not believe or cannot assume they have white privilege. In the first group, capturing most white Americans, I include a great number of Hispanic whites and assimilated Asian-Americans who are not particularly invested in the politics of multiculturalism; the second group, of course, is overwhelmingly black but includes a significant number of Hispanics and Asians who are darker skinned or otherwise invested in racial identity politics. The resistance of the first group, as I'll explain, is essentially passive, while that of the second group is active. But the common reason for their failure to be moved (other than perhaps to go out and buy something) is the fact that commercial culture automatically strips the politics of race and ethnicity from nonwhite icons and culture. Even gangsta rappers aren't politically black in a sense that anyone over thirty-five would recognize. This brings us to the nub of it.

People with white privilege are massively motivated to ditch old-fashioned cultural whiteness. They can see the handwriting on the walls of a global economy in a nonwhite world. They smell the coffee. But they cannot accept that the new transracial cultural map should or could alter the social reality of white privilege. They gladly concede cultural privilege; they are oblivious to any implied political concessions. Power, as Frederick Douglass said, concedes nothing without a demand. All the browning of mainstream culture demands is a credit card, or not to change the channel.

People without white privilege are massively motivated to find affirmation and validation in the triumph of transracial culture. They swell with pride and amazement as each new development moves from breakthrough to commonplace. But they cannot take any of it seriously to heart unless it is accompanied by a measure of redress for a history of denial of our humanity that goes back to slavery. Without some kind of assurance that the society that is now so open to accept Oprah and Michael is just as ready to embrace anyone who looks like them but isn't a TV or basketball star, they cannot lower their emotional or intellectual defenses.

And me? I see myself as a black man who cannot assume possession of white privilege, although I have had the regular benefit of earned, borrowed, and reflected white privilege due to educational and professional accomplishments and relationships. I have always felt not so much suspended between black and white worlds as living in both with one world superimposed upon the other, each exerting a compensating gravitational pull on my gut. I survive and even thrive by controlling my focus on things, grouping the objects in my chosen field of vision as I move through this compound universe of cultural objects and values. In some senses, but especially in popular culture and lifestyle, all Americans simultaneously inhabit multiple worlds, materializing and dematerializing from one dimension or another at will, provided they have the cash and, for nonwhites, a certain degree of earned, borrowed, or begged white privilege.

One of the things I thought I saw, as an African-American, when I was first infected with this vision of a deeper meaning in the browning mainstream, was nothing less than the triumph of African-Americans in America's popular culture. As the history I've attempted to lay out shows, black Americans have been central to the invention of American cultural identity since the country was founded, and for just as long they have been denied recognition and open access to positions of respect and authority in that culture. Like most African-Americans, I too get flush with awe and swell with pride every time there's another "biggie"—Tiger at the British Open, Audra McDonald at the Tonys. I also like to claim a little bit of Hispanics like Jennifer Lopez as they score their own "biggies," like a hit record and hit movie in the same week, if only because (literally in her case, as a fellow Bronx native) we come from the same or similar positions as outsiders to the Anglo-white mainstream. I even get off on the triumphs of people I don't particularly admire—the artist formerly known as Puffy and O. J. come to mind—as they get away from outrages still carrying the benefit of doubt and aura of celebrity that were until very recently reserved only for famous rich white people. Soon after O. J.'s acquittal, I told anyone who'd listen that the artificial blackening of his face on the cover of *Time* magazine, while egregious, was not representative of the final media verdict on the not-guilty Hall of Famer. I told everybody that O. J. would retain a respectful, if infamous, celebrity status for as long as he could keep his nose relatively clean (i.e., not kill anybody except in self-defense) and that over time it might even slowly recover. I was right.

But unlike the majority of black folks, who are indifferent, dismissive, or hostile to the idea that there's some positive value in our triumph in popular culture, I don't require a similar triumph in the struggle against inequality in order to recognize that coup for what it is: a validation in our near-sacred free marketplace that's been long, long overdue. Nothing in this book is meant to even suggest that, because Eddie Murphy is a movie star and America can't get enough of J. Lo's capacious behind, the essential struggle for social equality and against the institutional racism that supports white privilege can or should now be suspended or even relaxed. Black people can't afford to think that way, and we can't let white folks reach that conclusion, either. But nor should we let the necessity of continued struggle blind us to what Eddie Murphy, and so many others I've mentioned, have won, and the fact that they won it for all of us, whether that was their intention or not.

There is a rough but significant correlation, even equivalence, between black alienation from the good news in commercial media and the general African-American state of denial of economic and social progress over the same period. Some polling data reveal among African-Americans a belief that things are getting worse, when most of the important socioeconomic indicators show nothing but improvement that is, in some categories, striking. While a set of statistics concerning the number of black men in prison are always rolled out to justify the pessimistic perception, African-Americans have actually been closing gaps in income and education that had long been thought unclosable. My vision for this book is not concerned with making the case for black socioeconomic progress in the last decades of the century. I refer to the discrepancy only to illustrate the emotional quality of reasoning that attends black assessments of our position in society. Perception may be reality for groups or individuals, but perception can be and usually is highly selective, based on emotional criteria, and this should be recognized. Personally, I choose to incorporate more of the positive data into the perceptions driving my reality because so far they're consistent with my experience. You don't have to embrace the tenets of the tedious black "movement" conservatives to maintain a healthy distance from finding identity in victimhood. All you have to do is find a way to make your mortgage and SUV payments on time. I still remember my father proudly flipping the half-empty stubs of his GM-Chevy car payment book in my face and telling me that "this is what every good American is supposed to have."

But let's keep this simple. At the end of the day, I think all the privately proud but publicly and intellectually indifferent brothers and sisters should apply what I'll call the Halle/Denzel utility test. Take a piece of paper and draw a line down the middle. Title one column "With" for "With American Skin," and title the other "Without." Near the top of the "With" column, write the following:

> I get up every morning knowing I face a struggle to succeed and be rewarded commensurate with my efforts and talents because I am black. I can't expect to enjoy the full range of privileges that automatically come with white skin on a consistent basis; on any given day, in a particular situation, I might be stripped of any illusion of privilege I've worked to achieve. Still, I go forward.

Now copy the same paragraph at the top of the "Without" column. Only add the following sentences:

Oh, and adding insult to injury, and making my life really boring, there are no prominent figures in popular culture who look like me. If I want to be entertained, my choice is between earnest but undercapitalized black media and other all black venues that, as hard as they might try and as talented as they might be, remain somewhat marginal to the larger culture to which I still belong; or mainstream state-of-the-art media and other venues in which people like me are rarely seen, much less in leading roles, and in which the cultural contributions of my communities are very rarely represented.

Now, to the "With" column, add:

When I come home, I can kick back, turn on the TV, and be sure there are at least three movies starring people like me somewhere on cable. Even if not all of it makes it to the level of *The Matrix* (now become a franchise with Laurence Fishburne). If I check out the ball game, a majority of the players and half the commentators will be black or Hispanic. In all the top dramatic series on television, there will be nonwhites, mostly blacks, in feature roles out of proportion to our presence in the population. I can expect to find blacks or other people of color in leading roles in most high culture venues that I might peruse. It's still rough, but I'm comforted not only by regular opportunities to see (insert: Halle or Denzel) in a Hollywood movie and to suspend disbelief that we could be the lovers in this story, but also by the fact that *millions of white people are coveting someone who looks like me, too*. It is so commonplace, that I've begun to take it for granted.

Simple and tongue-in-cheeky as it is, the Halle/Denzel utility test gets to an important truth: African-Americans have received a sizable gross gain in consumer welfare from the revolution in mainstream culture. For little or no additional cost, we have much more to chooose from and much less to shun. Just because the millennium of equality and justice hasn't arrived doesn't mean things haven't been moved a sizable distance in the right direction. And if having an extensive supply of black stars to gawk at on *Entertainment*

Tonight serves to make us politically complacent, then shame on us; we have no one to blame but ourselves and the hypocritical mismatch between what we say we want and what we settle for.

Staying on the plus side of the ledger a bit longer, it's hard to escape the conclusion that corporate transracialism in media and marketing undermines white supremacy by slowly but steadily devaluing white privilege in commercial popular culture and by granting certain previously withheld privileges to nonwhites. Among the fifty points of white privilege catalogued by Wellesley College's Peggy McIntosh in her classic 1991 essay "On the Invisibility of Privilege" are several that go directly to white privilege in the marketplace:

No. 6. I can turn on the television or open to the front page of the newspaper and see people of my race widely represented.

No.7. When I am told about our national heritage or about "civilization," I am shown that people of my color made it what it is.

No. 12. I can go into a music shop and count on finding the music of my race represented, into a supermarket and find the staple foods which fit with my cultural traditions, into a hairdresser's shop and find someone who can cut my hair.

No.13. Whether I use checks, credit cards, or cash, I can count on my skin color not to work against the appearance of financial reliability.

No. 26. I can easily buy posters, postcards, picture books, greeting cards, dolls, toys, and children's magazines featuring people of my race.

If you live in one of the major metropolitan areas where 90 percent of your particular nonwhite privileged group lives—New York, Atlanta, or Washington if you're black, Miami, San Antonio, or Los Angeles if you're Latino—these privileges have been granted to some significant if not absolute degree by the combination of market forces and technology. Some of them come as a result of changes that weren't as fully realized in 1991. For example, while white people may still have some invisible advantage of credibility at the checkout counter (No. 13), the near universal reliance on electronic payment and identification systems controls all transactions, and it's color-blind. All they care about when they look at my face is that it matches the picture on my driver's license. Most of the time they don't even look at my face—they just tell their computer to talk to my bank's computer; neither machine knows or cares that I'm black.

As for No. 7, the media marketplace's role in articulating history, heritage, and culture is dominated by just two forces: PBS and cable. Ken Burns's documentaries on the Civil War, baseball, and jazz have both rewritten the role of blacks in American history and American heritage and have dominated the ratings, such as they are for serious stuff. On cable HBO's trophy case for movies like *The Tuskegee Airmen, Introducing Dorothy Dandridge,* and *Miss Evers' Boys* will soon need new shelves. The History Channel was the primary outlet for some of the books I cited in this book, including James Miller's history of rock and roll, David Halberstam's *The Fifties,* and Neal Gabler's story of how immigrant Jews invented Hollywood and the American dream. I can say without doubt that privilege No. 7 has been granted.

The greatest gains for nonprivileged nonwhites from the browning of mainstream culture, I think, come less from the increase in privileges like those just mentioned than from the erosion, from a white person's point of view, of a much greater number of McIntosh's enumerated privileges, due to the operation of the forces I've been discussing. Hence the passive indifference, passive resistance, and even passive aggression with which a majority of whites respond to the new state of affairs. They sense, correctly, that the market is coercing them into undermining certain aspects of their own privilege *with their own money,* and they can't (or don't seem to have the will to) do much about it. But before I treat the white balance sheet and offer conclusions about the consolidated national ledger as a result of the last twenty years of race in commercial culture, I must return to the debit side of the books from the perspective of many African-Americans and others whose sentiments might best be characterized as "multicultural-nationalist."

As Chapter 8 details, the black media and marketing industry has been a clear victim of the commercial mainstreaming of African-Americans and black culture. The damage goes far beyond the changed fortunes of a number of specific black companies. Make no mistake: Entrepreneurs like the Gardner family (Soft Sheen Products), Robert Johnson (BET), and Tom Burrell (Burrell Advertising) all received good prices for selling all or part of their businesses to publicly traded firms. All these firms continue to be entirely black run and, so far, are thriving.

The loss has really been the steady erosion of black identity as the organizing principle for community development and socioeconomic advancement. Black leadership in the post–civil rights era has relied on a kind of entrepreneurial vision of black identity for achieving its lofty and worthy long-term goals. This "commercial blackness" is really a brand of consumerism that links individual consumption choices to advances toward group social goals. Commercial blackness, as codified and amplified by black-owned media and marketing messages, is supposed to provide the galvanizing muscle behind the periodic boycott threats leveled by civil rights leaders like Jesse Jackson and Kweisi Mfume of the NAACP. Commercial blackness is putting the power and wealth of black celebrity clearly in the service of the black leadership agenda. Commercial blackness would be helping to build the kind of Afrocentric value system that some influential leaders and thinkers feel is the only hope for collective self-esteem and civic renewal.

But the triumph of depoliticized black culture and icons in mainstream media has marginalized the influence of even the most successful commercially black venues. The NAACP's periodic boycott threats are utterly hollow. Major television network executives I've interviewed on the civil rights group's recent push to increase diversity in the industry say—on deep background, of course—that their biggest fear is not an actual boycott but bad press coverage of a boycott threat. The NAACP would never actually call for a boycott of, say, ABC because the risk of an embarrassing failure is far too high. We believe in the stars of Monday Night Football, on and off the field, far more than we believe in Kweisi Mfume. And I seriously doubt that the NAACP would get any support from the black talent associated with Monday Night Football or the NFL. That goes double for any boycott of the NBA on NBC. Needless to say, choosing instead to boycott a show that blacks would readily boycott would make no sense because they're already not watching it.

The availability of a full menu of nonpolitical black culture for the gorging is a natural suppressant of black political and economic nationalisms. Those who would lead African-Americans by addressing their group identity simply have much more difficulty breaking through. Unless you are an acknowledged media master like the Reverend Al Sharpton, you can pretty much forget about it. Now that most old-line leaders and their legacies have been retired or stripped of their legitimacy, African-Americans find themselves in a new and uncertain place where individual choice is exalted to an historically unprecedented degree while traditions of sacrifice for collective action are nearly ignored. This state of affairs puts the black community of interest on ground that is as uncertain as it is brand new.

The door to black participation in mainstream commercial culture is almost wide open, but the price of admission is the negation or denial of the political value of group identity, if not its very existence. As one who came of age with the civil rights movement, albeit as a mostly passive participant, and with the process of naming and defining black identity, I recognize that this is no small price to pay.

But it's worth it. The sacrifice of commercial blackness reflects the cold hard fact that the nature of the struggle has changed. The black triumph in commercial culture on these terms raises the central question of post–civil rights multiculturalism as it applies to black identity: How do we move as a society toward valuing all members as individuals if we insisted on special recognition of group identity? Clearly, sooner or later group identity would have to go; a great deal of our loss is the expiring of jettisoning it on our own terms, on a timetable of our own choosing. Corporate America, for its own reasons, has forced our hand. Then again, I doubt seriously that we would or could have done it on our own. As *Washington Post* sports columnist Michael Wilbon, who is black, told me in an interview:

> We want to have it both ways. But we can't say, on one hand, that we're pissed off when whites say the NBA is too black, then turn around and say we're pissed off because whites say, "We don't see color." I mean, all of this double-standard bullshit is not all on white people. We have our own bullshit. I realize some people have never accepted the theory of integration, but the whole idea was to be seen as a person first. Isn't that what Martin Luther King died for?

The game has changed. For years I've been convinced that the future is not about black people leading black people, in the old mold that was first stamped for black preachers and teachers. The future is about black people leading all Americans, especially white Americans. That leadership will be accepted only if it comes from individuals who only happen to be black. Just ask Colin Powell. Like him or not, his chances of getting elected president, however narrow, are infinitely better than Jesse Jackson's ever were. Trans-racial popular culture has created a new mold for black leadership, one that is based on individual example rather than on group allegiance. Tiger Woods may have no politics that an old-school black nationalist would recognize, but he leads white people and not just on the golf course. Just the fact that he leads people to buy things is powerful, because consumption conditions identity. A white woman may well cross a deserted street or clutch her pocketbook when a stranger who looks just like Tiger comes walking by. But when she sees the same brother behind the counter of a wine store or across the desk at the insurance office, and his presentation bears even a superficial resemblance to that of Woods, she may be more inclined to buy because of the extraordinary comfort level that Tiger has established in the world. And if you can imagine somebody like Tiger Woods selling you a car, how about somebody like Oprah getting your vote for Congress or even president? You heard it here first.

"Familiarity," said Wilbon, "does more than breed contempt; it can and does also breed acceptance." The civil rights movement helped O. J. Simpson get into the University of Southern California, where he became a star, but it was the dawn of blacks in mainstream pop culture that made him familiar. Rodney King's videotaped beating—which became famously commercial—didn't prevent a white jury from acquitting his assailants, triggering the 1992 L.A. riots, but it did make him familiar, indicting and convicting the law enforcement system in the court of public opinion and making King himself an icon for a time. The familiar King story set the stage for Johnnie Cochran to make the justice system itself the defendant in the O. J. Simpson trial, making himself a black media star in the process. In this made-for-TV movie, supporting roles were played by a Japanese-American judge, a seemingly racist white cop straight out of central casting, and a black assistant DA who confesses to coming close to having an affair with his white partner. It was a hell of a show, and yet close on the heels of Simpson's acquittal, the whole thing seems like an ordinary plot on *Ally McBeal* or *The Practice*. O. J.'s ratings across all media changed the course of the news business (creating Court TV and bolstering the growth of all-news cable shows like CNN and MSNBC). The most popular sitcom in America at the time created a comic black character in Cochran's image, while Cochran became *the* civil suit lawyer to the new "stars" of racial oppression like Amadou Diallo and Abner Louima. Both of their tragic stories are television movies just waiting to happen. Yet none of it would be possible without the kind of *individual* familiarity that modern American celebrity requires. The very political story of Diallo's murder or Louima's ordeal would not be commercial without the familiar precedent of Rodney King and, the familiar presence, even to people who despise them, of Johnnie Cochran and Al Sharpton.

A year or two after Diallo, a black woman lawyer representing the White House—a real political change—gets fifteen minutes of international media fame defending President Clinton by facing down the mostly white male Republican impeachment team. Cochran goes on to parlay his burgeoning stardom into a merger, creating the most powerful civil litigation firm in the country, with his name up front. The same month the Clinton lawyer, Cheryl Mills, takes an executive position at a women-oriented emerging cable-Internet firm.

What all these developments show is that a browning commercial culture creates unprecedented opportunities for prepared black individuals—at the price of cutting traditional black leadership out of the loop. The slew of black judges, prosecutors, and defense attorneys popping up on TV don't seem to hold NAACP membership cards or belong to any movement beyond their own values and ambitions. What the "race" thinks, as articulated by people whose job it is to speak for African-Americans, isn't commercial. But what Johnnie Cochran, or Henry Louis "Skip" Gates, or any of a growing number of black star *individuals* thinks *is* commercial, whether or not it's actually news.

The game has changed, and while the rules of play may still be unfamiliar, the potential for victory is far greater because so many more people can get into the new game. If African-Americans aren't a monolith, then monolithic (in aspiration) institutions of black identity have little present and even less future. I think that is a good thing. What is problematic is commercial popular culture's bias toward giving the white majority what it craves to identify with in black culture and celebrity without threatening its comfort zone of white privilege, or even pointing to its existence. A white guy can have a few beers and growl "Whasssuuuup" with his all-white friends in an all white bar without having to give any consideration to the community that inspired that bit of culture. A white woman can buy the look of Halle Berry's makeup without altering any unknowingly racist perceptions of Halle Berry or people who look like her. The same white men who watch NBA stars all Sunday afternoon can, on Monday, approach me, a six-foot-seven black man, and say, "You look like a basketball player." To which my standard reply is, "Really? Which one?" before leaving them to marinate in their own ignorance.

But even here there's more operating in the direction of change than might meet the eye. For starters, for all their sins throughout history, one has to give white Americans credit for learning from experience. As I said earlier, like it or not, it's impossible for them to escape the impacts of a browned commercial culture. White men are the very template for the Borg of *Star Trek* fame; they will adapt to what they cannot assimilate by force. As whiteness continues to lose its overall premium in commercial culture, more and more whites are forced to take stock of their investment in whiteness. Most of this examination is taking place in academic and intellectual circles and barely touches the average white person over, say, thirty-five. But other adaptations are taking place in under-thirty-five America. One of the most telling is the rising rate of interracial marriage, up some tenfold since 1960, with most of the increase coming since 1980. To be sure, in 1980 just 5 percent of whites were married to someone of another race or of Hispanic origin. But more striking than the marriage numbers (which will take several more decades to move deep into the double digits) are the figures on attitudes. Somewhere in the early 1990s the proportion of white Americans who approve of mixed black and white marriages crossed into the majority. In 1997 it was 61 percent. The factors behind this trend of course are varied and complex, but I don't think they can be positively correlated with growing political liberalism or social sensitivity. Rather, I think they owe more to a kind of desensitization that comes from the declining premium on whiteness and the declining discount on nonwhiteness in commercial popular culture.

During my reporting I had a long dialogue with an economist about the possible implications of a decline in the *cultural* utility of whiteness that's unaccompanied by any apparent decline in the *social* utility of whiteness. We came away intrigued by the possibility of a hypothetical new white man. He's an economically confident knowledge worker (computer programmer, investment banker) with an Asian wife and a black girlfriend (or vice versa).

He not only doesn't mind mixing with nonwhites of the same social class, he increasingly values such "diversity" in his life, up to a point. Moreover, he doesn't need to rely on whiteness for his economic or social well-being. And even if he did, he couldn't rely on it very much because he's competing against nonwhite imported talent, and with much lower barriers to competition from qualified domestic minority talent. In his sector of the economy, lily-white unions or protective civil service bureaucracies never held particular sway. He has reached the point of diminishing marginal returns to whiteness.

Who knows, our hypothetical white man might be dreaming of seeing his child play in the NBA. Or more pragmatically, he'd like to raise children who are capable of fitting into a racially diverse world, or at least the major metropolitan urban environment in which he lives. As I said, it is the nature of all men but especially white men to adapt under pressure. The browning commercial culture pressures white people and even nominally white institutions to reconsider their identity.

A friend of mine, a black woman married to an Italian-American man, told me the story of her daughter's decision to compete for a college scholarship from an Italian-American ethnic organization. Her essay, "My Italian-American Experience," won a thousand-dollar prize. Her mother was elated, but her father worried that his child might be hurt or embarrassed if the organization found out that she was "black" despite her Italian surname. But he needn't have worried. The contest officials said, in effect, that as long as she had one drop of Italian blood, she was Italian. Imagine, we laughed out loud, the old one-drop rule being applied to make a black person officially, at least for the purposes of this award, Italian! After the laughter we recalled the "black-Italian" father-and-son characters on the old NBC *Homicide* drama, played by Yaphet Kotto and Giancarlo Esposito (who in fact is black and Italian). And we wondered aloud how to tell whether art was imitating life or vice versa.

What the story suggests is that while white privilege still obtains in America, it's becoming a luxury that's less and less fashionable and more and more costly to maintain. What price white privilege when even in tony Newport, Rhode Island, at the height of "the season," a high-powered stereo in a top-down jeep with "Check it ouuuut . . . funk soul brother" reverberates over and over again between the mansions? If that Italian-American group chose to wall themselves off to racially mixed Americans of Italian descent, it would increasingly cost them the affinity of a new generation; there are only going to be more Giancarlo Espositos in America, not fewer. The most likely place they learned this reality was sitting before the television set.

I have never claimed that transracial pop culture represents a trend toward political racial equality. But it has undeniably leveled the playing field in terms of cultural value judgments. Simply put, nonwhite cultural tropes in the mainstream and their nonwhite practitioners cannot easily be put down or marginalized on the basis of race, because their appeal is too broad. Moreover, I think, at a certain level it's hard to deny that as the trend in pop culture is self-sustaining, it must eventually be replicated in society itself.

Perhaps, in the end, what really matters about today's moment is where we go from here, because so much is now "been there, done that" in commercial perceptions of race, culture, and identity. Not coincidentally, the racial barriers in both culture and society that are falling fastest and hardest are those that are inconsistent with the fundamental shift in multinational relationships known as the "global economy." As Latin America in general and Mexico in particular become our most important trading partners, and as 150 years of engulfment (Mexico, Puerto Rico) and immigration finally succeed in making us one people, the idea of racial differences between Latinos and white Americans is becoming obsolete. The trend is the same with Asians, especially well-educated Asians, because the incorporation of their talent will be critical for the growth and competitiveness of American society for many decades to come. Whiteness will be redefined to incorporate so-called Hispanics and Asians and, to a lesser extent, even Americans of non-Hispanic African descent.

The only open question, for me, is whether whiteness will eventually redefine itself out of existence in America, taking blackness along with it. Logically it could happen when social and economic whiteness has entirely outlived its usefulness. People say it can never be done. I don't know the future, but I do know who's picking up the check, and I can't imagine corporate capital supporting the cost of whiteness past its economic retirement age. Never forget: The underlying motivation for the institution of political whiteness has always been economic first and social second. Hence no economic return, no more whiteness.

Interestingly enough, whiteness can be retired only in the moment when it fully embraces its arbitrary opposite, blackness. The triumph of African-Americans in a self-sustaining transracial commercial popular culture will one day be seen as the final catalyst to the wholeness of identity embodied in the phrase "One race, human, one culture, American." In writing this book, that phrase was my unspoken prayer and meditation.

Notes

Introduction

1. Albert Murray, after historian Constance Rourke, in Omni-Americans, pp. 16
2. Herbert S. Agar, U.S. writer, *A Time for Greatness,* from Macmillan *Dictionary of Quotations.*

Chapter 1: The Color and the Dream

1. Charles Dickens, *American Notes and Pictures from Italy* (London: Oxford University Press, 1957), 90.
2. Ibid.
3. Ken Emerson, *Doo-Dah, Stephen Foster and the Rise of American Popular Culture* (New York: Simon and Schuster 1997), 69.
4. Davy Crockett, *Davy Crockett's Own Story* (The Citadel Press, 1955), 178.
5. Michael Lind, *The Next American Nation* (New York: Free Press, 1995), 47.
6. Ibid., 47–48.
7. Richard Dyer, *White* (London and New York: Routledge, 1997), 9.
8. Ibid., 122.
9. Ibid., 27–28.
10. Emerson, *Doo-Dah,* 58.
11. Ibid., 59.
12. Ibid., 60.
13. Ibid.
14. Ibid., 58.
15. Interestingly, Emerson points out, in his own time Crockett himself was a well-known blackface devotee and even figured in the literature. "The blackest thing about much early blackface music may have been the burnt cork, and frequently it disguised none other than Davy Crockett. In one verson of 'Zip Coon,' Zip succeeds Andrew Jackson

and offers Davy the vice-presidency: 'Zip shal be President, Crockett shall be vice,/ And de dey two togedder, will hab de tings nice.' Crockett played the fiddle and relished blackface. He took in a show in Philadelphia and opined . . . that the performer who jumped Jim Crow . . . 'makes as good a nigger as if he was clean black, except the bandy-legs.'" Ibid., 71.

16. Ibid., 62.
17. Ibid., 65.
18. Ibid., 107.
19. Ibid., 107.
20. Ibid., 180.
21. Ric Burns, *New York: A Documentary,* Public Broadcasting System, Fall 1999.
22. *All Things Considered,* National Public Radio, March 20, 2000.
23. Ann Douglas, *Terrible Honesty: Mongrel Manhattan in the 1920s* (New York: Farrar, Straus and Giroux, 1995), 357.
24. Ibid., 366.
25. *Bulletproof,* with Damon Wayans and Adam Sandler, Universal Pictures, 1996.
26. Jody Rosen, "Rapping in Whiteface (for Laughs)," *New York Times,* April 23, 2000.
27. Audra McDonald, "How Glory Goes," Nonesuch Records, 2000.

Chapter 2: Color Under Cover from the Great War to the Cold War

1. Ann Douglas, *Terrible Honesty: Mongrel Manhattan in the 1920s* (New York: Farrar, Straus and Giroux, 1995), 371.
2. Ibid., 358.
3. Ibid., 359.
4. Ibid., 374.
5. Far from one-hit wonders, the Baha Men have proven to be sophisticated in extending their brand into a number of other markets and venues. For example, they do the theme song of the popular *Stanley* children's cartoon on the Disney Channel, which promotes the show with a video featuring the group.
6. Laurence Bergreen, *Louis Armstrong: An Extravagant Life* (New York: Broadway Books, 1998), 164.
7. Ibid., 164–65.
8. Douglas, *Terrible Honesty,* 362–63.
9. Ibid., 384–85.
10. Ibid., 385.
11. Bergreen, *Louis Armstrong,* 214; my italics.
12. Douglas, *Terrible Honesty,* 391.
13. Ibid., 394–95.
14. Susan J. Douglas, *Listening In: Radio and the American Imagination* (New York: Random House, 1999), 18.
15. Ibid., 94.
16. Ibid., 98–99; emphasis added.
17. Ibid., 108.
18. Ibid., 113.
19. The term *Hispanic* was put into official usage by the federal government only in the 1970s, creating a unique ethnic category, the only ethnicity treated like a racial minority for policy purposes. Until the 1970s census enumerators counted Hispanic citizens as "white," unless they were too apparently Indian looking. To this day about 51 percent of Hispanics identity themselves as "white" on the census racial question.

20. Neal Gabler, *An Empire of Their Own: How the Jews Invented Hollywood* (New York: Crown Publishers, 1988).

21. *Hollywoodism: Jews, Movies and the American Dream,* Associated Producers in association with Canadian Broadcasting Corp., A&E Network, Channel and 4 Television Corp; executive producers Michael A. Levine and Monty Montgomery, 1988.

22. Ibid.

23. Ibid.

24. Geoffrey Ward and Ken Burns, *Jazz: A History of America's Music* (New York: Alfred A. Knopf, 2000), 254.

25. Ibid.

26. Douglas, *Terrible Honesty,* 359.

27. Douglas, *Listening In,* 207.

28. Roland Marchand, *Advertising and the American Dream: Making Way for Modernity* (Berkeley and Los Angeles: University of California Press, 1985), 35.

29. Ibid., 192–93.

30. Ibid., 4.

31. Ward and Burns, *Jazz,* 282.

32. Ibid.

Chapter 3: The 1950s Set Up the 1960s and 1970s

1. David Halberstam, *The Fifties* (New York: Random House, 1993), 522.

2. James Miller, *Flowers in the Dustbin: The Rise of Rock and Roll, 1947–1977* (New York: Simon and Schuster, 1999), 44.

3. Ibid., 144.

4. Ibid., 29.

5. Ibid., 30.

6. Ibid., 50.

7. Halberstam, *Fifties,* 470.

8. Ibid., 468.

9. Miller, *Flowers in the Dustbin,* 51–52.

10. Greil Marcus, *Mystery Train: Images of America in Rock and Roll* (New York: Penguin Books, 1997), 34.

11. Miller, *Flowers in the Dustbin,* 37.

12. Halberstam, *Fifties,* 458.

13. Ibid., 459.

14. Miller, *Flowers in the Dustbin,* 112, 113.

15. Ibid., 158.

16. Ibid., 112.

Chapter 4: Marketing in Color

1. Roger Enrico and Jesse Kornbluth, *The Other Boy Blinked: How Pepsi Won the Cola Wars* (New York: Bantam Books, 1986).

2. Richard Harrington, "WHO IS HE? Somewhere over the Rainbow with the Enigma of the '80s," *Washington Post,* March 18, 1984.

3. Jay Cocks, "Why He's a Thriller: Michael Jackson's Songs, Steps and Sexy Aura Set a Flashy Beat for the Decade," *Time,* March 19, 1984.

4. In 1982, in a bow to nascent political correctness, *Billboard* renamed the rhythm-and-blues chart the "black music" chart.

5. Elizabeth Comte, "How High Can David Stern Jump?" *Forbes,* June 7, 1993.

6. Bob Kravitz, "NBA Bounces Back with Signs of Renewed Life," *Houston Chronicle*, February 28, 1985.

7. Richard Harrington, "Lionel Ritchie: He Writes the Songs," *Washington Post*, May 27, 1984.

8. Mark Heisler, "Even with All the Fame, Only Bo Knows Bo," *Los Angeles Times*, January 16, 1990.

9. The 0.5 is the runted unfortunate Gary Coleman, of *Diff'rent Strokes* fame, who showed up in a "Best and Worst Dressed" cover in 1980.

10. Harvey Araton, "A Valuable Lesson: Fleeting Fame," *New York Times*, October 31, 1999.

11. Stuart Elliott, "Gotta Talk Like This, It's a Reflection of Buyers' Speech," *New York Times*, March 9, 1992.

Chapter 5: Transracial America Sells

1. "Black Cinderella and the Beauty-Challenged Sisters," *Sunday Times* (London), August 31, 1997.

2. Claire Blickley, "Belle of the Ball," *Toronto Sun*, November 2, 1997.

3. In the sense of the term coined by Michael Lind in *The Next American Nation* (New York: Free Press, 1995).

4. Ibid.

5. A sampling of thirteen issues of the *Times* between November 1979 and December 1980 found just five images of color in display advertising in all sections excluding entertainment (movie, music, and performance ads). Interestingly, three of the five were media celebrities—television journalists Ed Bradley and Lem Tucker and then–Yankee star Reggie Jackson—and all appeared in the same July 14, 1980, issue.

6. That is, nonwhites are already represented in ads for movies, music, theater, and live performance in New York in proportion to their share of the U.S. population.

7. Minority Markets Alert, *Mass Circulation Magazine Ads Reflect Minority Population, Lifestyle Shifts* (New York: EPM Communications, March 1997).

8. Screen Actors Guild surveys of television, theatrical, and commercial casting, 1996 and 1998.

9. George Gerbner, "The 1998 Screen Actors Guild Report: Casting the American Scene," December 1998; online at www.sag.org/special/americanscene.html.

10. Ibid.

11. To be sure, blacks were shut out of Oscar nominations earlier that year, creating a mini-crisis over whether Hollywood was trying to squeeze blacks off movie screens.

12. In five of the six years between 1994 and 2000, film and television production set new records, according to the Mayor's Office of Film, Theater and Broadcasting. Including commercials, production companies poured $2.52 billion into the city's economy in 1999.

13. Interestingly, while Braugher was hailed in the mainstream as "the best actor on television" for his work, neither Braugher nor *Homicide* ever won an Image Award from the ten-thousand-plus NAACP members who vote the awards. *Homicide* never developed a particularly strong black following, either, to the great disappointment of its creator, veteran television producer Tom Fontana. "I would think in terms of an image—Andre Braugher, Yaphet Kotto, Clark Johnson—these are guys that you want," Fontana told me.

14. Race's only mention is at the expense of Hall of Famer Ty Cobb, when other players point out he was a racist and not a man they wanted to share baseball heaven with.

15. Technically, Banderas isn't "Hispanic" within the bizzare U.S. classification system since he is from Spain, the colonizer, not from Latin America, the colonized.

16. Interestingly, *Generations,* the first and only overtly interracial soap opera, heavily promoted as such by NBC, failed miserably in the early 1990s. Critics suggested it was too self-conscious of its racial content to satisfy the fantasies of daytime drama audiences.

17. Cynthia Joyce, "The Strange New Stirrings of Old Navy Nation," *Newsday,* July 12, 1998.

18. Margo Jefferson, "Looking at What Black Looks Like," *New York Times,* June 11, 1997.

19. Minority Markets Alert, *Mass Circulation Magazine Ads.*

20. Interestingly enough, however, there is no corresponding Asian or Hispanic hair-and-beauty industry of any scale.

21. At least not since the demise of the unique racial classification system that flourished primarily in Louisiana in the last third of the nineteenth century.

22. I tried to get Beals to talk about race and her career for my column during the media blitz surrounding *Devil in a Blue Dress.* After weeks of spinning me around (while no doubt trying hard to get her to consent to exposure in the nation's biggest newspaper), her public relations representative simply blew me off.

23. Larry Platt, "They Bad," *New York Times Magazine,* November 14, 1999.

24. John A. Hall and Charles Lindholm, *Is America Breaking Apart?* (Princeton, N.J.: Princeton University Press, 1999).

25. Ibid., 50.

26. Lind, *Next American Nation,* 259–60.

27. Ibid., 260.

Chapter 6: Youth Culture Leads the Way

1. *Youth Views: Newsletter of the Gallup Youth Survey,* vol. 6, no. 2 (October 1998).

2. Ibid.

3. "Kids in 2010," *American Demographics,* September 1999.

4. MTV poll released December 3, 1997.

5. Neil Howe and William Strauss, *Millenials Rising: The Next Great Generation* (New York: Vintage, 2000).

6. "Marketing Street Culture: Hip-Hop Style to the Mainstream," *American Demographics,* November 1996.

7. Ironically, perhaps, because they recognize that today Nader and Buchanan are not really poles apart but are merely separated by a few degrees on the ideological circle.

8. In tone the Sunny Delight commercial is eerily similar to the groundbreaking 1998 Cisco Systems campaign that droned the same "Are you ready" mantra over shots of mostly youthful nonwhite "foreigners" from around the world who are joining us on the Internet, ready or not.

9. "Marketing Street Culture: Hip-Hop Style to the Mainstream," *American Demographics,* November 1996.

Chapter 7: Majority Minority

1. "A Patel Motel Cartel?," *New York Times Magazine,* July 4, 1999, 36–39.

2. Ibid., 39.

3. Ibid.; emphasis added.

4. Ibid.

5. "For Women Great and Small, Briefs Can't Get Much Briefer," *New York Times*, August 13, 2000, Styles, 1–6.

6. Ibid.

7. Hispanic households, with an average of 3.6 people per home, are 40 percent larger than the U.S. average, and they spend 23 percent, about $20, more per week at the supermarket, according to a 1993 report by Strategy Research, a Miami market research firm.

8. Glenn Collins, "The Americanization of Salsa," *New York Times*, January 9, 1997, D1.

9. Ibid.

10. Ibid.

11. Yumiko Ono, "Marketers Whip Up Weird Ethnic Blends," *Wall Street Journal*, November 9, 1994, B1.

12. The stories included a long feature about the prominence of black comedians in film, a loving profile of choreographer Katherine Dunham, yet another take-out about Latin American bands, a review of a Senegalese dance troupe at a prominent venue, and a review of a novel about modern life in India.

13. "Victory to the Low and Slow," *New York Times*, May 21, 2000.

14. "Ethnic Voices Call the Tune in the Cities," *New York Times*, February 6, 1994, Arts & Leisure, section 2, 1.

15. Ibid., 26.

16. Ibid.; emphasis added.

17. *Emerging markets* is also used to refer to the economies of what used to be called third-world countries, with a political-correctness quotient very similar to the domestic usage.

18. Orlando Patterson, "Race by the Numbers," *New York Times*, May 8, 2001; emphasis added.

19. Ibid.

20. Michael Lind, "The Beige and the Black," *New York Times Magazine*, August 16, 1998, 38–39.

21. Michael Lind, *The Next American Nation* (New York: Free Press, 1995).

Chapter 8: The Rise and Fall Ethnic Marketing

1. Earl G. Graves, *How to Succeed in Business Without Being White* (New York: Harper-Collins, 1997), 19, 20.

2. Travis Poling, "Hispanic Agencies Score in English and Spanish Markets," Associated Press, June 17, 2000.

Index

About the Author

LEON WYNTER has followed the transformation of American identity in the multiracial marketplace for more than twenty years as a journalist and essayist. He created the *Wall Street Journal's* monthly "Business & Race" column and wrote it from 1989 to 1999. His commentaries on race, popular culture, and life have been heard on National Public Radio's "All Things Considered," since 1993. And he published two dozen essays in the *Wall Street Journal, Washington Post,* and *New York Newsday,* among others.

Wynter was corporate lending officer for a major New York bank when his first essay, on gentrification and identity in Fort Green, Brooklyn, was published in the *New York Times* in 1979. He soon joined the staff of the *Washington Post* where he covered education and racial change in suburban Prince George's County, Md. From there he moved to the Washington bureau of the *Wall Street Journal* where he covered the federal banking beat on Capitol Hill, as well as government telecommunication and technology policy.

Wynter is a graduate of Yale (1974, Psychology) and received an MBA from New York University's Stern School of Business (1979, Economics).